Identity and Nation Building in Everyday Post-Socialist Life

This book explores the function of the 'everyday' in the formation, consolidation and performance of national, sub-national and local identities in the former socialist region. Based on extensive original research including fieldwork, the book demonstrates how the study of everyday and mundane practices is a meaningful and useful way of understanding the socio-political processes of identity formation both at the top and bottom level of a state. The book covers a wide range of countries including the Baltic States, Ukraine, Russia, the Caucasus and Central Asia; and considers 'everyday' banal practices, including those related to consumption, kinship, embodiment, mobility, music, and the use of objects and artefacts. Overall, the book draws on, and contributes to, theory, and shows how the process of nation building is not just undertaken by formal actors, such as the state, its institutions and political elites.

Abel Polese, senior researcher at the Institute for International Conflict Resolution and Reconstruction of Dublin City University and Tallinn Law School of Tallinn University of Technology.

Jeremy Morris is an associate professor in Global Studies, Aarhus University, Denmark.

Emilia Pawłusz is an early stage researcher in the School of Governance, Law and Society at Tallinn University, Estonia.

Oleksandra Seliverstova is a Marie Curie Fellow at the School of Governance, Law and Society of Tallinn University, Estonia.

Routledge Contemporary Russia and Eastern Europe Series

For a full list of titles in this series, please visit https://www.routledge.com/ Routledge-Contemporary-Russia-and-Eastern-Europe-Series/book-series/ SE0766

68 **The Return of the Cold War**
Ukraine, the West and Russia
Edited by J. L. Black and Michael Johns

69 **Corporate Strategy in Post-Communist Russia**
Mikhail Glazunov

70 **Russian Aviation, Space Flight and Visual Culture**
Vlad Strukov and Helena Goscilo

71 **EU-Russia Relations, 1999–2015**
From Courtship to Confrontation
Anna-Sophie Maass

72 **Migrant Workers in Russia**
Global challenges of the shadow economy in societal transformation
Edited by Anna-Liisa Heusala and Kaarina Aitamurto

73 **Gender Inequality in the Eastern European Labour Market**
Twenty-five years of transition since the fall of communism
Edited by Giovanni Razzu

74 **Reforming the Russian Industrial Workplace**
International management standards meet the Soviet legacy
Elena Shulzhenko

75 **Identity and Nation Building in Everyday Post-Socialist Life**
*Edited by Abel Polese, Jeremy Morris, Emilia Pawłusz
and Oleksandra Seliverstova*

Identity and Nation Building in Everyday Post-Socialist Life

Edited by Abel Polese, Jeremy
Morris, Emilia Pawłusz
and Oleksandra Seliverstova

LONDON AND NEW YORK

First published 2018 by Routledge

2 Park Square, Milton Park, Abingdon, Oxfordshire OX14 4RN

52 Vanderbilt Avenue, New York, NY 10017

Routledge is an imprint of the Taylor & Francis Group, an informa business

First issued in paperback 2019

Copyright © 2018 selection and editorial matter, Abel Polese, Jeremy Morris, Emilia Pawłusz and Oleksandra Seliverstova; individual chapters, the contributors

The right of Abel Polese, Jeremy Morris, Emilia Pawłusz and Oleksandra Seliverstova to be identified as the authors of the editorial material, and of the authors for their individual chapters, has been asserted in accordance with sections 77 and 78 of the Copyright, Designs and Patents Act 1988.

All rights reserved. No part of this book may be reprinted or reproduced or utilised in any form or by any electronic, mechanical, or other means, now known or hereafter invented, including photocopying and recording, or in any information storage or retrieval system, without permission in writing from the publishers.

Notice:
Product or corporate names may be trademarks or registered trademarks, and are used only for identification and explanation without intent to infringe.

British Library Cataloguing-in-Publication Data
A catalogue record for this book is available from the British Library

Library of Congress Cataloging-in-Publication Data
Names: Polese, Abel, editor.
Title: Identity and nation building in everyday post-socialist life / edited by Abel Polese, Jeremy Morris, Oleksandra Seliverstova and Emilia Pawlusz.
Description: Abingdon, Oxon ; New York, NY : Routledge, 2018. | Series: Routledge contemporary Russia and Eastern Europe series ; 75 | Includes bibliographical references and index.
Identifiers: LCCN 2017006084| ISBN 9781138736412 (hardback) | ISBN 9781315185880 (ebook)
Subjects: LCSH: Nationalism—Former Soviet republics. | Group identity—Former Soviet republics. | Nation-building—Former Soviet republics. | Post-communism—Former Soviet republics.
Classification: LCC DK293 .I34 2018 | DDC 306.20947—dc23
LC record available at https://lccn.loc.gov/2017006084

ISBN: 978-1-138-73641-2 (hbk)
ISBN: 978-0-367-88552-6 (pbk)

Typeset in Times New Roman
by diacriTech, Chennai

Contents

List of figures	vii
List of contributors	viii
Acknowledgements	ix
Introduction: on informal and spontaneous national identities	1

PART I
Music and cultural events   15

1 **Formal and informal nationalism: jazz performances
   in Azerbaijan**   17
   ANETA STRZEMŻALSKA

2 **Can musicians build the nation? Popular music and
   identity in Estonia**   34
   EMILIA PAWŁUSZ

3 **The Georgian National Museum and the Museum of
   Soviet Occupation as loci of informal nation building**   52
   ALISA DATUNASHVILI

PART II
Consumer practices   71

4 **Made in Ukraine: consumer citizenship during
   EuroMaidan transformations**   73
   TETIANA BULAKH

vi *Contents*

5 National food, belonging, and identity among Russian-speaking migrants in the UK 91
ANNA PECHURINA

6 Consumer citizenship and reproduction of Estonianness 109
OLEKSANDRA SELIVERSTOVA

PART III
National discourses in everyday life 129

7 How to pronounce 'Belarusian'? Negotiating identity through naming 131
ANASTASIYA ASTAPOVA

8 Nuanced identities at the borders of the European Union: Romanians in Serbia and Ukraine 146
JULIEN DANERO IGLESIAS

9 Can nation building be 'spontaneous'? A (belated) ethnography of the Orange Revolution
ABEL POLESE 161

Conclusion: identities for the everyday 176

Index 180

Figures

3.1 Façade of the Simon Janashia Museum of Georgia: first banner on the right side advertises 'Museum of Soviet Occupation'.   59

3.2 On the left wall is the list of people shot by Communists; there is a also cannon and Wagon (imitation), where occupation victims were shot. A picture of Georgian Cadets shot during Russian invasion is on the floor, and there is a red spotlight – 'blood' – on the wagon with holes – 'shooting marks'. Altogether this creates an immediate emotional effect and creates unequivocally negative associations that are continued in the main exhibition hall.   63

3.3 Main exhibition hall, divided by the prison cell doors and massive pillars covered with concrete; together with the dimmed lights and dominant black and grey colours the exhibit makes an oppressive impression.   63

3.4 (Left) 'Sir John Oliver Wardrop. The UK's first Chief Commissioner in Transcaucasia, Active supporter of Georgia's independence and sovereignty.' (Right) 'Friedrich Werner von Schulenburg. Consul of Germany in Georgia. Co-author of the text of founding charter of Democratic Republic of Georgia.' This shows the Georgian–European relationship to emphasize Georgia's desire to be part of Europe.   65

3.5 Georgian national costume, 'chokha', presented as belonging to Kakutsa Cholokashvili, the leader of the first Georgian Republic government. One of the stumbling blocks between museumelis and exhibition authors: the chokha did not belong to Cholokashvili. To present it as such means to lie to visitors, which is unacceptable for the museum.   66

Contributors

Anastasiya Astapova, University of Tartu, Estonia.

Tetiana Bulakh, Indiana University Bloomington, US.

Alisa Datunashvili, Tbilisi State University, Georgia.

Julien Danero Iglesias, CEVIPOL – Université libre de Bruxelles / University of Glasgow, UK.

Emilia Pawłusz, Tallinn University, Estonia.

Anna Pechurina, Leeds Beckett University, UK.

Abel Polese, Institute for International Conflict Resolution and Reconstruction, Dublin City University and Tallinn Law School, Tallinn University of Technology.

Oleksandra Seliverstova, Tallinn University, Estonia, and Free University of Brussels (VUB), Belgium.

Aneta Strzemz˙alska, European University at Saint Petersburg, Russia.

Acknowledgements

We had not realized how far we were going until the necessity arose to think of an edited volume on alternative aspects of identity constructions. Some of us were just coming out of a project on nation building in the former USSR, some others were busy with other volumes and their PhD theses. At the department of Political Science of Tallinn University, where three of the four authors work, we had received a lot of feedback over the years on the project TENSIONS (FP7, Marie Curie ITN grant no.316825) that we wish to acknowledge for allowing us to devote time to this book. The odd thing was that, when travelling to specialized workshops, topics such as consumption and national singing and their role in identity production were often received much more positively than in our home department, a thing that pushed us to look further for more feedback. These meetings gave us also the chance to interact with extremely pleasant people working on similar topics, and we attempted to launch a call for papers. An innocent call for papers posted on some mailing lists sparked so much interest among scholars and publishers that we thought the times were mature for a volume on everyday nationalism in the former USSR. We are therefore grateful to Peter Sowden at Routledge, who supported the idea from the very beginning, and in particular to the authors of our chapters, for their hard work and capacity to submit on time, reflect on our feedback and end up with a product that we are happy to present here.

The way this book was developed was influenced by the feedback that we received at the workshop 'Lived Experiences of the Everyday Nation', organized by Peace Research Institute Oslo (PRIO) on June 9-10, 2016. We are grateful to its organizers Mette Strømsø and Marta Bivand Erdal and also to the key speakers Marco Antonsich and Michael Skey. It is also the result of regular interaction with colleagues working on similar topics who have always been very keen to share their work or provide us with constructive feedback or simply with inspiring ideas. We wish to thank, in random order: Donnacha Ó Beacháin, John Doyle, Eileen Connelly, Karolina Stefanczak, Gezim Visoka, Giorgio Comai, Chiara Loda, Raivo Vetik, Peeter Muursepp,

x   *Acknowledgements*

Tanek Kerikmae, Archer Chocha, Vlad Vernagora, Firouzeh Nahvandi, Sarah Murru, Rajan Kumar, Ajay Patnaik, Sally Cummings, Rick Fawn, Raquel Freire, Licinia Simao, Heiko Pleines, Bruno De Cordier, Simon Tordjman, Ilona Baumane, Markku Lonkila, Jan Kohler, Diana Lezhava, Erhan Dogan, Filippo Menga, Pal Kolsto, Rico Isaacs, Aleksandr Prigarin and Jon Fox. May we be forgiven by the ones we have forgotten here.

Introduction

On informal and spontaneous national identities

In 2014, as a consequence of the Russian–Ukrainian conflict, an interesting tendency rapidly emerged among Ukrainians. In March a civic campaign was initiated by two local activists, eventually leading to strong restrictions on Russian products, regionally first, then at the national level. Just within the first month a boycott of Russian goods spread first throughout Western Ukraine and then in Kiev. Some large supermarkets, attentive to consumer behavior, decided to limit their range of Russian products or entirely cease selling merchandise produced in Russia.[1] Some smaller retailers started to facilitate identification of Russian and Ukrainian products by placing small flags on price labels. According to TNS,[2] by September 2014, the boycott was supported by 57% of the Ukrainian population, with 46% of them actually refusing to buy Russian products.

While most of its tangible effects were economic, the refusal to buy Russian products, it was suggested, served primarily as a way for Ukrainians to express their patriotism and feelings towards their country (Vershitskaya 2014). It was an affective movement by an imagined community, by which that community became somehow more 'real'. Just as the realpolitik annexation of Crimea by Russia and the role of Russia in the military conflict in Eastern Ukraine changed consumer patterns of the majority of Ukrainians and brought changes in Ukrainian legislation, the boycott was a measurable, tangible and perhaps the only practical response of Ukrainians to share and show some sense of national accord. Boycotting products coming from the 'aggressor-country' and at the same time trying to give more support to local Ukrainian products could be considered acts of civic responsibility and loyalty to the state and its people, usually defined as consumer citizenship and defined as 'production of national identity by way of shared consumption practices' (Foster and Özcan 2005: 5). Identification of an enemy has often been a major step in the construction of national identity. What is particular to this case is that identity manifested itself through an action (or rather, lack thereof) related to everyday life. Confrontation of a perceived enemy, as well as expression and reproduction of a national identity was performed on supermarket shelves and, in parallel, in people's minds. Thus through ordinary consumption practices ordinary people obtain a crucial political role

2   *Introduction*

in securing consolidation of a national community and state in critical times (Cohen 2003).

The goal of this book is to demonstrate that everyday practices are a meaningful, and useful, site for understanding socio-political developments in the process of identity formation both at the top and bottom level of a society. Inspired by a number of previous studies on other world regions (Edensor 2002, 2006, Fox 2016, Skey 2015) we use 'everyday' here in a meaning encompassing any kind of quotidian and 'banal' practices, possibly related to consumption, kinship, embodiment, mobility, music, use of objects and artefacts. By showing the links between macro studies on nation and state building in the former Soviet region with micro, bottom-up research into the everyday, the book explores how official and unofficial discourses of national, ethnic or civic categorizations traverse lifestyles, consumer practices, leisure time activities, and individuals' engagements with cultural products.

Every day we are confronted with, and have to make choices about, mundane issues that nonetheless influence our life. We go to work, buy food and drinks, spend leisure time, go on holiday, meet friends at cafes, watch movies and read books according to seemingly individual criteria that are shaped by our personal experiences, by our individual but also shared perception of events and by our both private and socially-mediated aspirations. Not all criteria we endorse are rational; we might choose a product or a place because it brings memories of our childhood, because we feel an irrational desire to experience that particular thing.

There is a growing body of scholarship maintaining that these choices are influenced by our identity, cultural background and subliminal political messages that we may receive through 'banal' practices. This book maintains that taking a contrarian view is equally important. First, subliminal messages are conveyed but not automatically accepted. By performing national identity through consumption or through shared participation in a cultural event we do not necessary accept the message but rather rebroadcast it, put our own stamp of identity on it. After all, the very notion of performance carries with it the idea of individual difference and distinction. Second, the question of 'reproduction' of shared national identities is equally problematic. People are acted upon by a state but also act, in forms that have been debated but originate in Giddens' structuration theory (1984). In other words, people have the agency to construct a narrative on national identity from the bottom up of a society performing what Eriksen called informal nationalism (1993). This agency, when originated and performed by ordinary people, is the main subject of this book.

The loci of national identity

When performing our everyday practices, we often adopt a position in favour, or against, something else. Identity, and performance of identity, is not alien to this process, because by doing or not doing we define who we are, and who

Introduction 3

we are not. By choosing to consume a certain product or not, we perform and reproduce (Douglas 1996). We identify with a certain community, we empathize with a certain approach or ideology or we reject another. National identity works in the same way and identification with a certain (national) community may push us to make choices that influence our consumption and life patterns. Starting from Billig's Banal Nationalism (1995) scholars have paid progressive attention to the capacity of a state or a political elite to construct, or influence national identities through everyday actions (Goode and Stroup 2015, Menon 2012; Jones and Merriman 2009). Political narratives are performed not only through formal or traditional instruments of nation building, such as school policies, they are also inculcated, reproduced and consolidated through hidden, subconscious or unperceived dynamics. Indeed, in a recently edited volume on the post-Soviet region, attention is paid to what are identified as 'nontraditional' tools and approaches in the construction of national identity (Isaacs and Polese 2016). The approaches suggested in the book allow us to construct a first account of the factors that can influence national identity going beyond a political-centric narrative. Attention is paid, in this respect, to phenomena other than those originated by the political elites, in a manner that had informed the term 'spontaneous nation building' some years before (Polese 2009a, 2009b). The idea of spontaneous nation building is:

> [A] construction of national identity conceived, performed, and engaged with by people or organizations of people; for instance, the construction of national identity through the perpetuation of national songs, popular art, singing, and dancing despite the possible lack of support from state authorities ... second, just as nation-building measures might not have the desired effects and impact on a given population, there might be some measures that, conceived of at the central level, were not intended to primarily influence identity construction but nevertheless end up strongly affecting identity in a country. (Polese and Horak 2015: 2)

Indeed, in their work Isaacs and Polese (2015, 2016) have made a first attempt to look at national identity construction through the lenses of non-traditional channels. Second, they introduce a complementary discourse. Whilst previous studies concentrate on phenomena that were not necessarily born as nation building tactics by elites, the main focus of the current book are phenomena that originate at the bottom of society and that receive increase attention and popularity and end up being considered an identity marker for a significant portion of the population.[3]

This book is an attempt to bring this discourse even further. Not only do we look at non-traditional loci of nation building, we also examine process as constantly renegotiated by ordinary people through everyday actions and performances

4   *Introduction*

The informal faces of identity construction

Nation building and identity formation are conceived in this book as part of a synergy between elite forces, providing 'instructions' on identity markers to choose, and bottom-up (or informal) ones, reacting to these instructions and, in many cases, renegotiating identity, selecting markers and performing identity in a way that is not necessarily the one that state institutions are interested in. We start from the idea that formal actors of nation building (state, its institutions, political elites), provide instructions through formal and official channels but are not alone in this task. There are a number of unrecognized, unnoticed and non-formalized actors that act, in a way that has been defined as informal or spontaneous, for a redefinition of a national identity more in line with what the people themselves 'want'.

As a result, the everyday, informal and unregulated has remained formally separated from the study of political processes, an issue that this book is intended to redress. In other words, processes originated by local and bottom-up actors, once the number of actors becomes higher, come to have a political significance and can actually be seen as an indicator of the success of a given policy or measure but also can nullify the work of political institutions. This assumption rests on the works of James Scott who, through his studies of unorganized resistance, defined a concept of infrapolitics that are composed of:

> [F]oot dragging, poaching, pilfering, dissimulation, sabotage, desertion, absenteeism, squatting and flight ... why risk an open land invasion when squatting will secure de facto land rights? Why openly petition for rights to wood, fish, and game when poaching will accomplish the same purpose quietly? ... [A]nd yet the accumulation of thousands or even millions of such petty acts can have massive effect for warfare, land rights, taxes and property relations. (Scott 2012: xx)

Renegotiation of national identities at the local level has already been demonstrated (Richardson 2008; Rodgers 2007). The novel further step is to use Scott's framework to ask what happens when a state or a political elite proposes some identity markers that are either rejected or renegotiated by local actors or ordinary people. Official narratives of the state might contend that this only is the 'real identity', constructed around a number of markers and narratives. However, once a significant number of actors rejects or renegotiates this identity, we maintained that this brings about a measureable change in how identities are lived, reproduced and passed to other generations (see Polese 2010, 2014).

Another key concept that we engage with here is the framework provided by Michael Billig in his study of everyday nationalism. The idea is that banal nationalism can be taken as a framework that works in established states, as opposed to hot nationalisms of states 'in the making'. We would like to

Introduction 5

overcome this distinction by emphasizing that the routine and quotidian identity expressions and the ecstatic (when the flag is consciously waved) are intertwined in real life, in people's experiences. While arguably, depending on the political and social context, one of them becomes more prominent and reported, this does not mean that the other disappears. By extending the thesis of Billig to non-Western states, we bring back the agency of people in the major socio-political processes, which however is not the focus of Billig. Billig's main contribution to the recent literature on nationalism was about switching the focus from hot nationalism to cold or banal nationalism, showing that nationalism exists also in consolidated, peaceful nation-states. However, when he talks of the ways nation is displayed and presented to its citizens, his definition of nation and national identity is rather fixed and the fact that such categories may be accepted/rejected or interpreted differently by members of a nation is not taken into account. In a framework that was then critically engaged with by Michael Skey (2009) and more recently by Jon Fox (2016), it is suggested that people are not a homogeneous national audience, passive receivers of banal nationalism enacted by the state, but instead consume, and experience it in different ways. In the same vein, Antonsich (2015), in his study of ethnically diverse Italian youth, suggested that banal nationalism unwittingly overlooks the individual in reproducing the nation. The goal of this book is to attend to the diversity and agency in people's experiences and actions pertaining to identity construction. It emphasizes the heterogeneity of the definition of nation, which is traceable in the everyday acts of ordinary people.

Although acknowledging Billig for the everyday framework, the chapters in this book are inspired by the works of Eriksen and in particular his distinction between formal and informal nationalism. In an article published in 1993, Eriksen distinguishes between two categories of actors that participate in the construction, and reconstruction, of national identity narratives. In his study on Trinidad and Mauritius nationalisms, he raises the question of a nationalism that needs to cope with an ethnically diverse society in which political elites must create an autonomous, non-colonial ideology of credible authentic nationhood. They must try to infuse citizens with patriotic sentiment relating to a nation that did not even exist a generation ago (Eriksen 1993: 4). He thus distinguishes between the role of state institutions and what he calls civil society that, in our view, could be extended to highly informal mechanisms or simply ordinary people (and informal associations of citizens) to show that nationalisms arise despite the state or develop independently from state-fed narratives and thus can be considered just as valid as state-led ones.

This last point is what we embrace and wish to bring forward in the rest of this book. We maintain that state and non-state narratives on national identity move through distinct, but complementary channels and both contribute to the construction of the 'national'. On the one hand, we have official state narratives that have been taken into account by a number of studies. On the other hand, and this is the main innovation of this book, we acknowledge and

6   *Introduction*

explore the role and agency of ordinary citizens, their 'unorganised struggle' (Scott 1984) for recognition and their capacity to create movements and institutions and identify markers that are then endorsed by a growing number of fellow citizens and become part of a national narrative on identity in a given place.

Notes on the everyday

The past years have witnessed an exponential interest in studies of the 'everyday'. Using a framework critically engaging with what Billig termed as 'banal nationalism', scholars have explored different layers and modalities of identity constructions. We are indebted to Edensor (2002), who explored Scottish identity through the study of different aspects of everyday life (movies, media, popular culture). Identity is thus not a top-down product but an ongoing practice of masses. However, by showing how ideas about nation are reproduced in everyday life Edensor, like Billig, overlooks the role of people as creators and rather considers them only performers of a nation. Another relevant study is by Foster (2002) who, in his ethnographic perspective on nation building, analyzed the role of consumption practices and in particular consumption of media products in the formation of imaginative national community in Papua New Guinea. He, following Hobsbawm's lead, focuses on top-down strategies of gluing the national community and on bottom-up actions of people, which are seen as commonly followed patterns in daily consumption. Another important elaboration of Billig's framework was recently provided by Skey (2011), who introduced the concept of 'ecstatic nationalism', suggesting that a critical revisiting of nation-building theories could lead to the conceptualization of a variety of new tools for the study of identity construction. In post-socialist spaces, this has translated into a variety of attempts to introduce new approaches or revisit existing ones with the goal of providing new directions in the study of identity building in the region (Bassin and Kelly 2012; Isaacs and Polese 2015, 2016). Still, we believe that the everyday dimension in post-socialist spaces remains largely unexploited and its potential to understand current socio-political processes of the region unexplored, especially when it comes to identity.

Indeed, most studies on identity seem to be structure-oriented. In contrast, it must be possible to 'bring back human agency' and systematically account for how individuals actively organize and live out, or at least, abide in ideas of nation and national identity. Indeed, a large majority of nationalism-related studies (Smith, Gellner, Guibernau, also Billig) tend to focus on high-magnitude events such as wars, ethnic conflicts or new state building, forgetting the little, micro processes which sustain the idea that we live in a world of nations in the daily life and consciousness of people (Thompson 2001). These claims possibly inspired reflections by Fox and Miller-Idriss (2008) and Brubaker et al. (2006) and then Fox (2016) on the theoretical 'turn to the everyday' in identity studies and their suggestion to employ multiple methods

Introduction 7

in an effort to go beyond disciplinary boundaries in identity studies. This, in their view, would allow us to capture identity construction in many aspects, from discourses to bodily expressions and gestures.

In our proposal for an equally innovative approach, however, we cannot neglect previous efforts that have guided us in this direction. In this respect, a number of scholars have been examining the role of middle actors, mostly schools and teachers, in conveying a sense of identity to the national community. Although not specifically focusing on the everyday, they have opened the way to a reflection on the role of human agency, of schoolteachers and administrators renegotiating an official narrative on national identity at the local level (see Janmaat 2000, Polese 2010, Rodgers 2007, Richardson 2008). This has possibly led more recent studies to examine the way taken for granted categories, such as ethnic or national, are being renegotiated and sometimes contested by ordinary people (Knott 2015, Kulyk 2014, Pawłusz and Seliverstova 2016, Seliverstova 2017). Such works mainly focused on post-socialist or UK contexts and provided new insights on people's association with the state, nation or country they live in. For instance, people can strongly identify themselves with a nation even when not favouring national symbols and its official narrative. In such situations most likely they will look for and produce new alternative markers of national identity. Similar critiques to mainstream political science understandings of identity and methods used for its research were put forward by Knott (2015) in her analysis of Romanian identity in Moldova and Russian identity in Crimea. She argues that national identity is relational and interactive, therefore simple census categories do not reflect the lived experience(d) identity of its bearers. She suggests that the census categories which many studies operate with reflect the nation-building project of the state, rather than the complex identification mechanisms individuals employ, often unintentionally.

Pawłusz and Seliverstova (2016) expanded this perspective further, focusing specifically on the inability of mainstream top-down, macro-oriented approaches to capture the complexity of identity formation. Rather than advocating ethnography as a sole method for identity studies 'from below', they propose extending anthropological and sensitivity into mainstream political science/political sociology, which in their view, might shed light on everyday, implicit, practical aspects of national identity construction, and thus complement more macro-oriented quantitative and mainstream qualitative approaches.

Structure of the book and main themes

We see everyday practices as a territory through which individuals establish, negotiate and embed references to concepts of citizenship, statehood and national self-definition. Studying everyday practices is relevant and useful to understand how the elite-led official nation-building narrative trickles down to the society and how it becomes altered, negotiated or challenged. Moreover, it

8 Introduction

also reveals some spontaneous, tacit, informal factors that influence people's perceptions of national identification, yet are not immediately visible if the study of nation building is limited to the lead taken by officialdom. With this in mind, we have organized this book into three separate sections that engage with distinct aspects of everyday construction of identities.

The first part is concerned with the construction and reproduction of identities through cultural products, events and leisure activities. We will look at the way themes related to the nation and sense of belonging penetrate popular culture like making and consuming music, festivals and cultural events. We will also look at more established cultural institutions such as museums and the informal agency museum workers have in creating exhibition narratives for the public. The bulk of chapters in this section show how actors and individuals related to different cultural sectors (musicians, museum workers, curators, educators) can often work as nation builders (intentionally or not) and influence the way ordinary citizens imagine and engage with the concept of the nation.

The first chapter, by Aneta Strzemżalska, looks at the role of jazz music in the redefinition of Azeri identity. She looks at the increased role of jazz festivals since the 2000s, many of which attracted world-renowned musicians to the point of earning Baku the definition of Jazz Mecca, the only place in the world where 'jazz-mugam' is performed. In her view, this jazz-centred narrative of Azerbaijan is evidence of music being a tool of promoting at the governmental level modern Azerbaijani culture, which has developed under the influence of Islamic and European cultures, Iranian and Turkic heritage as well as Russian influences. At the same time, the meaning of jazz is contested at the everyday level. The chapter locates the role of jazz in the Azerbaijani political environment and an overview of music festivals, events in Baku and other Azerbaijani cities. Strzemżalska explores why jazz has come to represent Azerbaijan, how it has been appropriated and produced, and how memory and tradition have taken on particular significance in different historical periods.

The following chapter by Emilia Pawłusz explores how rock musicians become agents of perpetuating ideas of nationhood. In contrast to traditional scholarship on music and nationalism, which focused either on folk music or classical composers as particularly tied to the notion of national culture, this chapter investigates popular music as a platform for negotiating narratives of collective belonging. The focus on the agency of popular musicians draws attention to the questions of 'who' builds the nation and 'how' (instead of the classic 'what' the nation is). The study shows that elite (top-down) and informal (bottom-up) nation-building actors are not clear-cut, exclusive categories. A group of ordinary citizens who form a successful and popular band which takes national identity, ethnicity and heritage as its main inspiration and context of their music can become important actors of nation building that affect how people, especially youth, relate to the nation. The argument is illustrated with a case study of Metsatöll, an Estonian band commonly referred as a folk metal group, which combines classic heavy metal music with folk songs and traditional Estonian instruments. Based on ethnographic observations of the band's performances, analysis of the songs' lyrics and iconography, as well as communication with one of the musicians/songwriters in the band, the chapter explores how various narratives of national belonging traverse the musical work of Metsatöll and situates them within the context of nation building in Estonia and the post-Soviet space (Vetik 2012).

The section concludes with a chapter on identity construction through national museums. In her study of the *Georgian National Museum and the Museum of Soviet occupation*, Alisa Danutashvili looks at the construction of national museums in post-Soviet Georgia as embedded in an official discourse of the Georgian political elites with regards to identity formation in the country. In her ethnography of the museum she looks at the way the Georgian National Museum contributes to the construction of a narrative on Georgian national identity. Created in 2004, the Georgian National Museum has a symbolic significance since its constituency was largely Georgia's 'Rose Revolution' and the anti-Russian discourses generated. In this respect, the museum has provoked two opposing positions. On the one hand, it has been built as a place to demonstrate Georgia's modernity and rupture with the past. On the other hand, this has been perceived as a challenge, or even threat, to Georgian traditional values and 'Georgianness'.

The second part of the book examines modes and patterns of consumption in the redefinition of identity in post-socialist settings. Consumption lies at the intersection of economic and social phenomena. On the one hand, it is a way to endorse, or not, market forces. Purchase of certain goods is a feedback mechanism to companies and economic actors. On the other hand, symbolic consumption can be seen as a proxy of acceptance, or rejection, of identity markers proposed from the elite of a state.

In her chapter, Tetiana Bulakh, explores how ideological transformations are translated into tangible consumer practices through the concept of consumer citizenship in contemporary Ukraine. The study interrogates the manifestation of state and national belonging through consumer choices, namely, the boycott of Russian products, renegotiation of national symbols in commodities, and consumer nationalism or patriotic consumption, which aims to rediscover and support local Ukrainian producers. By doing this, she argues that a new interpretation of citizenship is shaped among middle-class Ukrainians. It combines Ukrainian exceptionalism with a so-called identity of newly emerged 'European Ukrainians'.

The following chapter explores the role of national food consumption in a space that can be symbolically located between post-socialist spaces and the West. In her account of consumer practices in the UK, Anna Pechurina looks at the connection between national food and food consumption practices to the sense of national belonging and identity. In particular, she examines a number of unique food provision strategies that are recognized and sometimes reconstructed by migrants from post-socialist countries and discuss how

10 *Introduction*

the attachments to familiar and national food are articulated by migrants and migrant communities in a new to them cultural context. Using the concept of foodways (Caldwell 2009, Petridou 2001, Rabikowska and Burrell 2009) her study looks at several types of migrants' food cultures including practices related to everyday food consumption, such as buying, cooking and sharing traditional meals as well as performances and media discourses of post-Soviet and Russian food that redefine it in diasporic terms as a so-called 'ethnic' branded cuisine, and discusses the complex relationships between everyday lives, relationships, culture and identity.

The section ends with a chapter by Oleksandra Seliverstova exploring the nexus between consumer citizenship and the reproduction of Estonianness within the context of the problem of newly emerging multi-ethnic societies that potentially undermine the consolidation of rediscovered nations returning to Europe (in this case a form of Nordic Europeanness). Estonia has seen no major conflict but tensions between the main ethnic group and Russians have been widely documented (Vetik 2012). She explores the contrasting views of Estonianness present in Estonia. On the one hand, there is a tendency to ethnicize the country and suggest that being an Estonian is equated to being ethnically Estonian, thus excluding a large community of Russians and other ethnicities there. On the other hand, she goes beyond this narrative by using the lens of everyday life practices to contend that in a number of (undocumented) cases, often invisible to most approaches on identity studies, Russian speakers have a more active role than is usually argued in the construction of Estonian nationhood. Her case, like the other chapters in this section, focuses on the process of national identity formation to suggest that nation building is not an exclusively state-driven process, but one to which different non-state actors contribute.

National discourses and everyday life politics

The final section of the book examines the interaction of language politics, bordering and othering, and the visible-invisible markers that vernacular, lingua franca, spellings and the geographical definition of national spaces represent for imagined nations.

The first study, by Anastasiya Astapova, looks at naming as a locus for perfomance of national identity. Her chapter focuses on current arguments regarding naming Belarus, forming further derivatives from the name, and the right ways of spelling and pronouncing them in different languages. Different variants of the country's name as well as slight differences in the forms' pronunciation become the matter of frequent vernacular discussion, while in the official arena the question remains untouched. This tendency corresponds to the clash between civil nationalism proposed by official Belarus and formed by the consent of the majority and ethnic nationalism, remaining the alternative and rather marginalized choice of the minority. The latter oppose the official discourse, searching for the unique ethnicity-related representation for their country, including self-naming; the further the Belarusian name is from 'Russian' the more authentic it seems to them. They try to separate everything related to the young nation from its Russian colonial past, as 'Belarusian' currently seems too similar to 'Russian' to be independent. Meanwhile, the official discourse avoids these arguments not to undermine its ties with Russia – essentially due to the economic dependence on 'the elder brother'. The choices between ethnic and civic nationalism and, correspondingly, the importance of naming points to a clear social split in Belarus, the country often called 'a denationalized nation' due to the assumed low ethnic self-conscience of the majority of its population. Based on interviews and observation, this chapter examines the problems and ideologies behind the politics of naming in Belarus compared to other post-colonial countries where naming becomes crucial too.

The second chapter by Julien Danero Iglesias explores identities of borderplaces. He looks at the changes brought about by EU enlargements of 2004 and 2007. He calls on the process of 'rebordering' and a number of new obstacles to travel to EU countries to look at the discourse of 'ordinary citizens' and provides an account of how national identity can be approached through a bottom-up perspective. On the basis of a theoretical framework influenced by Rogers Brubaker's 'triadic nexus' (1996) he shows how commitment to Romanian identity can be understood as an instrumental attachment to the extent that Romanian citizenship allows the benefits of EU citizenship and the ability to cross the border. However, the chapter goes further than this simple rational explanation to show the emergence of multicultural, multiple and multi-layered identities. Indeed, in a second section, the chapter shows how identity constructions are deeply influenced by how Romanians in Serbia and Ukraine compare with Romanians on the other side of the border and with the majority of the country in which they live. As a result, the border can be considered one of the main everyday identity markers in their discourse. Indeed, ordinary Romanians constantly put forward an 'us' by comparing it with an 'other' that influences the construction of a 'nuanced' Romanian national identity that is dependent on the border and the everyday context of their lives.

In what he calls a 'belated' ethnography of the 2004 Orange Revolution in Ukraine, Abel Polese focusses on phenomena that have gone unnoticed, underreported or ignored, in a continuation of the critical approach suggested by Hobsbawm and Rude (1968) and recently applied to the study of the informal or the 'invisible' (Knott 2015, Pawlusz and Seliverstova 2016, Pawlusz and Polese 2017, Polese 2016). The chapter sees the 2004 events as a crucial moment of identity construction in post-independence Ukraine. It proposes it as a moment of consciousness of being Ukrainian and an historical moment in the creation, identification or invention of identity markers. In a fashion that has been used by other scholars (Bilaniuk 2005, Crescente 2007), Polese focuses on the everyday to illustrate how Ukrainians started living their everyday identity in a different way and construct or identify markers

12 *Introduction*

that were not used before. These markers then spread out from ordinary people to the society at large and were tacitly accepted, or even endorsed, by the elites through public narratives or simply behaviours that confirm the importance of these markers to Ukrainian identity. In turn the chapter explores everyday language politics, civic engagement, and the othering of Russia.

Notes

1 For boycott coverage see: http://korrespondent.net/ukraine/politics/3363518-bolee-polovyny-ukrayntsev podderzhyvauit-boikot-rossyiskykh-tovarov-opros
2 A worldwide market research group, present also in Ukraine. For further details see www.tns-ua.com/ua/
3 What constitutes a significant portion of the population has been discussed by Walker Connor in his question, 'When is a nation?' There is no way to call a 'finished nation' an entity where 70, 80, 90 percent of the people adopt a certain national identity since this is a constantly ongoing process that will probably never get to 100 percent. By the same token, we believe there is no possibility to quantify how many people we need to accept an identity marker before this is accepted as a national identity marker.

References

Antonsich, M. 2015. The 'everyday' of banal nationalism – Ordinary people's views on Italy and Italian. *Political Geography,* 54, 32–42, doi:10.1016/j.polgeo.2015.07.006
Bassin, M., Kelly, C. eds. 2012. *Soviet and post-Soviet identities.* Cambridge: Cambridge University Press.
Bilaniuk, L., 2005. *Contested tongues: Language politics and cultural correction in Ukraine.* Ithaca and London: Cornell University Press.
Billig, M. 1995. *Banal nationalism.* London: Sage.
Brubaker, R. 1996. *Nationalism reframed: Nationhood and the national question in the new Europe.* Cambridge: Cambridge University Press.
Brubaker, R., Feischmidt, M., Fox, J., Grancea, L. 2006. *Nationalist politics and everyday ethnicity in a Transylvanian town.* Princeton, NJ: Princeton University Press.
Caldwell, M. 2009. *Food and everyday life in the postsocialist world.* Bloomington, IN: Indiana University Press.
Cohen, L. 2003. *A consumer's republic: the politics of mass consumption in postwar America.* New York: Vintage Books.
Crescente, J. 2007. Performing Post-Sovietness: Verka Serduchka and the hybridization of identity in Post-Soviet Ukraine. Conference paper presented at the Soyuz Symposium, 25–28 April 2007.
Douglas, M. 1996. *Thought styles: critical essays on good taste.* Thousand Oaks, CA: Sage.
Edensor, T. 2002. *National identity, popular culture and everyday life.* Oxford: Berg Publishers.
Edensor, T. H. 2006. Reconsidering national temporalities: Institutional times, everyday routines, serial spaces and synchronicities. *European Journal of Social Theory* 9, 525–545.
Eriksen, T. H. 1993. Formal and informal nationalism. *Ethnic and Racial Studies* 16(1), 1–25.
Fox, J. E. 2016. The edges of the nation: a research agenda for uncovering the taken-for-granted foundations of everyday nationhood. *Nations and Nationalism* 23(1), 26–47. doi:10.1111/nana.12269

Introduction 13

Fox, J. E., Miller-Idriss, C. 2008. Everyday nationhood. *Ethnicities* 8(4), 536–563.
Foster, R. J. 2002. *Materializing the nation: Commodities, consumption, and media in Papua New Guinea.* Bloomington, IN: Indiana University Press.
Foster, R. J., Özcan, D. 2005. Consumer citizenship, nationalism, and neoliberal globalization in Turkey: The advertising launch of Cola Turka. *Advertising and Society Review* 6(3).
Giddens, A. 1984. *The constitution of society: Outline of the theory of structuration.* Cambridge: Polity Press
Goode, J. P., Stroup, D. R. 2015. Everyday nationalism: Constructivism for the Masses. *Social Science Quarterly* 96(3), 717–739.
Hobsbawm, E., Rudé, G. 1969. *Captain swing: A social history of the great agrarian uprising of 1930.* London: Lawrence and Wishart.
Isaacs, R., Polese, A. 2015. Between 'imagined' and 'real' nation building: Identities and nationhood in post-Soviet Central Asia. *Nationalities Papers* 43(3), 371–382.
Isaacs, R., Polese, A. 2016. *Nation building in the former USSR: New tools and approaches.* London: Routledge.
Janmaat, J. G. 2000. *Nation-building in post-Soviet Ukraine: Educational policy and the response of the Russian-speaking population.* KNAG.
Jones, R., Merriman, P. 2009. Hot, banal and everyday nationalism: Bilingual road signs in Wales. *Political Geography* 28(3), 164–173.
Knott, E. 2015. What does it mean to be a kin majority? Analyzing Romanian identity in Moldova and Russian identity in Crimea from below. *Social Science Quarterly* 96(3), 830–859.
Kulyk V. 2014. Ukrainian nationalism since the outbreak of EuroMaidan. *Nova-Istra* 3 (4), 94–122.
Militz, E., 2016. Public events and nation-building in Azerbaijan, in *Nation-building and identity in the post-Soviet space: New tools and approaches*, edited by R. Isaacs and A. Polese. London: Routledge.
Pawłusz, E., Polese. A. 2017. "Scandinavia's best-kept secret." Tourism promotion, nation-branding, and identity construction in Estonia (with a free guided tour of Tallinn Airport). Nationalities Papers, 1–20. doi: 10.1080/00905992.2017.1287167
Pawłusz, E., Seliverstova, O. 2016. Everyday nation-building in the post-Soviet space. Methodological reflections. *Studies of Transition States and Societies* 8(1), 69–86.
Petridou, E. 2001. The taste of home, in *Home possession: Material culture behind closed doors*, edited by D. Miller. Oxford: Berg, 87–107.
Polese, A. 2009a. Une version alternative de la «révolution orange»: transformations identitaires et 'nation building spontané'. *Socio-logos* 4. Available online at http://socio-logos.revues.org/2315 [accessed 10 August 2016].
Polese, A. 2009b. Dynamiques de nation building et évolution d'une identité nationale en Ukraine: le cas d'Odessa. PhD Thesis, Universite libre de Bruxelles.
Polese, A. 2010. The formal and the informal: Exploring 'Ukrainian' education in Ukraine, scenes from Odessa. *Comparative Education* 46(1) 45–62.
Polese, A. 2014. Between 'official' and 'unofficial' temperatures: Introducing a complication to the hot and cold ethnicity theory from Odessa. *Journal of Multilingual and Multicultural Development* 35(1), 59–75.
Polese, A. 2016. *Limits of a state: How informality replaces, renegotiates and reshapes governance in post-Soviet spaces.* Stuttgart: Ibidem.
Polese, A., Horak, S. 2015. A tale of two presidents: Personality cult and symbolic nation-building in Turkmenistan. *Nationalities Papers* 43(3) 457–478.
Rabikowska, M., Burrell, K. 2009. The material worlds of recent Polish migrants: Transnationalism, food, shops, and home, in *Polish migration to the UK in the 'new' European Union after 2004*, edited by K. Burrell. Aldershot: Ashgate, 211–232.
Richardson, T. 2008. *Kaleidoscopic Odessa: History and place in contemporary Ukraine.* Toronto: University of Toronto Press.

14 *Introduction*

Rodgers, P. W. 2007. 'Compliance or contradiction'? Teaching 'history' in the 'new' Ukraine. A view from Ukraine's eastern borderlands. *Europe-Asia Studies* 59(3), 503-519.

Scott, J. C. 1984. *Weapons of the weak: Everyday forms of peasant resistance*. New Haven , CT: Yale University Press.

Scott, J. C. 2012. *Two cheers for anarchism: Six easy pieces on autonomy, dignity, and meaningful work and play*. Princeton, NJ: Princeton University Press.

Seliverstova, O. 2017. Consuming' national identity in western Ukraine. *Nationalities Papers* 45(1), 61–79.

Skey, M., 2009. The national in everyday life: A critical engagement with Michael Billig's thesis of Banal Nationalism. *The Sociological Review* 57(2), 331-346.

Skey, M. 2011. *National belonging and everyday life*. Basingstoke: Palgrave.

Skey, M. 2015. 'Mindless markers of the nation': The routine flagging of nationhood across the visual environment. *Sociology*. DOI:10.1177/0038038515590754

Thompson, A. 2001. Nations, national identities and human agency: Putting people back into nations. *The Sociological Review* 49(1), 18-32.

Vershitskaya, Y. 2014. Boykot made in Russia: patriotizm v denezhnom izmerenii. UNIAN, 1 August. Available online at Available online at www.unian.net/politics/946421-boykot-made-in-russia-patriotizm-v-denejnom-izmerenii.html [accessed 30 January 2016].

Vetik, R. ed. 2012. *Nation-building in the context of post-communist transformation and globalization: The case of Estonia*. Frankfurt am Main, Berlin, Bern, Bruxelles, New York, Oxford, Wien: Peter Lang.

Part I
Music and cultural events

1 Formal and informal nationalism
Jazz performances in Azerbaijan

Aneta Strzemżalska

Azerbaijani jazz[1] is a phenomenon that possesses an undeniably political meaning. The genre took root as a result of teleological official policy of the Soviet Union, and over time, it took hold in local Azerbaijani culture, as people began to combine it with folk melodies and play *mugham* harmonies.[2] Jazz performances and festivals, which are organized and/or supported by the Azerbaijani government, usually take place at the highest level: the creative accomplishments of local jazz musicians, who are often internationally competitive, are recognized by music critics. At the same time, despite the fact that many cafes and restaurants offer 'jazz', it is almost impossible to hear this trend in music in the nation's capital, where instead of jazz, one simply hears pop songs played in jazz arrangements.

Taking into account discursive construction of 'Azerbaijani jazz', there are two types of jazz prevalent in the cultural space of Azerbaijan. One is classical government-supported jazz, similar to Western jazz but with a local *mugham* flavour. The other is a stylization of jazz, in which jazz is reminiscent of pop songs, played in the trendy restaurants of Baku with the use of jazz harmonies. From the beginning, Azerbaijani jazz was created and popularized by official authority, and was and is included in the national ideology of the independent republic. This fact, along with the differentiation of Azerbaijani jazz, prompts a discussion on the interconnection between government and citizens, and the penetration of daily life into national ideology.

Following Billig's (2005) idea of 'banal nationalism' – a conceptual model of national identity, which refers to the methods by which the idea of a particular nation is constructed and perpetuated, both in society as a whole and in the minds of individual citizens, in this chapter, I raise the question of the interrelationship between official cultural politics and everyday practices. Taking into account the specific contradiction between political establishment and the perception of jazz as a 'form of oppositional art', I describe the process of the nationalization of this musical genre, and discuss how jazz performances fit into Azerbaijani national ideology. Moreover, I analyze how Azerbaijani jazz is interpreted and used by average city dwellers to meet personal goals, including strengthening their social or economic position. In this way, I touch upon the subject of the interrelation between quasi-jazz performances and national ideology.

18 *Aneta Strzemżalska*

The material used in this chapter is the result of my fieldwork, which took place in Baku and its surrounding territories from July 2015 to April 2016 (a total of three months). My main research methods include participant observation of jazz practices, as well as interviews with representatives of the jazz community in the capital of Azerbaijan, including jazz performers and audiences, scholars, publicists, employees of concert halls and cafes where musicians perform, and the employees of governmental institutions that are responsible for the cultural development of the country.

Research starting point

A number of studies on the topic of nationalism, even those which examine the emotional and quasi-religious aspects of nationalism (Anderson 1983, Smith 1986, Kapferer 1988), prefer to write off formal practices and symbols without considering how they are perceived by citizens. This approach does not contradict, but rather adds to a more common view on the processes by which modern states are formed: that nationalist ideologies are above all constructed to fulfil the requirements of the bureaucratic institution of government (Gellner 1983, Giddens 1985). While the political elite play the main role in constructing national identity and without leaders this process cannot take place, there is no single ideology that can successfully build a modern nation if it is not approved of and/or adopted by a large group of citizens.

Moreover, the idea that official ideology is in conflict with the convictions of common people and their daily actions is popular. This approach, the opposition of citizen (informal) practices with State ones, was implemented by Thomas Eriksen in his article titled 'Formal and Informal Nationalism' (Eriksen 1993). Eriksen defines two types of nationalism, formal and informal, using a dualistic model of the perception of reality, and citing results of comparative research in the Republic of Trinidad and Tobago, and the Republic of Mauritius. The first type of nationalism is characterized by its cultural homogeny and the political consensus of its citizens. It fulfils the requirements of a modern national government and is realized as a bureaucratic apparatus headed by the political elite. Informal nationalism, on the other hand, is realized in collective events, such as ritual ceremonies, international sporting events, musical performances and organized civil society.

The bipolarity of the social and political space, the official system versus the citizens, is at the foundation of the majority of research on the topic of nation building. Among these works are those dedicated to the study of separatist movements, diasporas, and ethnic groups. These works echo Fredrik Barth (1969), arguing that national identity is formed in clashes with 'others', and that nationalistic ideologies form as a reaction to a specific official policy. As shown in many works, this discussion undoubtedly explains some processes. However, it does not take into account situations where the opposition of official (governmental) and unofficial (civilian) ideologies and practices do not have a place, where citizens do not stand against the system, but rather use it to accomplish their own goals.

Formal and informal nationalism 19

Both anthropologists and political scientists have raised the issue of the interaction and permeation between and official and unofficial nationalisms on the post-Soviet territory. Often, new post-Soviet republics are viewed as a *bricolage*, simultaneously built on formal governmental structures inherited from the socialist system, and informal institutions (Grzymala-Busse and Jones Luong 2002, Kaliszewska and Voell 2015). The pluralism of institutions of power leads to the combination of the centre of social and political research from formal structures to civilian ones. Some scholars cast doubt on the concept of government as a set of well-defined institutions and individuals, who keep control over a defined territory and act together as a united political subject with clear boundaries between government and society (Grzymala-Busse and Jones Luong 2002). This has led a growing number of scholars to chase the concept of a defined division between government and society (Collins 2004, Dubuisson 2013).

The saturation of the daily life of people and the actions of governmental structures is characteristic for any modern society, and especially for those countries in which a strict authoritarian regime rules (Brubaker 1996, Horák 2005). Therefore, it would be inaccurate to think that the actions of the political elite and regular citizens do not intersect. Even a person who could never live in a different societal or political situation, much less learn about one, and who does not explicitly accept ideological practices or messages, still exists in the realm of the political. Political ideology shapes the lives of all citizens in order to overlap nation and state boundaries (Polese and Horák 2015: 458). They are forced to (and even strive to) come to terms with political ideology, if they want to find their place in society, start a family and develop professionally (Fox and Miller-Idriss 2008). Therefore, the connection between government and society must be considered, even in cases when, at first glance, its existence is not obvious. As in Eric Hobsbawm's later works, he shows that although nationality and nationalism are constructed from above, they 'cannot be understood unless also analyzed from below, that is in terms of the assumptions, hopes, needs, longings and interests of ordinary people, which are not necessarily national and still less nationalist' (Hobsbawm 1990: 10).

The rest of this chapter is divided into five sections. The next section is a brief history of the jazz development in Azerbaijan. Touching on the issue of top-down popularization of jazz in the USSR, it engages with the statement on teleological politicization of the musical phenomenon. The following two sections give some characteristics of free jazz movements in the first years of existence of independent Azerbaijan, and elaborate on how the musical tendency came under the control of formal institutions. The last two parts concentrate on jazz performances as seemingly free from national ideology, and explain why the phenomenon plays such a crucial role in building national identity.

'Proletarian jazz': forerunners of Azerbaijani jazz

Azerbaijani jazz was popularized in Baku in the 1920s, when Azerbaijan was still a part of the USSR. The October Revolution was the beginning of

20 *Aneta Strzemżalska*

turbulent cultural, social and political changes, as well as a short period of possible contacts and interactions between the Russian/Soviet and Western worlds of music. It is thanks to these connections that New Orleans melodies and rhythms made their way through its largest cities from the cultural centres of Europe during the last years of the Russian Empire.

Since New Orleans melodies and rhythms attracted mass attention from music listeners, Soviet power decided that instead of fighting jazz, it would use jazz to its own benefit. Therefore, 'proletarian jazz' was created in order to 'cheer up' millions of workers. It is to this end that in the middle of the 1930s dozens of state jazz orchestras (gov. jazz – in Russian *gosjazz*) were formed (Фейертаг 2014: 56). The first gov. jazz concert took place in November 1938 in the Bolshoi Theatre in Moscow featuring the State Jazz Orchestra of the USSR, under the leadership of Victor Knushevitskiy. Other orchestras formed at the same time in different corners of the empire, including the Armenia State Jazz Orchestra in the South Caucasus (directed by Artemi Ayvazyan), the Georgia State Jazz Orchestra (directed by Revaz Gabichvadze), and the Azerbaijan State Jazz Orchestra in 1938 directed by Tofig Guliyev (azer. Tofiq Quliyev, 1917–2000).

Tofig Guliyev developed professionally in Moscow: he graduated from the Moscow State Tchaikovsky Conservatory, and for several years worked with Alexander Tsfasman (1906–1971), the director of the first Soviet professional jazz collective – AMA-Jazz.[3] It was only after this that the administration of the Russian Association of Proletarian Musicians (RAPM),[4] the most prominent music management organization in the USSR, requested he transfer his Moscow experience to his home: by their order Guliyev, and the conductor Niyazi (azerb. Niyazi Tağızadə-Hacıbəyov, 1912–1984) organized many capable Baku musicians and founded the first gov. jazz in Azerbaijan. For the most part, young musicians, among whom were authentic jazz players, played dance and easy music, but rarely with a national flavour. Guliyev, who had a superb knowledge of his native folklore, for the first time in the history of Azerbaijani music tried to combine jazz with *mugham*. Baku music scholars describe how during his performances of American swing music, the composer asked one of his saxophonists to improvise in the harmony of *chargakh* (double harmonic major scale) (Бабаева and Фархадов 2010: 79).

The meaning of Guliyev and the role of other Azerbaijani 'jazz luminaries', including Rauf Hadjiev, (azerb. Rauf Hacıyev, 1922–1995) director of the Estrada Orchestra of Azerbaijan (founded in 1955), and Tofig Ahmedov (azerb. Tofiq Əhmədov, 1924–1981), conductor and director of the Estrada Orchestra of Radio and Television, were not straightforward, despite the merit of the musical national stage. The problem is that jazz in its wider sense, as a musical genre and lifestyle, was unlikely to exist in early Soviet Baku. One of the most talented young Azerbaijani composers speaks on this issue:

> Tofig Guliyev was a wonderful composer, a real favourite of the people. He had a superb sense of harmony and he simply used several jazz

techniques in his works. For example, he (Guliyev – AS) and **Niyazi** would give the saxophonist ten seconds to improvise. But it was so seamless that people didn't even notice it was improvisation: they thought it was part of the song. (T., m., 28 years old, composer)

Another composer in the work of *estrada* orchestras evaluates 'how a song element was written in gov. jazz:

> It's important to look at this from the perspective of arrangement, not improvisation. The arrangement is very rich, and this Azerbaijani music sounds as though it was done, let's say, by an American arranger. And everything sounds great, the harp, the violins, the saxophones. In those days there were fabulous arrangers, and even today we could really learn something from them. (S., m., 57 years old, composer)

In conclusion, the work of *estrada* orchestras can be understood as one of the successful 'state-ideological projects', rather than a full-fledged contribution to the genre of jazz. First of all, this is because in the large collectives that gained exclusive rights to exist in the 1930s, it was impossible to play spontaneously, and improvise freely. Moreover, 'jazz big bands', renamed *estrada* orchestras after the war, were made over to fit the 'aesthetic norms of musical socialist realism'. The predominance of a song and dance element over musical imagination gave way to big bands performing light music that did not require any intellectual engagement, and at the same time, did not allow musicians to develop, especially the jazz of whom went beyond the limits of the 'proletarian taste' (Бабаева and Фархадов 2010: 90–91) In spite of this, Guliyev, along with other directors of Baku orchestras, was able to infuse a national tone in symphonic and pop songs of the time. They brought together a large number of musicians, equally well-versed in both jazz and Azerbaijani traditions, which created fertile ground for the appearance of 'Azerbaijani jazz'. I will discuss the rise and the nature of this phenomenon in the next section.

Jazz in Baku in the early 21st century

Over the course of several years of tumultuous geopolitical changes, including the fall of the USSR and the Nagorno-Karabakh War, the cultural life of Baku as the capital of a newly independent state was restored at the same time that the political and economic situation in the country began to stabilize. The tipping point was the conclusion of the major oil 'Contract of the Century' in 1994. International hydrocarbon export companies signed the agreement, and as a result, multimillion-dollar foreign investments increased in the republic. The large earnings from 'black gold' extraction led to industrial progress in Azerbaijan. The country was filled with foreigners once more, but this time mainly from Western Europe, the United States and Turkey.

22 *Aneta Strzemżalska*

As a result of the large inflow of 'intellectually enthusiastic middle and upper management' during the second half of the 1990s, jazz clubs opened in large numbers in Baku.

> There was this belief that since foreigners were coming, it meant foreigners loved jazz. (...) That was when there weren't enough days in the week to work. The whole week was already booked, and we'd keep getting offers to perform, either play somewhere else, or somewhere another club just opened. We played a lot of places. They weren't called jazz clubs, but you could listen to jazz there. We worked at this place, White Club, that's where the funicular is, across from the Mugham Center. Then there was Room 103, a real posh place by the Maiden Tower, right under that beautiful building where the Tom Ford store is now. The late Emil Mammedov played there too (Ibragimov – AS). The clubs opened, and everybody wanted jazz. (M., m., 61 years old, musician)

The revival of jazz in Baku prompted the opening of the first, and for a long time, the only typical jazz club. The Caravan Jazz Club on Aziza Alieva Street, across from the Puppet Theatre, opened its doors on October 4, 1997. It was established by Muslim Eldarov (azerb. Muslim Eldarov, 1956–2003), who was one of the founding directors of the Association of Creative Youth of Azerbaijan sponsored by private businesses (today known as the 'Yeni Gallery' Baku Center of Art). Fans of improvisation remember the Caravan as a club 'with a liberated atmosphere of pure jazz', 'without any officialdom at the tables'. The jazz life of Baku concentrated around the Caravan because of the quality musical arrangement, relaxed and friendly atmosphere, and the circle of regular listeners.

> The place itself, it's the word energy, whether you like it or not, because the energy was there, and it was very underground. There was a bar where you could have a good cocktail or just sit down. There was this interesting life there. The musicians played magnificently and there were sessions. It was the only place of its kind in Baku. And then it was gone. They just wiped it out. It was replaced by a super expensive boutique where no one went. (F., f., 45 years old, publicist)

The Caravan Club was in operation for around ten years, until 2006, while gradually losing its significance at a time when other places were becoming more popular. Nuri Ahmedov (azerb. Nuri Əhmədov, b. 1942) was the director of 'AzEuroTel', and the director of the Baku Communications College, one of the best secondary schools in the country in the 1980s. He founded the Baku Jazz Center on Rashid Behbudov Street in 2004.

The businessman was interested in jazz since his teen years, listened to the works of Tofig Guliyev, Rauf Hadjiev, Vagif Mustafazadeh, Rafig Babayev and Vagif Sadykhov, and hung out with his friends on the central streets of Baku in trendy, bright clothes, like *stilyagi* wore. As a member of the Baku

Formal and informal nationalism 23

intelligentsia with a large amount of financial freedom, Ahmedov planned to create a place where young, talented, upcoming musicians, who had nowhere to realize their potential, could practice. Ahmedov rented a space in the building of the Academy of Music, in their opera studio, with the help of Farhad Badalbeyli (azerb. Fərhad Şəmsi oğlu Bədəlbəyli, b. 1947), the composer and rector of the Hajibeyov Baku Academy of Music (formerly known as the Azerbaijan State Conservatoire).

The main goal of the enterprise was to unify and revive the Baku jazz community and support young performers. To this end, a musical program was realized at the Jazz Centre: it hosted paid concerts and international collectives. The club also became a place to practice for all those who needed it.

> It was the only place where we could come and no one would tell us we were using the lighting and the facilities. In this sense it was really convenient and hospitable to musicians. (R., m., 34 years old, musician, remarking on the Jazz Centre's programs)

Moreover, the Centre included a recording studio, published *Jazz Dunyasi*, the first jazz journal in Azerbaijan, and created a website that shared information on all of the events happening in the Azerbaijani jazz world. In addition, Ahmedov was a patron to many musicians: he sponsored professional album recordings in international studios, and he paid for tours, and the publication of many books and albums. Thanks to Ahmedov's support, the Jazz Centre became the central hub of jazz in the 2000s and its golden age took place in the years 2005, 2006 and 2007, when under its auspices the Baku International Jazz Festival was organized.

Jazz festivals: the nationalization of jazz

Baku international jazz festivals have been taking place since 2002. In the beginning, they were called the Caspian Jazz and Blues Festival and were held by American Voices, an organization that existed as part of the American Consulate in Baku. According to my informants, local members of the jazz community were not very pleased that international organizers were dominating their cultural space, 'underestimating the rich Azerbaijani experience with improvisation'. As a result of several confrontations with members of American Voices, Nuri Ahmedov and the Jazz Centre, with the support of the Ministry of Culture and Tourism, took responsibility for holding yearly 'jazz days'.

The Baku International Jazz Festival (azerb. Bakı Beynəlxalq caz festivalı) was very successful both musically and organizationally from the first year of its existence. Many world-famous and magnificent jazz players participated (including Joe Zawinul, Al Jarreau, Herbert Jeffrey Hancock, Billy Cobham and Deborah J. Carter) along with a whole lineup of local jazz stars, like Aziza Mustafazadeh, daughter of the popular Vagif Mustafazadeh.

24 *Aneta Strzemżalska*

Evening concerts were accompanied by jam sessions and master classes, filling Baku with a rich jazz culture:

> So, this festival in 2005 immediately advertised itself as a real jazz festival. Until then the American consulate held the festivals, but that was, you know, mediocre. The community wasn't happy. It was only in 2005 that it got interesting, 2006 and 2007 too. Those festivals weren't just a series of concerts like they've become now. It was real jazz culture, some kind of demonstrations, print production, master classes during the day, evening concerts, and at night, sessions. Constant socializing between our musicians and foreign ones, playing together. I remember we didn't even have time to sleep. I would get home really late, around 5 in the morning. Something like that. Took a shower. Slept a bit. Sometimes I wouldn't even have time to sleep. Emotions, I didn't feel like it. And then again, we'd film from 10–11 AM, talk. The city was in full swing, the concerts were in the very centre of the city (in Fountains Square – AS), people sat on benches, on the sidewalks. It was something, a real. (A., m., c.50 years old, journalist who worked at a leading radio station in the 2000s)

Informal jazz festivals took place in Baku until 2007, then 'they closed up shop'. The Ministry of Culture and Tourism (MCT), one of the sponsors of the event, accused Nuri Ahmedow of fraud. After his defamation, jazz festivals lost their informal status, and MCT became the main organizer in cooperation with the Heydar Aliyev Fund in collaboration with the first lady Mehriban Aliyeva (azerb. Mehriban Əliyeva, b. 1964). After that, the character of the jazz culture of Baku gradually changed. Firstly, this was because the number of venues where professional performers could practice was significantly reduced. The Jazz Centre lost its significance and its ability to support itself, which led it to close in summer 2015. Yet other jazz clubs did not open in its place. Secondly, local jazz players' professional performances stopped being profitable due to a general decline in interest in such a complex art. In order to survive, they began to require support from the government. Because of this, professional improvisation practices became dependent on official structures and were limited to several concerts as part of the above-mentioned Baku International Jazz Festival.

Due to the support of official structures, jazz in Azerbaijan is primarily developing on the path of 'Azerbaijani jazz'. 'Jazz-*mugham*', which is a 'fusion of *mugham* lyrics and jazz dynamics, a synthesis of traditional *mugham* melodies and modality with a variety of jazz harmonies and rhythms' (Бабаева and Фархадов 2010: 63), has caused intellectual controversy in the Baku jazz community. Many members of the jazz community consider it a 'made-up idea' and 'the subject of speculation and profanity'. They believe there is an absence of a single world jazz-*mugham* standard. Despite the fact that the majority of local music historians deny 'jazz-*mugham*' as an independent style

Formal and informal nationalism 25

of music, local authorities actively use the term to create Azerbaijani cultural propaganda and sponsor new projects in this vein.

Thanks to financial sponsorship, a new community of professional jazz players, mainly from the pianistic school, is forming. They are creating works with new stylistic features and successfully representing their country, mostly in international venues, and rarely for the local public. On the other hand, many cafes and restaurants have been appearing in the capital, where commercial jazz, similar to pop, is played, and is seemingly free from governmental financial support, as well as from national ideology. This will be discussed in the next section.

Jazz pop

Rumours of a new jazz club had been circulating in Baku for some time. Some hinted that it would open on the Western side of the bank, not far from Yarat.[5] Others had suggested that the club should open close to the Baku Academy of Music, since jazz enthusiasts are used to listening to their favourite performances in that part of the city. I also heard more sceptical opinions, most often from those who were deeply involved in the jazz scene. They argued that 'there won't be anything (there will be no club – AS), since there is no one in Baku to listen to real jazz' (A., m., 49 years old, journalist), and that 'there is no audience who would understand complicated improvised moves' (R., m., 51 years old, musician). There were conflicting opinions, but at last, a club opened.

The owners and joint managers of the new establishment are Rauf Aleskerov, who was the main manager of the former Jazz Centre starting in 2011, and Camilla Ahmedova, the niece of Nuri Ahmedov, the founder of the Jazz Centre. They openly emphasized the connection between the two clubs, and considered the Jazz Club (written specifically in English) to be the successor of the Jazz Centre. For the new project, they chose a restaurant in the prestigious five-star Sapphire Hotel in the very heart of the city, only a few steps away from the main avenue – Nizami Street. A decently stocked bar occupied the centre of the medium-sized venue. A stage was behind it. A trumpet player and double bass player were depicted on a small podium. The space designated for musicians was quite modest, and instead of a grand piano, there was a smaller electric piano. Small portraits of famous performers on the walls were supposed to be reminiscent of the jazz spirit of the venue, along with a corresponding menu that disguised tasty cocktails and European cuisine with 'jazzy names' like Blue Moon.

In spite of its several jazzy attributes, Jazz Club was in no way reminiscent of a cosy place where people could come to simply listen to improvisation and enjoy elegant music. Neither the walls, covered with gold wallpaper, nor the glowing chandeliers, nor the big round tables with elegant tablecloths and beautiful modern dishware, come close to the usual jazz atmosphere. However, the repertoire in many ways was analogous to the interior, which became clear as soon as the club opened.

26 *Aneta Strzemżalska*

The new club's grand opening ceremony was planned for the middle of November 2015,[6] and officially continued for two days (unofficially, four days). The most spectacular of them was the first day, Saturday. Entrance was by invitation only, and the organizers called each guest to invite them personally. The guests included high-ranking officials from ministries and other governmental organizations, directors of large firms, reporters, doctors, engineers and, of course, the artists themselves.

The musical arrangement of the grand opening ceremony was different each day. On Saturday, the program primarily featured local pop culture stars, with the exception of performances by famous local jazz musicians like Emil Afrasiyab (azerb. Emil Əfrasiyab, b. 1982) and Isfar Sarabski (azerb. İsfar Rzayev-Sarabski, b. 1989), the work of whom is supported by official structures.

The star of the evening was the young band Orient Xpress. This group's music is different from that of many other famous groups in that it cannot be called pop. A characteristic feature of Orient Xpress performances is a mix of musical genres including rock, free jazz, fusion, electronica and ethno-music. The group's leader, Anar Yusufov (azerb. Anar Yusufov, b. 1988), vocalist and keyboardist, spent several winter Fridays in a row successfully entertaining Jazz Club guests. He confesses that 'as a freelance composer, I've completely stopped categorizing music by style, since I've understood that different genres are different palettes that can be used to express an idea' (A.K., m., 28 years old, musician).

Along with the two groups mentioned above, other young pop singers demonstrated their vocal talents at the grand-opening ceremony. They included Sabina Babayeva (azerb. Səbinə Babayeva), who took first place in Euro Vision 2012, Rilaya (azerb. Rilaya, birthname azerb. Valeriya Huseynzade), Tofig Hasansoy (azerb. Tofiq Hasansoy), Emil Aliyev (азерб. Əmil Əliyev) and Farid Askerov (azerb. Fərid Əskerov). The latter two, Emil Aliyev and Farid Askerov, soon became the main component of the Jazz Club's program: their performances entertained guests of the establishment every weekend and sometimes even on weekdays. Although both artists regularly made appearances on the stage of the Jazz Club, neither of them claims to be jazz vocalists as such. In an interview with a local channel, Emil openly admitted that he 'doesn't do jazz' and performs 'beautiful pop-music', mainly at weddings, which is his main source of income (Mamedova 2016).

Emil's situation is not an exception: performances at events like weddings, birthdays, and parties pay well, in contrast to performances in cafes and clubs. It is not rare that a popular musician might work several parties in one night. On the other hand, although performances in the Jazz Club are not that different from those at weddings, they pay far less money, but are considered more prestigious. Therefore, they strengthen a musician's place on the local market, discussed later in this section.

The second day of the grand-opening ceremony was different from the first in every way: the ambience and the cultural program left no doubt about the fact that we are in a jazz club. On the second day, mostly professional jazz musicians performed, including Salman Gambarov (azerb. Qəmbərov Salman, b. 1959), Jamil Amirov (azerb. Cəmil Əmirov, b. 1957), Elchin Shirinov (azerb. Elçin Şirinov, b. 1982) and the above-mentioned Emil Afrasiyab. In comparison with the first day of the opening, it seemed that there were fewer official guests present, such as representatives of various government establishments, organizations, and large companies. However, there were more jazz enthusiasts, including quite a few friends of the musicians themselves. Because of this, it seemed that the guests were not as interested in the possibility of 'making an appearance', and 'being in the right place', as they were in the artistic side of the event and simple conversation. A significant number of the visitors preferred to stand by the bar, socialize and even dance, rather than sit at the ceremonial round table as is custom at such events. The atmosphere was more free and relaxed than it was on Saturday.

The division of the Jazz Club program into evenings featuring either professional jazz musicians or popular music was noticeable from the moment the club opened. It was not accidental and was the foundation of the artistic concept of the establishment. The organizers planned that on weekdays, when there are fewer guests, there would be jazz performances, and on the weekends there would be 'lighter, entertaining' music. Rufat, a director of the club, explains that there is not enough interest in ambitious music, the governmental institutions do not support them, so they cannot afford organizing 'real jazz performances everyday (R., m., 41 years old, club director).

Despite the fact that the Jazz Club managers considered themselves improvisation enthusiasts and patrons, their establishment became a venue for the popularization of music of different genres, and jazz was no longer a priority. Starting on Friday (sometimes even Thursday) through Sunday, the place seemed like a typical trendy restaurant, where a middle-aged member of the Azerbaijani middle class could go mainly to dine and socialize; the music was only a backdrop for a pleasant meal with family or friends. During the first few days of the club's existence, the cultural program that the general director had promised to jazz fans quickly became unrealistic: jazz performances were rare, because they were not in high demand nor were they lucrative. And although the Jazz Club occasionally organized decidedly jazz events, like, for example, an evening in memory of Emil Mammedov,[7] when local performers reminisced about the art of their close friend and gifted musician between sets, many of my informants complained that the club did not become 'a real jazz place'.

The social status of jazz

Many representatives of Baku's wide artistic circles alluded to the superiority of jazz over other styles of popular music, putting it at the level of classical music. As a result, the jazz community emphasizes the necessity of obtaining formal instruction on composition at a jazz department of a university, and perfecting

28   *Aneta Strzemżalska*

one's technique. It was also considered important to possess deep knowledge and a rich life experience, since only they could guarantee an understanding of music that would allow for improvisation and participation in jazz-sessions.

> In order to find a 'common language' with new musicians during jams, you need to meet world musical standards, in order to recognize works from the very first note, and be fluent in different styles and manners of jazz. In this sense, real jazz is undeniably intellectual and refined. (S., m., 60 years old, music critic explaining the essence of the genre)

Jazz was characterized as an 'intellectual' genre of music, and jazz musicians as 'intellectuals'. The high social status of improvisation was pointed out in almost every discussion I had on the cultural life of the city. Inviting jazz pianists to art show openings and the birthdays of high-ranking people was considered to be in good taste. The Yarat Contemporary Art Space, mentioned at the beginning of this section, occasionally organizes jazz concerts with American musicians, and seminars about the historical development of the genre and its stylistic features. Elementary instruction in jazz is also a part of a minor program at the prestigious Baku University. Not only does the Azerbaijan Diplomatic Academy (ADA University) (azerb. ADA Universiteti) hold classes on the major musical genres, it hosts jazz evenings (like, for example, the Evening in Memory of Vagif Mustafazadeh) and concerts.

> ADA University invited me to an event once [said Rilaya, a singer]. There were about a thousand students, the rector, and all of the teachers there. It was the beginning of the school year. And the rector wanted us (Rilaya and her group the Fusion Band – AS) to play jazz and what not. I noticed that they - the kids were bored. So see the difference, adults want jazz, more serious music, and young people aren't interested. And when I started playing Rihanna, 'Please, Don't Stop the Music', they started dancing. And the rector was glad they liked it, and were actually having fun. The rector really loves jazz. He even gave me an exam. When we first met, he asked me what kind of jazz I love, and what jazz I would sing. I was kind of nervous, but I named a couple of jazz performers who I love and whose songs I sing. That was for young people, but in general I have a more adult following. (R., f., 27 years old, musician)

Attempts to interest youth in 'high culture' and deepen their knowledge of jazz led to a superficial understanding of the genre. It did not so much fit the taste of the listeners, as it did enjoy a good reputation, and therefore attracted the attention of people living in the city. Many of my informants hinted at this, especially when we first met and I told them about my research topic. For example, one employee at the Heydar Aliyev Centre (azerb. Heydər Əliyev Mərkəzi), one of the most prestigious Baku venues for large-scale concerts

Formal and informal nationalism   29

and exhibitions for high-ranking bureaucrats, assured me that she really loves jazz. When asked what she particularly likes about it, she confessed that she doesn't listen to music at home, but enjoys going to jazz parties, since they 'always have a great atmosphere, pleasant and elegant' (N., f., 26 years old, manager).

Thus, because of the prestigious social position of jazz, or because jazz is perceived that way in the capital of Azerbaijan, the genre is a product that attracts the attention of listeners, and in turn sells well. Rufat, the above-mentioned director of the Jazz Club that used jazz as a brand to open a trendy restaurant with live music, confessed this openly. Jumshud is yet another manager of a fashionable restaurant who confirmed this fact. Gate 25 (also called the 25th Floor by Russian-speaking residents of Baku) is on the 25th and 26th floors of a modern skyscraper with a magnificent view of the city centre and Baku Bay. The fashionable spot started unfolding in spring 2016 and was designed for prosperous Baku residents. Young guests, mostly successful businessmen, high-ranking officials and diplomats, belonging to the middle class with a stable professional and family life, were fond of smooth jazz, sometimes blended with electronic music. Since 'light jazz music' is highly requested, many musicians who are just starting out advertise themselves as jazz performers. It is with this goal in mind that the Heydar Aliyev Palace (azerb. Heydər Əliyev Adına Saray)[8] hosted a gala concert in spring 2016 featuring jazz, in the emic understanding of the word, with vocalists and bands of the younger generation.

> I came up with the concept for the event myself. The thing is that in Baku there still haven't been major jazz concerts, only festivals. And we have many young and powerful vocalists who play different music, from pop to folk, and of course, jazz. I'm well aware because I graduated from the conservatory as a vocalist. And young people need help to develop, but they need an appropriate platform to do so. And so we came up with this concert. It's called jAzzeri Bands. See, look at the font, and … this is a logo. I want to use this concert to popularize the uniqueness of our Azerbaijani jazz. The key is its synthesis of jazz and mugham, and the city really loves it. I was worried the idea wouldn't take hold, but we already sold plenty of tickets. (M., f., 26 years old, director, musical director and event organizer)

Thanks to its high social status, Azerbaijani commercial jazz similar to pop music has gained popularity among a large number of the residents of Baku. Audiences of events that use jazz are primarily made up of members of the middle class, 30 years of age and older. The demand for 'light jazz music' has prompted the development of a professional community around the craft, and the appearance of new 'jazz bands' and 'jazz cafes'. The 'jazz scene' in Baku is growing right before our eyes, although it can be hard for the outside

30   *Aneta Strzemżalska*

observer to identify, since the music played has significant stylistic differences from what is usually considered jazz.

Like in the period of late socialism, also today jazz takes on varied and often contradictory meanings (Юрчак 2014: 326–328), and occupies an important place in the social and political space of Azerbaijan. This is due to the mythologization of the origin and development of jazz as a symbol of the battle with foreign power (in this case Soviet), as well as the perception of performances as acts of refined, complex creation, or 'the music of intellectuals' in Western style. Baku is still referred to as the 'Jazz Mecca'. Azerbaijani musicians and international performers participate in international jazz festivals held in Azerbaijan.

Conclusion

Two forms of jazz can be defined in the cultural space of Baku. The first is 'Azerbaijani jazz', also known as 'jazz-*mugham*', which is characterized by performing traditional New Orleans jazz with *mugham harmony*. Since the concept of 'jazz-mugham' does not have the academic basis to become a separate genre of music, this term mainly has an emotional-patriotic character. It is one of the forms of culture that is supported and developed at the official level in order to later represent the country in prestigious international arenas. Because of this, Azerbaijani jazz music has taken on the role of national cultural heritage. It has become a subject of pride, whose unique qualities are driven by not only its original form as mentioned above, but by a mix of jazz and mugham, and by purposeful information politics. Thanks to propaganda and statements by 'people of culture', jazz is now considered 'intellectual' and 'oppositional' art with a rich historical past, which gave rise to its high social status.

The second type of jazz performances can be thought of as jazz pop. It is reminiscent of popular songs in jazz arrangement, and is performed mainly in restaurants for an affluent, middle-aged and older public. The development of jazz pop is dictated by market relations. The music that pays more is played more, and in part, performers do not have an alternative. They need to fulfil the requirements of their clients, in order to provide for themselves and their families. Just as 'Azerbaijani jazz' performances are directly supported by the government, quasi-jazz performances cannot be considered independent. One characteristic of any authoritarian system, including Azerbaijan's, is the deep politicization of social and cultural life, or rather, the penetration of politics in daily life.

Official Azerbaijani cultural politics is determined to popularize only those forms of culture that meet the requirements of national ideology, and on the other hand, to ignore those art forms that do not fit the image of the country. Consequently, official power has a whole series of ways to control the cultural space of the country. The process of making the nation by making people national (Fox and Miller-Idriss 2008: 536) in authoritarian regimes also includes censorship, fear, insecurity and as mentioned above, market relations.

Formal and informal nationalism 31

Political ideology quite strongly governs the actions and morals of Azerbaijan's citizens. An excellent example is the spread of jazz practices in daily life. Although jazz pop is not on the list of national forms of art, it is protected by the government and expanded by official power. It is only under these conditions that performing jazz can be noticeably profitable: it increases social status and the income of both musicians and the owners of venues where these performances take place.

In this way, jazz pop, by being the solution to goal-oriented government politics, is an example of Azerbaijani citizens' participation in the process of constructing the national idea. Thus, jazz can be considered a compromised cultural form that does not fit into the dualistic perception of the post-Soviet place, since it absorbs elements belonging to both official and unofficial nationalism; conclusive division of formal and informal nationalism is not applicable. Thomas Eriksen emphasizes that both ideologies are just as 'authentic', since they possess the ability to create a feeling of community, which can transform into effective political action. However, these ideas possess various structures and characters, and they have different aims: governmental practices, in contrast with civilian practices, frequently do not correspond with the experience and requirements of a large part of society. Because of this, both types of nationalism simply contradict one another (Eriksen 1993: 6).

In Azerbaijan we deal with a case when contradiction of governmental and civic ideologies and practices do not have a place. In this case, the interaction between both sides takes on a polyphonic quality, enabling the appearance of new types of practices: different ideas and meanings are created that contribute to the formation of alternative identities in the framework of one national idea. As Alexei Yurchak notes, the division of Soviet culture[9] into official and unofficial, '*ofitsioz*' and 'underground', is not a winning scientific approach, since a large number of cultural phenomena include elements that are simultaneously on both sides of this division (Юрчак 2014: 40). Due to that it is valid to examine 'nationalism from below', but not in the ways in which nations have become a taken-for-granted part of the landscape of things (Billig 1995: 38, Edensor 2002: 88). Nationalism is produced and reproduced in everyday life by ordinary people, who are active participants of the nation-building process, and who as much as elites decide the shape of nationhood (Fox and Miller-Idriss 2008, Isaacs and Polese 2015, Seliverstova 2017). This work is just such an attempt.

Notes

1   When using Azerbaijani jazz without quotation marks, I mean Jazz music that is played by Azerbaijani musicians. By the phrase 'Azerbaijani jazz' in quotation marks I mean those works, which, in the opinion of Azerbaijani experts on the promotion of local culture, are considered examples of a new genre in world music.
2   *Mugham* (azerb. muğam) – musical poems that are considered the foundation of Azerbaijani folk music. The performance of a *mugham* is free meter and rhythm improvisation, based on consecutive use of voice registers, limited within the boundaries of the specific harmony.

32 Aneta Strzemżalska

3 In 1928 'AMA-Jazz' became the first jazz collective to play on Moscow Radio, and the first Soviet ensemble to record on a gramophone record.
4 RAPM existed from 1913 to 1932. The Composers' Union was founded in its place.
5 The Yarat Contemporary Art Space (azerb. Yarat Müasir İncəsənət Məkan) is a non-commercial organization founded in 2011 by Aida Mahmudova, the niece of the first lady of Azerbaijan, Mehriban Aliyeva. It supports the development and professional advancement of contemporary art in Azerbaijan as well as abroad. One of the center's main goals is to create a creative platform for both beginning and experienced artists. To this end, the organization hosts a series of ground-breaking events that attract a large group of progressive Azerbaijani youth.
6 The Jazz Club at the Sapphire Hotel existed for only a few months. It was closed in March 2016 when a high-ranking official living several floors above it complained. I was told in confidence that he was 'bothered by the loud, annoying music'. The Jazz Club reopened several months later on June 2016, but this time at the Dalga Beach Aquapark Resort, located opposite of the Absheron Peninsula, about 40 km from the Baku city centre.
7 Emil Mammedov (azerb. Emil İbrahim Məmmədov, 1975–2011) was a famous jazz pianist and composer, the art director of the Jazz Centre. He died in Germany after a long-term illness. He was a close friend of many in the Baku art world. Jazz musicians honor his memory by organizing evening memorial events on the anniversaries of his birth and death.
8 The palace stage is one of the largest and most reputable in the republic. Along with concerts and other cultural programs, it hosts governmental events, such as the ceremonial inauguration of Heydar Aliyev in 1993 and 1998, and the ceremonial inauguration of Ilham Aliyev in 2003 and 2008.
9 The present political situation in Azerbaijan is in many senses a continuation of the Soviet system. For more on this topic, see R. R. Garagozov (2012) Azerbaijani history and nationalism in the Soviet and post-Soviet periods: Challenges and dilemmas. *Dynamics of Asymmetric Conflict.* 5(2), July 2012, 136–142.

References

Anderson B. 1983. *Imagined communities: Reflections on the origin and spread of nationalism.* London: Verso.

Barth F. 1969. *Ethnic groups and boundaries. The social organization of culture difference.* Oslo: Universitetsforlaget.

Billig M. 1995. *Banal nationalism.* London: Sage.

Brubaker R. 1996. *Nationalism reframed: Nationhood and the national question in the new Europe.* Cambridge: Cambridge University Press.

Collins K. 2004. The logic of clan politics, evidence from the central Asian trajectories. *World Politics,* 56(2), 224–61.

Dubuisson, E. M. 2013. Dialogic authority: Kazakh aitys poets and their patrons, in *Ethnographies of the state in Central Asia: Performing politics,* edited by M. Reeves, J. Rasanayagam, and J. Beyer. Indianapolis and Bloomington, IN: Indiana University Press, 56–77.

Edensor T. 2002. *National identity, popular culture and everyday life.* Oxford: Berg.

Eriksen, T.H. 1993. Formal and informal nationalism. *Ethnic and Racial Studies,* 16, 1–25.

Fox, J. E., and Miller-Idriss C. 2008. Everyday nationhood. *Ethnicities,* 8(4), 536–556.

Gellner, E. A. 1983. *Nations and nationalism.* Ithaca, NY: Cornell University Press.

Giddens A. 1985. *The nation-state and violence: Volume two of a contemporary critique of historical materialism.* Berkeley, CA: University of California Press.

Grzymala-Busse, A., Jones Luong P. 2002. Reconceptualizing the state: Lessons from post-communism. *Politics and Society*, 30(4), 529–554.

Hobsbawm, E. J. 1990. *Nations and nationalism since 1780: Programme, myth, reality*. Cambridge: Cambridge University Press.

Horák S. 2005. The Ideology of the Turkmenbashy Regime. *Perspectives on European Politics and Society*, 6(2), 305–320.

Isaacs, R., Polese A. 2015. Between 'imagined' and 'real' nation-building: Identities and nationhood in post-Soviet Central Asia. *Nationalities Papers*, 43(3), 371–382.

Kaliszewska, I., Voell, S. eds. 2015. *State and legal practice in the Caucasus: anthropological perspectives on law and politics*. London: Ashgate.

Kapferer B. 1988. *Legends of people, myths of state: Violence, intolerance, and political culture in Sri Lanka and Australia*. Washington, D.C.: Smithsonian Institution Press.

Polese, A., Horák S. 2015. A tale of two presidents: Personality cult and symbolic nation-building in Turkmenistan. *Nationalities Papers*, 43(3), 457–478.

Seliverstova O. 2017. 'Consuming' national identity in western Ukraine, *Nationalities Papers*, 45(1), 61–79.

Smith, A. D. 1986. *The ethnic origins of nations*. Oxford: Blackwell Publishers.

Бабаева, Ф., Фархадов, Р. 2010. *Рафик Бабаев: От темы к импровизу*. Баку: Letterpress.

Мамедова, Н. 2016. Эмиль Алиев: 'Я вынужден этим заниматься, потому что надо жить ...' (Интервью). In Baku.ws. Available at: http://baku.ws/71553-emil-alievya-vynuzhden-etim-zanimatsya-potomu-chto-nado-zhit.-intervyu.html [accessed 1 June 2016].

Фейертаг, В.Б. 2014. *Джаз от Ленинграда до Петербурга. Время и судьбы*. СПб: Лань, Планета музыки.

Юрчак, А. 2014. *Это было навсегда, пока не кончилось. Последнее советское поколение*. М.: Новое литературное обозрение.

2 Can musicians build the nation? Popular music and identity in Estonia

Emilia Pawłusz

Introduction

On the 23rd of August, 2014 Estonia, Latvia and Lithuania celebrated the 25th anniversary of the Baltic Way, a human chain in which two million people had joined hands from Tallinn to Vilnius to show the region's solidarity and draw international attention to the political situation of the Baltics under the Soviet Union. Tallinn commemorated the anniversary with an event on the Freedom Square, during which photographs from 1989 were shown, and popular artists performed well-known national songs that mobilized Estonians in the late 80s for the civic movement popularly called 'the Singing Revolution'. The second part of the event was a concert of two Estonian bands, one of them Metsatöll, an internationally recognized folk metal band active for almost 20 years. Heavy metal music, although a big music market, is usually considered underground, alternative and absent from mainstream radio stations. It is often associated with massive sound, amplified distortion of guitars and hyper masculinity of the musicians. Having such a picture in mind, I was surprised when I saw how enthusiastic the audience was when listening to Metsatöll on the anniversary concert. Although the event took place in a concert hall in Tallinn where the audience was supposed to sit, many people stood up, danced and sang along, proving that Metsatöll's music is known well beyond metal fans. The band uses traditional folk instruments and the lyrics of their songs often talk about Estonian heritage and the national past. Having toured abroad, in particular with Scandinavian folk metal bands, it is presented as a modern adaptation of Estonian folk music, which has long been a cornerstone of Estonian national identity narrative.

This chapter uses the case of the Estonian folk metal band to analyze the role of popular music as a vehicle of nation building. It argues that popular music artists can be viewed as nation builders who through their musical pieces, performances and discourses (re)create certain representations and narrations of the nation (in accordance or not with the elite notion of the nation). If the artist is internationally successful, he/she may be, similarly to successful sportsmen, a reason for national pride. Moreover, the chapter highlights that it is not only through lyrics that the nation 'is made' in music; musical performances, direct affective and bodily experiences of music at concerts, the discourses (outside lyrics) the musicians themselves create, and finally the public and media reception of the music and musicians all influence how audiences make sense of musical pieces and performers vis-a-vis their identities (cf. Revill 2000, Wood and Smith 2004, Wood et al. 2007, Wood 2012).

Traditionally, the connection between music and national identity has been explored in two major directions. One strand of literature focused on folk music and its 19th-century romantic discovery as a repository of 'national character' (Wilson 1973, Bohlman 2011, Baycroft and Hopkin 2012). Another body of literature investigated how classical composers often took the role of nation builders and how some of their pieces came to represent high culture of a nation (Curtis 2008, Frolova-Walker 2007). Recently, it has been shown that also popular music, although often based on the pattern and style of the Anglo-American music industry, can channel, evoke or reproduce themes related to the sense of locality, and ethnic or national belonging (Larkey 1992, Cloonan 1996, Connell and Gibson 2003, Whiteley et al. 2004, Biddle and Knight 2007). This chapter is a further move in this direction. Footing on the ideas of Billig (1995) to look for banal mechanisms of nationalism and Isaacs and Polese's (2016) to see nation building beyond the state, this chapter investigates popular music, its creators and reception as a prolific site to explore how official identity narratives are processed, amplified or challenged through the artistic medium which surrounds and engages people in their everyday lives (Edensor 2002, Fox and Miller-Idriss 2008, Skey 2011, Antonsich 2015). Popular music, broadcast and accessible through traditional and new social media is an 'invisible', even 'banal' site of identity building that accompanies the everyday, even if we do not pay direct attention to it.[1] Having an individual dimension, music affects people on discursive, auditory and emotional levels (Stokes 1994, Billig 1995, Revill 2000, Wood and Smith 2004). Furthermore, music informs attitudes, perceptions of the social world and the sense of self, especially for young people (Bennett 2000).

The basis for this chapter is my ethnographic fieldwork done in Estonia between 2014 and 2016, during which I observed five concerts of Metsatöll, ranging from a usual club concert, to a rock festival and national celebrations. I also analyzed lyrics, visuals (album covers, fan art, music videos and concert photographs), and online materials (band's official webpage, interviews and album reviews in *Postimees*, the biggest national newspaper). Finally, I contacted one of the members and corresponded with him for two months which allowed me to get insights into his interpretations of the band, as well as his perception on what the Estonian identity is today.

Before delving into the empirical data, the chapter discusses the different approaches to the relationship of music and the nation. Then it presents the case study of Estonia, starting from the historical context of 'singing nationalism' and the role of music in Estonian nation building. Finally, it turns to the case of Metsatöll to illustrate how the band attempts to reconcile 'taken for granted' romantic national identity with modern, global music business.

36 *Emilia Pawłusz*

Music and national identity

Music and arts have been critical for the establishment of national cultures and ultimately, national citizens (Curtis 2008). Scholars agree that music itself cannot be nationalist, nor it is a simple expression of national(ist) feelings. Rather, it can be seen as a tool to create, sustain and mobilize national sentiments. Music *makes the nation* (Curtis 2008, Bohlman 2011) by mapping onto people's recognition of places, geographical sites and cultural boundaries (Stokes 1994, Wood 2012). It is the reception and interpretation, rather than the music itself, that make a musical piece 'national'. As many scholars argue, music is primarily about the feeling and individual bodily experience rather than only lyrics (Revill 2000, Wood et al. 2007, Wood and Smith 2004). Thus music (from lyrics to performances, sounds and emotional atmospheres) constitutes an interesting way into the study of national identity beyond its official and discursive aspects as it shows that individuals perform and experience national identity in certain situations with varying intensity, and do not necessarily 'have' it.

Research into the relationship between music and national identity has focused on two major processes. First, scholars investigated various regional forms of the 19th-century idealization and appropriation of peasant songs and dances as representation of innate 'national character' of the whole nation (Wilson 1973, Baycroft and Hopkin 2012, Bohlman 2011, Djumaev 2005). Public rituals and festivals engaging folk music and folklore heritage have been a vehicle of convincing populations of tangibility and reality of nationhood (Hobsbawm and Ranger 1983, Kuutma 1996, Adams 2010, Cojocaru and Dimova 2013, Pawłusz 2016), as well as a platform of its contestation (Creed 2011, Dimova and Cojocaru 2013). A prominent body of literature analyzed the phenomenon of turbo-folk in the former Yugoslav states, as a shared cultural memory of Yugoslavia and, often, a form of national populism (Hudson 2003, Baker 2010, Čvoro 2014).

Another strand of literature investigated the role of national composers (such as Wagner, Grieg or Kreek) as nation builders who through their music aimed at creating a national culture that would orientate people towards a polity (Kõlar 2004, Engelhardt 2008, Curtis 2008, White and Murphy 2001, Frolova-Walker 2007). Within nationalism studies scholars noted the role of national anthems as 'embodiment of nation in song' (Anderson 1991: 132–133, Connell and Gibson 2003, Bohlman 2011), a symbolic vehicle of nation building (Mach 1994, Eyck 1995), and sometimes a site of competing national ideologies (Daughtry 2003).

Recently, scholars have looked into how music represents or revives socio-cultural identities against the backdrop of glottalization. This includes studies into the intersection of popular music and locality, in particular, various musical styles (for example, 'Brit-pop'), instruments or performances considered 'national', 'ethnic' or 'a national brand' (Strachan and Leonard 2004). The prevailing argument is that although production of music has been

Can musicians build the nation? 37

enormously homogenized, the national, geographic and cultural context of music still matters for creators and audiences alike and the global is mediated and experienced through the local (Larkey 1992, Cloonan 1996, Connell and Gibson 2003, Whiteley et al. 2004, Biddle and Knight 2007). Neo-folk and folk rock have been researched as worldwide phenomena that answer identity challenges stemming from globalization, as well as regional and national identity dilemmas (Ramnarine 2003, Strmiska 2005, Cepeda 2010, Winter and Keegan-Phipps 2013). This 'back-to-roots' trend has been present in the post-Soviet region, too. On one hand, it reflects the global condition of a sense of 'identity loss'. On the other hand, it taps into the local nation-building processes on at least two levels. First, it is a part of the officially endorsed musical representations of the nation aimed at reminding local populations of their national identity (Wanner 2004, Spinetti 2005) but also staging newly regained nationhood for international audiences, for example at Eurovision (Baker 2008, Ismayilov 2012, Jordan 2014). Second, the search into 'locality' and 'authenticity' has also been visible in bottom-up and popular music creation (Johnson 2006, Wickström 2008, Wood 2012).

This chapter joins the body of literature on popular music and furthers the idea that contemporary popular musicians, with traditional and social media as powerful transmitters, can affect how people perceive issues of identity and belonging and position themselves vis-a-vis space, history and geopolitics. Song lyrics, musical performances and discourses in which musicians make connections between music, identity and politics create new channels through which local renditions of the past can be conveyed to national audiences and beyond (Ashby 2015). Listening and creating music is a form of identity performance (Spracklen et al. 2014); it:

> [C]onstructs our sense of identity through the direct experiences it offers of the body, time and sociability, experiences which enable us to place ourselves in imaginative cultural narratives (Frith 1996: 125).

The focus on the agency of musicians draws attention to the questions of 'who' builds the nation and 'how' (instead of the classic 'what' the nation is). It shows that ordinary citizens are not passive receivers of elite-proposed nationalism but can play an active role in negotiation of nationhood (Thompson 2001, Antonsich 2015, Knott 2015). Regardless if their voice is co-opted by the state or challenges the elite-imposed idea of national identity, musicians and popular culture personalities can be seen as 'middle-level' actors, in between elites and ordinary citizens, who have the agency of forming and popularizing national mythologies, landscapes and inclusion-exclusion narratives. Listening and performing music may work as an informal site of nation building (Eriksen 1993, Isaacs and Polese 2015, 2016, Polese 2016) which goes in parallel to official nation building and penetrates many aspects of everyday life, leisure, public spaces, television, Internet, social media, etc. (Edensor 2002,

38   *Emilia Pawłusz*

Fox and Miller-Idriss 2008, Skey 2011, Pawłusz and Seliverstova 2016, Seliverstova 2017). The focus on ordinary citizens who become recognized as pop culture icons or cultural elites draws attentions to the fact that the formal (elite) and everyday (ordinary people) are not binary or homogeneous categories and there is a range of 'middle' actors whose interpretations of the nationhood become viral and thus affect how the nation is understood and experienced in a society. The case study of Metsatöll serves as an illustration of this process – when ordinary citizens become recognized as nation builders and re-create national identity anew.

Music and politics in Estonia

The ability of music to build and mobilize collective identities has been observed everywhere in the world. Still, there are some cases where this process is more evident and influential in the wider context of the nation building process. Estonia, similarly to Latvia and somewhat less, Lithuania, has been known for its strong incorporation of folk songs and dances, as well as choral music, in the idea of the Estonian nation (Kuutma 1996, Lippus 2006, Brüggemann and Kasekamp 2014, Pawłusz 2016). Estonia's nation-building process can be described largely with Gellner's (1983) 'Ruritania model' in which the culture of the folk becomes the basis for the future national culture. A great illustration of this processes is the national song celebration, a 150-year-old tradition of choral singing festivals in which amateur ensembles from all over the country gather to perform national songs, some of which were also sung during 'the Singing Revolution' (Šmidchens 2014). The appreciation of folklore as the basis for the national culture can also be read from the fact that Estonia has a special higher education institution, Viljandi Culture Academy, that teaches traditional handicraft, music and dance with the aim to sustain the Estonian native culture. The town of Viljandi every year hosts also 'Viljandi Folk', an international festival of world music in which the notions of heritage and authenticity are mediated (Kuutma and Kästik 2014). In its official branding Estonia uses the image of 'the singing nation', the heritage of traditional singing (est. *regilaul*) and the vibrancy of modern-day folk music to establish distinctive markers of national identity for local and international audiences (Pawłusz and Polese 2017). When I came to Estonia to do research on post-Soviet nation building and music, I first focused on the choral singing festivals which in various forms take place all over the country. I soon realized that nationally-themed music is not limited to choral singing and folk, and popular music, including rock and metal bands, increasingly pick up on national or ethnic themes, too.

Edward Larkey (1992), in his analysis of pop music in Austria, distinguished four stages of development of popular music: consumption of popular music coming from hegemonic centers of entertainment industry, imitation of the style by local artists, de-anglicization of the imported music and re-ethnicization, namely establishment of local styles as independent and legitimate centers of creativity. The model suggests that the initial copying of Anglo-American models gradually becomes adapted to local contexts and consumer tastes. Moreover, local touches to well-known musical styles might be what 'sells' certain artists as familiar yet different from mainstream Anglo-American music. I argue that similar processes might be observed elsewhere and in other music genres. In the Soviet Bloc, Western music (along with the homegrown rock and roll, blues and jazz) had a profound socio-political impact, alienating people from the Soviet state and its official culture (Ryback 1990), as well as popularizing the everyday images of the West. In the late nineties/early 2000s, however, it might be said that this non-critical consumption of Western cultural products to a certain degree lost its attractiveness. The 'empowerment of locality' has been visible in 'reterritorialization' of music, for example, music in local languages is now what is seen as less mainstream and 'cool' (cf. Allaste and Kobin 2012).

In the rock and metal scene, the nineties brought a great differentiation of styles and sub-genres, including Europe-born folk metal. Typically, folk metal is characterized by:

> [T]he concurrent performance of heavy metal music with the integration of folk music, mythological and/or cosmological stories, vocal performances in non-English languages, a focus on historical events or historical figures and lyrics or images that identify with a specific nation or group of people (Marjenin 2014: 2).

In Europe and North America 'Viking metal' that uses Nordic heritage elements has emerged as the most prominent branch of folk metal (Lucas 2014, Marjenin 2014, Ashby 2015). The Estonian band Metsatöll has toured with major stars of Viking metal and therefore is also classified as a representative of it; however, the band prefers to refer to Estonia's Ugro-Finnic identity, rather than Nordic heritage at large.

The official website of Metsatöll informs that the band has released over 20 albums, singles and DVDs with the latest album coming out in 2015. Several times the band has been awarded the title of 'The Best Metal Act' at the Estonian Music Awards. In 2011 they gained an official acknowledgment by the Estonian president for singing in the Estonian language and acquainting the world with Estonia, its culture and language. The mainstream success (beyond the metal audience) of Metsatöll is also visible in the fact that the band is often presented in official promotional materials about Estonia. It is described as 'Estonian folk metal band whose identity is based on the 13th-14th century Estonian fight for freedom and Estonian folk heritage' (Estonian Institute, *The World of Estonian Music,* 2015). In the next sections selected characteristics of the band's music, discourses and performances will be reviewed in the context of nation building in post-Soviet Estonia.

40   *Emilia Pawłusz*

Folk songs, kannels and independence: Major features of Metsatöll's music

Metsatöll formed in 1999 and released a demo the same year. The current lineup of the band, four members (electric guitar, bass guitar, drums and folk instruments) formed in 2004. The name Metsatöll (est. *mets* – forest, *töll* – creature, being) is an archaic euphemism for wolf, which according to folklore tradition could not be named, as this would make the wolf appear. The band sings in Estonian, often employing archaic vocabulary and, occasionally, dialects of Estonian. The band has evolved from classic heavy to more folk-oriented metal. Folk instruments such as *torupill* (bagpipe), flutes, kannels, mouth harps and goat horns were incorporated. Moreover, the band successfully drew from Estonian runo songs (est. *regilaul)*, an archaic style of singing found amongst Finno-Ugric peoples (Lippus 2006, Kuutma and Kästik 2014).

Singing runo songs can be interpreted as an act towards making music 'Estonian' as they are popularly thought of as repositories of pre-modern 'authentic' Estonian identity. Since the mid-19th century *regilaul* was of great interest to folklorists and philologists who scrupulously archived thousands of folk songs as *Estonian* heritage. Some of the collected songs became the basis for the national epic *Kalevipoeg* ('Son of Kalev'). In Soviet times, *regilaul* became a synonym for authentic folk song, as opposed to Sovietized grandiose folklore (Šmidchens 2014, Kuutma and Kästik 2014). Nowadays, the archaic style of singing has gone through a revival in contemporary music as many composers, as well as, pop, folk and rock groups adapt it in their musical pieces. An example of a folk song from northern Estonia (archived in 1910) performed by Metsatöll in a metal version would be:

> This story I would sing,
> First sung by my father,
> Taught by my aunts,
> Used wisely by my brothers.
> I sing it the way I know,
> Like my father used to sing.
> (translation from Estonian by Metsatöll)

Apart from folk songs, the music of Metsatöll is inspired by two major topics. First, the band sings about calamities of war, patriotism and heroism, which are contextualized in Estonia's medieval and modern history. The lyrics talk about Estonians' fights for independence against German-speaking elite,[2] hardships of slavery and the necessity to protect the land of the ancestors against recurring invasions. This theme reiterates the official national narrative of Estonia and is a banal reminder of it – its main events, moral aspects, enemies and allies ('us and them'). Some of the songs refer explicitly to geographical places in Estonia, mapping the national territory and establishing the sense of embeddedness of the nation (versus other nations) in the imagined geography of the world of nations (Stokes 1994, Billig 1995).

The second major theme is the native beliefs and pre-modern cultural heritage. Estonians' native religion, having little or no connection to both Western and Eastern Christianity (thus German and Russian cultures respectively), has long been considered profoundly Estonian. In the mid-19th century native deities and beliefs were incorporated into the national ideology and became popular motives in literature. In the late 20th century the movement of Estonian native religion and *Taara* worshipers (*Taara* – the main god of Estonian mythology) was revived and registered (Rinne 2016). Currently, it is the biggest non-Christian religion uniting adherents of animist beliefs in Estonia (Vakker and Rohtmets 2008). The movement regards indigenous beliefs as the cultural and natural continuity and heritage of the people, prefers a native calendar over the Gregorian one (Metsatöll uses it also),[3] and underpins the Finno-Ugric connection of Estonians. Finno-Ugric identity is also present in official identity discourse. In 2011 'Tribal Day' (est. *hõimupäev*) was introduced as a national holiday to celebrate the Finno-Ugric heritage. This can be interpreted as an assertion of Estonia's distance from the Soviet Union and the Slavic world, as well as an attempt to construct a modern identity of Estonian nation-state. It also furthers the romantic notion of the nation as a historical entity embedded in one single ethnic heritage and ancestry and the state as the protector of it.

The song 'Hiiekoda' from the album of the same title (2004), which was a breakthrough to the international career of Metsatöll, provides a good illustration of the major themes in Metsatöll's lyrics. In the song an unknown hero is enraged by the slaughter of the community of people (Taara's tribe = Estonians) he identifies himself with, emphasizing the necessity to remember the past deeds and sacrifice of his ancestors, as well as to take revenge on the enemies for the oppression they caused on the peaceful folk. There is a distinct sense of 'us' and 'togetherness', fraternity and horizontal comradeship (Anderson 1991) which contribute to the notion of historical continuity of the nation, and one's sense of belonging to and responsibility for it. The song brings the distant past into the experience of the present.

'Hiiekoda'/ 'Sacred grove'
[Translation from Estonian by Metsatöll]

Death was spun into the homes
Of fortune's children
Into the farmsteads of Taara's
people [Estonians]
Into the forests of mother earth

I would rather fall for my
fatherland

I remember the war that like a
tempest ravaged my lands
I remember the sacred grove
where my father fell victim
I remember the sacred grove
where the blood of my brothers
flowed
(...)

42　*Emilia Pawłusz*

Than hang in a stranger's leash
I would rather fill the Devil's empty pouch
Than pay the church's tithe

I would rather fall in battle
Than pinch a stranger's penny
I would rather bury my sorrow in the soil
Than forget the manor's taunts [Baltic Germans]

I remember the war that took away my ideals
Barons were burned
Hangmen were slain
Prophecies of progenitors
Sufferings of lost ages

Taara's sons rise from ashes
Bold brothers of Vanemuine [god of music]
Uku's [god of thunder] proud war-wolves
Children of iron heavy from fury (…)

Overseers' forts were overthrown
Landlords were crushed
Grandfather-grandmother,
Sneered at by the manor-folk [Baltic Germans]

My land is my home, my sacred grove

The interpretation of Metsatöll's music is not limited to the history of Estonians' fight for independence in the Middle Ages. Some of the songs have been contextualized in the 20th-century political history of the country. 'Oma laulu ei leia ma üles'[4] ('I cannot find my song') has been the soundtrack of the Estonian historical drama TV series 'Tuulepealne maa' ('Windward Land') which tells a story of Estonia's first independence and interwar time, through the prism of the life of two young men. Based on my observation at Metsatöll's concerts, this is one of the most popular songs; it is received particularly enthusiastically and is known well beyond metal fans. The song was usually performed at the end of a concert which added to the growing emotional intensity of the performance. The popularity and magnitude of the song was clear as the people came close to the stage, danced, sang along, closed their eyes in the moment of 'feeling the music'. There was a sense of greater understanding and harmony between the band and the audience and amongst the audience.

Human geographers (Wood et al. 2007, Wood and Smith 2004, Wood 2012) argue that the experience of musical performance (even if ephemeral) that engages the body and emotional self is critical for understanding how the sense of identification is constructed. Wood et al. (2007) write:

> Musical performances are, then, about 'intimate' encounters with others; they are about sharing an emotional experience with other people, most of whom will never see each other again, let alone exchange the time of day. These are encounters where feeling, sensing, and tacit understanding are more prevalent than articulation and explanation (...). The sounds

Can musicians build the nation? 43

and rhythms of music constitute a nonverbal signifying system; they express precisely what we cannot express in language. (p. 883)

The intensity of music experience (like at Metsatöll's concert) shows that identity is always performed and embodied; it is the 'here and now', mediated through one's body, emotions and experiences through which the national in relation to the individual is created (Revill 2000).

Estonianness in musical performance: the example of the 'Course Upon Iron' concert

During their almost 20-year career, Metsatöll has performed on various state and national holiday celebrations such as the Baltic Way 25th anniversary in Tallinn in 2014, Veterans' Day and numerous midsummer concerts (night of 23/24 June; est. *Jaanipäev*).[5] The band's participation in national celebrations shows that in terms of identity narratives they do not represent a counter-culture to the state (in contrast to many metal bands) but to the contrary, their music resonates well with some 'taken for granted' assumptions of what Estonianness means (ethnic Estonian).

One of the major undertakings and distinctive performances of the band was their cooperation project with the National Male Choir (RAM) and one of the most known Estonian choral composers – Veljo Tormis. Tormis' music, which draws from Estonian and other Ugro-Finnic folk and shamanic traditions, was an important repository of Estonian identity during the Soviet times. Today, Veljo Tormis and Arvo Pärt are considered by Estonians to be their most important living composers (Daitz 2004). Metsatöll, RAM and Tormis created a spectacle based on the artwork of Tormis, 'Curse Upon Iron', arranged for rock performance. The band member whom I interviewed said that even though musically, there is not much that connects a classical composer and a rock band, Metsatöll and Tormis share similar interest – folksongs from 'our' tradition. He considers the opportunity to work with Tormis as something that could happen only when the band was no longer seen as 'a small heavy metal band, long-grease-haired-idiots', signaling the prestige of the cooperation. The joint project is narrated on Metsatöll's website in the following way:

CURSE UPON IRON is undoubtedly one of the better known works in Estonian choral music. Already in its original form, it contains all the primary characteristics of this particular project: shamanic chants, rhymes borrowed from *Kalevala*, the primeval power of runo-singing. To this we add some increasingly popular ethno-rockers and the 54 trained voices of the only full-time professional male choir in the world. (...) Metsatöll becomes grand choral music, Veljo Tormis turns into rock. One summer night in 2006, history was made in Estonia, and with this disc you can enjoy it all again. (Metsatöll's website, www.Metsatöll.ee/en/muusika/raua_needmine.html)

44   *Emilia Pawłusz*

The first concert of 'Curse Upon Iron' took place in the ruins of a medieval cloister of Pirita, a seafront district of Tallinn. It is not a music venue but primarily a place on the imaginary national map (ruined cloister as a site of resistance to Christianity). The event utilized a rich repertoire of symbols and meanings related to the ethnic nation: folk heritage themes, national colours in performers' outfits, and the national meaning of choral singing and choral compositions of Tormis. Through the performance the ethnic past was rendered real and tangible, yet in a different form. Similarly to Wood (2012) who observed how 'new Scotishness' is created at music festivals, I would argue that the cooperation project between what is 'old and known' as Estonian (choral singing, Veljo Tormis) and a contemporary rock band showed how a new way of being Estonian is created. The performers reconfigured familiar themes of romantic Estonianness for the purpose of the present, and embedded them in the reality of contemporary popular music. This shows how representations of the nation and experience of national identity are constantly remade in the everyday life, by various actors and in dialogue with the present, answering the question of 'who we are *today*' (Skey 2011, Wood 2012, Pawłusz and Seliverstova 2016).

Discourses and reception of Metsatöll

In contrast to most academic studies, in people's perceptions nations (or ethnic groups) are often taken for granted, as if national identity was a stable, self-evident characteristic of an individual (cf. Knott 2015). In the interview, one of the band members portrayed the nation as a historically shaped community of people with a profound, spiritual connection to the land that their ancestors have long inhabited. He sees local customs, native beliefs and attachment for the land as deeply Estonian values, (as opposed to the contemporary world which is superficial, and somewhat less 'real' and valuable than 'the old ways') and thus should be treated with certain reserve. My interviewee explained:

Q: Why is it important to sing about the past of Estonia? Why did you choose this topic?
A: The time is fictional, so, there is no past. We sing about Estonia, I make songs about us. Why do I choose topics like this? Maybe it would be a cliché, but I think, I don't choose topics, the topics choose me. (...) One function of the music has always been rebellion against the fictional development or progress of the human kind. Reminding people about their roots is a rebellion against those, who think, they can live without them. And if you have toes in a soil, you don't even care about the plastic wonderland, do you. (Interview, March 2016)

He further explained that music creation and reception is about being yourself, where often 'you' is a multiple, collective being. 'Metsatöll is about being

Estonian', he summarized. In his view, to be Estonian is to stand firmly in one's roots and heritage and to be connected to the land, understood as a nourishing mother. Furthermore, the Estonian nation is seen as a continuous collective being mentality rooted in history and land, preceding its political structures such as the state. This echoes the post-Soviet dominant (though not homogeneous) ethnocentric national identity discourse that informed Estonia's foreign, security, citizenship and minority rights policies (Kuus 2002, Mole 2012). Fledman (2001) argued there are two major narratives in Estonian public discourse, one of 'Return to Europe' after the experience of the Soviet Union, and the other one of 'Homeland', according to which Estonia is one of the oldest countries in Europe, characterized by an ancient language and a shared awareness of the indigenous population's ancient territory. Similarly, Pawłusz and Polese (2017) in their study of Estonian nation branding argued that in promotional rhetorics the ancientness of the nation is often juxtaposed with the young and fragile state. Metsatöll's music and discourse that emphasize cultural heritage and continuity of the nation through ages reiterate elements of the Homeland narrative. Simultaneously, 'the other' is not only the historical enemies (Russia, Germany) but also 'the global'. In their discourse it can be read that the band appreciates locality and ethnic roots as a way to contest globalization, capitalism and consumerism.

Although the symbolic meanings that listeners create around the music of Metsatöll can be diverse and multiple, in the media discourse the band has often been labeled as Estonian and patriotic. Their music has met with positive, sometimes even enthusiastic, reception and the fact that they revive romantic national identity has been pointed out in reviews. *Postimees*, the biggest national newspaper, wrote:

> Our governors should acknowledge and reward Metsatöll for that they have woken up the ancient power and the pride (of the fatherland). (*Postimees*, 15.01.2005, all translations from Estonian by Gerli Punison)
>
> Their activity is patriotically more meaningful for the young people than for example the domestic political show-off. (...) For a long time already Metsatöll has not been just a band but an Estonian musical phenomenon in itself, that is worth being proud of! (*Postimees*, 7.09.2006)

When Metsatöll's album *Iivakivi* ('The Fertility Stone', 2008) was released on 24 February (Independence Day), it was reviewed on *Postimees* as an album celebrating the nation's independence and continuity. Moreover, the wide appeal of the band amongst Estonians was highlighted:

> When the new album will be released on the 24th of February, it means a party for Estonians regardless if their home is Woodstock bar [popular rock pub in Tallinn] or Kadriorg palace [presidential palace]. (*Postimees*, 23.02.2008)

46   *Emilia Pawłusz*

Culture-focused magazine *Müürileht*, even if somewhat skeptical of the folk metal genre, appreciates the international 'breakthrough' of Metsatöll and call it the most famous Estonian band which 'plays a significant role in the Estonian cultural landscape, being representatives of the metal subculture, as well as the country' (*Müürileht*, 3.04.2014).

The potential role of Metsatöll as nation builders stems not only from the use of the Estonian language and its dialects, and the romantic national style of the music, but also the international success of the band. The band is appreciated for being 'cultural ambassadors' for Estonia, and like victories of national sport teams, their commercial success evokes the sense of national pride. I experienced this during one concert of Metsatöll when an Estonian acquaintance, not a big fan of metal otherwise, approached me after the show and exclaimed, 'They have toured America, they are the most famous Estonian band!'

Conclusions

This chapter argued that popular music may be studied as a site of identity construction where musicians, even if not always directly intending to do so, participate in the process of building the sense of nationhood. The study analyzed the case of the Estonian folk metal band as an example of a commercially successful group that gained recognition amongst diverse audiences in their home country and the status of informal national ambassadors. Being one of the few musical projects from Estonia that gained international popularity, the band is often presented as 'our' success, which evokes national pride beyond heavy metal fans. In their music the band draws from folk songs, uses self-made traditional instruments and through lyrics reiterates the ideas of romantic nationalism. Benedict Anderson (1991) wrote that nations' main dream is to be free; so sings Metsatöll. This discourse of native land, ancestral traditions, and nation's continuity has been strongly present in the Estonian political discourse after regaining independence and played a major role in the country's identity politics (Mole 2012). Although the band hardly refers to the state and prefers to talk about pre-state times in Estonia, it affirms the tangible existence of the nation, takes pride in its heritage (indigenous religion, folklore, country life) and assumes the collective responsibility to protect it. What is new is the medium of identity formation – popular music which is used to reconfigure 'old' elements of Estonian identity in the context of the present, perhaps bridging the experience of identity of Soviet and post-Soviet generations. Moreover, the appeal of the band as a popular national symbol may be strengthened by the idea that music is the cultural form that most strongly signifies Estonianness ('the singing nation').

The power of music to help us imagine the nation lies in several aspects: its bodily engagement, symbolic references and emotional appeal. Music, with its personal and bodily dimension, brings the abstract idea of 'us', a group or collective, onto the level of personal, tangible experience (Wood 2012). In the words of Frith (1996: 109), 'Music, like identity, is both performance and story, describes the social in the individual and the individual in the social, the mind in the body and the body in the mind'. Just as literature in the late 19th century helped to imagine the nation as a certain social fixity and the readers as members of this nation (cf. Anderson 1991), today's nationally-themed popular music provides a sense of 'ourness', nativeness and cultural distinctiveness. Folk metal and other ethno- or folk genres tap into the romantic imagining of the nation constructed at the formative period of national awakening, while at the same time they propose a more modern, globalized idea of national music and culture, adapted to reality of global music market and increasing internationalization of everyday life. The success of folk metal bands may be read as a global phenomenon which is meant to symbolically resist the perceived threat of global homogenization and empower locality, yet rests on economic resources, opportunities and models created within the mainstream music production.

The chapter also showed the significance of leisure time in constructing identity (Moser 2010, Spracklen et al. 2014). Both making and consuming nationally-themed music may be regarded as everyday life identity performances in which individuals make sense and rework their sense of collective identity. The case of the Estonian band illustrates how ordinary citizens have the agency to (re)create ideas of what it means to belong to the nation, proving that national identity is an ongoing process mediated every day in many informal ways.

Acknowledgements

I would like to thank Eleanor Knott, Marco Antonsich, Hannah Lyons, Manolis Pratsinakis and the editors of this volume for commenting on an earlier draft of this chapter.

Funding

The research was supported by the REA/EC under the Marie Curie program [grant number MCA- ITN-2012-TENSIONS].

Notes

1   Here I am thinking of how many times I heard popular songs with national themes on the radio, or as background music in shopping malls in Tallinn.
2   Baltic Germans were political, social and commercial elite from the 13th century until Estonia's first independence in 1918.
3   The Estonian native calendar assumes the Billingen catastrophe (dramatic change in the Baltic Sea levels which caused the emergence of a piece of land, today's Estonian terriotory) as the beginning of its chronology. For example, the year 2016 is 10,229 according to the Estonian native calendar. In the interview, one of the band members mentioned that 'For me (and for us) it was weird to spot Metsatöll's

48   *Emilia Pawłusz*

record-dates with a time from the year (what is also not precise, neither a fact) mythical Jesus from Nazareth was born'.

4   The song is actually a jazz piece, 'Take Five', composed in 1959 by Paul Desmond and performed by the Dave Brubeck Quartet. In Estonia it was first performed by a female singer Heli Lääts in 1967.

5   Midsummer is celebrated all over Estonia and is a public holiday since 1992. The 23rd of June is also a Victory Day (est. *Võidupüha*) in Estonia that commemorates a battle won over the Germans in 1919 during the so-called 'Estonian War of Independence' in the aftermath of World War I.

References

Adams, L. L. 2010. *The spectacular state. Culture and national identity in Uzbekistan.* Durham, NC: Duke University Press.

Allaste, A. -A., Kobin, M. 2012. From underground cultural boundaries in nineties to fluid networks at present. The context of youth (sub)cultural identities in Estonia. *Filosofija. Sociologija* 23(2), 93–201.

Anderson, B. 1991. *Imagined communities: Reflections on the origin and spread of nationalism.* London: Verso.

Antonsich, M. 2015. The 'everyday' of banal nationalism – ordinary people's views on Italy and Italian. *Policial Geography* 54, 32–42.

Ashby, S. 2015. 'Hold the heathen hammer high': Representation, re-enactment and the construction of 'Pagan' heritage. *International Journal of Heritage Studies* 21(5), 493–511.

Baker, C. 2008. Wild dances and dying wolves: Simulation, essentialization, and national identity at the Eurovision Song Contest. *Popular Communication* 6(3), 173–189.

Baker, C. 2010. *Sounds of the borderland: Popular music, war and nationalism in Croatia.* Farnham: Ashgate.

Baycroft, T., Hopkin, D. eds. 2012. *Folklore and nationalism in Europe during the long nineteenth century.* Leiden: Brill.

Bennett, A. 2000. *Popular music and youth culture: Music, identity and place.* Houndmills: MacMillan.

Biddle, I., Knight, V. eds. 2007. *Music, national identity and the politics of location: Between the global and the local.* Hampshire: Ashgate.

Billig, M. 1995. *Banal nationalism.* London: Sage.

Bohlman, P. 2011. *Focus: Music, nationalism, and the making of the new Europe.* New York and London: Routledge.

Brüggemann, K., Kasekamp, A. 2014. 'Singing oneself into a nation'? Estonian song festivals as rituals of political mobilisation. *Nations and Nationalism* 20(2), 259–276.

Cepeda, M. E. 2010. *Musical ImagiNation: U.S.-Colombian identity and the Latin music boom.* New York: New York University Press.

Cloonan, M. 1996. Pop and the nation-state: Towards a theorisation. *Popular Music* 18(20), 193–207.

Cojocaru, L., Dimova, R. 2013. 'Nature' and 'nation' in the republic of Moldova: Rebirth and rebuilding through the international festival of music 'Mărţişor'. *History and Anthropology* 24(1), 13–35.

Connell, J., Gibson, C. 2003. *Sound tracks: Popular music identity and place.* London and New York: Routledge.

Creed, G. W. 2011. *Masquerade and postsocialism: Ritual and cultural dispossession in Bulgaria.* Bloomington, IN: Indiana University Press.

Can musicians build the nation? 49

Curtis, B. 2008. *Music makes nation. Nationalist composers and nation building in nineteenth century Europe*. Amherst, NY: Cambria Press.

Čvoro, U. 2014. *Turbo-folk music and cultural representations of national identity in former Yugoslavia*. Surrey, UK: Ashgate.

Daitz, M. S. 2004. Integral vs. derivative use of Balto-Finnic traditional song in the choral compositions of Veljo Tormis. *Fontes Artis Musicae*, 51(3/4), 322–331.

Daughtry, M. 2003. Russia's new anthem and the negotiation of national identity. *Ethnomusicology* 47(1), 42–67.

Dimova, R., Cojocaru, L. 2013. Contested nation building within the international order of things: Performance, festivals and legitimization in South-Eastern Europe. *History and Anthropology* 24(1), 1–12.

Djumaev, A. 2005. Musical heritage and national identity in Uzbekistan. *Ethnomusicology Forum* 14(2), 165–184.

Edensor, T. 2002. *National identity, popular culture and everyday life*. Oxford: Berg.

Engelhardt, J. 2008. Late- and post-Soviet music scholarship and the tenacious ecumenicity of Christian musics in Estonia. *Journal Of Baltic Studies* 39(3), 239–262.

Eriksen, T. H. 1993. Formal and informal nationalism. *Ethnic and Racial Studies* 16(1), 1–25.

Estonian Institute. 2015. *The world of Estonian music*. Tallinn: Estonian Institute.

Eyck, F. Gunther. 1995. *The voice of nations: European national anthems and their authors*. Westport, CT: Greenwood Press.

Feldman, M. 2001. European integration and the discourse of national identity in Estonia. *National Identities* 3(1), 5–21.

Fox, J. E., Miller-Idriss, C. 2008. Everyday nationhood. *Ethnicities* 8(4), 536–563.

Frith, S. 1996. Music and identity, in *Questions of Cultural Identity*, edited by S. Hall and P. du Gay. London: Sage, 108–127.

Frolova-Walker, M. 2007. *Russian music and nationalism: From Glinka to Stalin*. New Haven, CT: Yale University Press.

Gellner, E. 1983. *Nations and nationalism*. Ithaca, NY: Cornell University Press.

Hobsbawm, E., Ranger, T. eds. 1983. *The invention of tradition*. Cambridge: Cambridge University Press.

Hudson, R. 2003. Songs of seduction: Popular music and Serbian nationalism. *Patterns of Prejudice* 37(2), 157–176.

Isaacs, R., Polese, A. 2015. Between 'imagined' and 'real' nation building: Identities and nationhood in post-Soviet Central Asia. *Nationalities Papers* 43(3), 371–382.

Isaacs, R., Polese, A. eds. 2016. *Nation building and identity in the post-Soviet space: New tools and approaches*. New York and London: Routledge.

Ismayilov, M. 2012. State, identity, and the politics of music: Eurovision and nation building in Azerbaijan. *Nationalities Papers* 40(6), 833–851.

Johnson, D. 2006. Music videos and national identity in post-Soviet Kazakhstan. *Qualitative Research Reports in Communication* 7(1), 9–14.

Jordan, P. 2014. *The modern fairy tale: Nation branding, national identity and the Eurovision Song Contest in Estonia*. Tartu: University of Tartu Press.

Knott, E. 2015. What does it mean to be a kin majority? Analyzing Romanian identity in Moldova and Russian identity in Crimea from below. *Social Science Quarterly* 96(3), 830–858.

Kõlar, A. 2004. Folk hymns as a source of Cyrillus Kreek's compositions. *Fontes Artis Musicae* 51(3/4), 315–321.

Kuus, M. 2002. European integration in identity narratives in Estonia: A quest for security. *Journal of Peace Research* 39(1), 91–108.

Kuutma, K. 1996. Cultural identity, nationalism and changes in singing traditions. *Folklore: Electronic Journal of Folklore* 2, 124–141.

Kuutma, K., Kästik, H. 2014. Creativity and 'right singing': Aural experience and embodiment of heritage. *Journal of Folklore Research* 51(3), 277–310.

50 Emilia Pawłusz

Larkey, E. 1992. Austropop: Popular music and national identity in Austria. *Popular Music* 11(2), 151–185.

Lippus, U. 2006. The Estonian tradition of folk hymn singing. In *Spiritual folk singing. Nordic and Baltic traditions*, edited by K. S. Bak and S. Nielsen. Forlaget Kragen, 41–66.

Lucas, O. 2014. A Finnish medley: Forging folk metal. *Ethnomusicology Review*, June 23. Available online at http://ethnomusicologyreview.ucla.edu/content/finnish-medley-forging-folk-metal [accessed 30 September 2016].

Mach, Z. 1994. National anthems: The case of Chopin as a national composer, in *Ethnicity, identity and music: The musical construction of place*, edited by M. Stokes. Oxford: Berg Publishers, 61–70.

Marjenin, P. A. 2014. The metal folk: The Impact of music and culture on folk metal and the music of Korpiklaani. MA thesis, Kent State University.

Mole, R. 2012. *The Baltic states from the Soviet Union to the European Union. Identity, discourse and power in the post-Communist transition of Estonia, Latvia and Lithuania*. New York and London: Routledge.

Moser, S. 2010. Creating citizens through play: The role of leisure in Indonesian nation building. *Social and Cultural Geography* 11(1), 53–73.

Pawłusz, E. 2016. The Estonian song celebration (Laulupidu) as an instrument of language policy. *Journal of Baltic Studies*, DOI: 10.1080/01629778.2016.1164203

Pawłusz, E., Polese, A. 2017. 'Scandinavia's best kept secret': Tourism promotion, nation branding and identity construction in Estonia (with a free guided tour of Tallinn airport). *Nationalities Papers*, 1–20. doi: 10.1080/00905992.2017.1287167

Pawłusz, E., Seliverstova, O. 2016. Everyday nation-building in the post-Soviet space. Methodological reflections. *Studies for Transition States and Societies* 8(1), 69–86.

Polese, A. 2016. *Limits of a state: How informality replaces, renegotiates and reshapes governance in post-Soviet spaces*. Stuttgart: Ibidem.

Ramnarine, T. K. 2003. *Ilmatar's inspirations: Nationalism, globalization, and the changing soundscapes of Finnish folk music*. Chicago and London: University of Chicago Press.

Revill, G. 2000. Music and the politics of sound: Nationalism, citizenship, and auditory space. *Environment and Planning D: Society and Space* 18, 597–613.

Rinne, J. 2016. *Searching for authentic living through native faith. The Maausk movement in Estonia*. Ph.D dissertation, Södertörn University.

Ryback, T. W. 1990. *Rock around the Bloc*. New York: Oxford University Press.

Seliverstova, O. 2017. 'Consuming' national identity in western Ukraine. *Nationalities Papers* 45(1), 61–79.

Skey, M. 2011. *National belonging and everyday life*. Basingstoke: Palgrave.

Šmidchens, G. 2014. *The power of song: Nonviolent national culture in the baltic singing revolution*. Seattle: Washington University Press.

Spinetti, F. 2005. Tradition and Tajik popular music: Questions of aesthetics, identity and political economy. *Ethnomusicology Forum* 14(2), 185–211.

Spracklen, K., Lucas, C., Deeks, M. 2014. The construction of heavy metal identity through heritage narratives: A case study of extreme metal bands in the north of England. *Popular Music and Society* 37(1), 48–64.

Stokes, M. ed. 1994. *Ethnicity, identity and music. The musical construction of place*. Oxford, Providence: Berg.

Strachan, R., Leonard, M. 2004. A musical nation: Protection, investment and branding in the Irish music industry. *Irish Studies Review* 12(1), 39–49.

Strmiska, M. 2005. The music of the past in modern Baltic Paganism. *Nova Religio: The Journal of Alternative and Emergent Religions* 8(3), 39–58.

Thompson, A. 2001. Nations, national identities and human agency: Putting people back into nations. *The Sociological Review* 49(1), 18–32.

Vakker, T., Rohtmets, P. 2008. Estonia: Relations between Christian and non-Christian religious organisations and the state of religious freedom. *Religion, State and Society* 36(1), 45–53.

Wanner, C. 2004. Nationalism on stage: Music and change in Soviet Ukraine. *Popular Music: Music and Identity* 4, 136–155.

White, H., Murphy, M. eds. 2001. *Musical constructions of nationalism: Essays on the history and ideology of European musical culture 1800-1945*. Cork: Cork University Press.

Whiteley, S., Bennet, A., Hawkins, S. 2004. *Music, space and place: Popular music and cultural identity*. Farnham: Ashgate.

Wickström, D. E. 2008. 'Drive-ethno-dance' and 'Hutzul punk': Ukrainian-associated popular music and (geo)politics in a post-Soviet context. *Yearbook for Traditional Music* 40, 60–88.

Wilson, W. A. 1973. Herder, folklore and romantic nationalism. *The Journal of Popular Culture* 6(4), 819–835.

Winter, T., Keegan-Phipps, S. 2013. *Performing Englishness. Identity and politics in contemporary folk resurgence*. Manchester, NY: Manchester University Press.

Wood, N. 2012. Playing with 'Scottishness': Musical performance, non-representational thinking and the 'doings' of national identity. *Cultural Geography* 19(2), 195–215.

Wood, N., Duffy, M., Smith, S.J. 2007. The art of doing (geographies of) music. *Environment and Planning D: Society and Space* 25, 867–889.

Wood, N., Smith, S.J. 2004. Instrumental routes to emotional geographies. *Social and Cultural Geography* 5(4), 533–548.

3 The Georgian National Museum and the Museum of Soviet Occupation as loci of informal nation building

Alisa Datunashvili

Introduction

Museums, in particular national museums, are an important place of memory. As Nora (1989) puts it they are 'lieux de memoire' often charged with the tasks to crystalize and maintain collective memory and create markers that help new interpretations and representations of collective markers for a given group. As such, they are also the place where nationalistic discourses may become more visible and help us discover the cultural intimacy (Herzfeld 2005) of a country, a group, often unveiling hidden sentiments or attitudes that remain long unnoticed. Like many counterparts, Georgia's museums are based on collections. The availability of original collections is crucial for a 'real museum'. Collections and exhibits and their selection criteria, presentation and interpretation show how and where the nation sees its place in the world of nations (Westerwinter 2008). But the modern approach in museology is to have a collection as a means but not an end (Hein 2000). Contemporary Western museums have become not only bearers of certain discourses of different elites and educational institutions accessible for every citizen, but a place for spreading and sharing scientific knowledge, a place for communication with, between and among societies. New technologies allow the creation of scenography to achieve 'an experience that is genuine'. Learning through experience is the end of modern museums (Hein 2000).

Innovation and introduction of novel approaches, learning tools and perspectives are the new challenge for museums all over the world, especially in the post-Soviet states. The nineteenth-century static expositions and narratives interpreted according to Soviet ideology are changing with introduction of new research methods and the influence of modern social theories and technologies in Georgia. To accomplish this task it is not enough to just change the scenography or install a new exhibition, but change the concept of the museum itself. This is not an easy task for the newly established postcolonial nation-state where museums acquire special importance as having one's own culture and history is considered to be a sign of being a 'genuine, authentic people' which deserves independence and self-governance (Handler 1988). Hence, political elites strive to not only fix and present a nation's 'authenticity'

Museums as loci of nation building 53

and 'otherness' in museums but to construct new identities through 'recalling' 'forgotten' parts of history and culture. In the early 1980s Benedict Anderson noted that after acquiring independence the newly established nations inherited the concept of political museums from their colonial ancestors (Anderson 1983).

Georgia is no exception. This chapter presents the case of the Georgian National Museum from the perspective of museum professionals – registrars, guides, exhibition managers/curators – in the context of everyday nationalism. Seeking a dialogue with a scholarship looking at possible gaps between official narratives, transmission of political ideas and their reception by the citizens that locates between 'real' and 'imagined' nation building (Isaacs and Polese 2015, 2016, Polese and Horak 2015), this study investigates the official narratives around the discourse by policymakers and those involved in the transmission of political ideas. Civil servants working in a museum or in other public institutions are charged with the task of transmitting ideas that might not necessarily coincide with their own perception of events or national facts (Pawłusz 2016, Pawłusz and Seliverstova 2016). This chapter explores the synergy between a nationalizing attempt by the political elites and the passive resistance by civil servants who, in some cases, cannot live with some changes. The main focus of this chapter is, thus, the dynamics and forces resulting from contrasting, and somehow conflictual, discourses of national identity performed by the elites and civil servants working in a museum. How do they express their 'individual' nationhood in their everyday practices? What happens if the new political elite tries to change the museum according to their discourse of nationalism? How do people working in the museum reflect on this change and what effect does it have on performing their job?

There is a consolidated body of scholarship exploring the role of national heritage and memory and its uses and instrumentalization with respect to national identity. Constructivist approaches see national heritage as produced to consolidate an official discourse on national identity (Ashworth and Larkham 2013, Smith 2006) and different uses of this discourse (Howard 2003). In this frame, museums are a central place of identity construction (Coombes 1988, Cummins 2004) and uses of the past (Brown and Davis-Brown 1998). Museums can be seen as a place for negotiation of a national identity discourse (Kaeppler 1994). Present-centred heritage is 'a recurrent theme in the recent literature on Heritage' (Graham and Howard 2008: 2). Bendix examines hegemony in making heritage (Bendix et al. 2012). Laurajane Smith speaks about 'authorized heritage discourse' considering management and maintenance and even visiting heritage sites as 'acts directly implicated in the occasional construction or reconstruction ... of social and cultural meanings' (Smith 2006: 12). This chapter focuses on people directly involved in these 'acts' and producing and reproducing nationhood. Although 'banal nationalism' introduced by Billig (1995) sheds light on daily expressions of nationalism, including newspaper articles, politician

54 *Alisa Datunashvili*

speeches, national festivals and memorials, and tangible and intangible heritage, people's agency in everyday nationalism was emphasized by Skey: 'Without the activities of people there are no national (or indeed any other, social) formations' (Skey 2011: 150). Moreover, everyday nationalism is examined by Antonsich as practiced through individual acts, habits and practices of ordinary people (Antonsich 2015). In this regard I consider the museum as a place where nationalism is practiced daily and its staff as 'practitioners' of nationalism.

Nationalism in post-Soviet Georgia

After the collapse of the Soviet Union Georgia experienced two wars (South Ossetia 1991–1992 and Abkhazia 1992–1993) and a civil war in 1989–90. National institutions hardly functioned. Corruption at every level of the state authorities was common practice. The non-violent, so called 'Rose Revolution', followed by reforms, was a big shift in Georgia's recent history: in November of 2003 Georgia's President Eduard Shevardnadze was forced to resign because of the mass protests in the capital city against election fraud. The new political elite introduced a governmental program which consisted of 10 clauses and was called 'For Integrated and Strong Georgia through Economic Growth, Long-Term Stability and Eurointegration'. The day before his inauguration the newly elected president Saakashvili made his speech on the tomb of David the Builder, who ruled Georgia in 11th century. This symbolic act in the presence of the Head of the Georgian Orthodox Church promised a new golden age under his rule: 'Georgia will be integrated, strong, it will be unified again and be an integrated strong state' (De Waal 2011: 5) Saakashvili's aim was to present modern Georgia as the descendant of medieval 'Great' Georgian kingdom and himself as the builder of 'new' Georgia. King David the Builder is one of the most important characters in Georgian's collective memory, known as the liberator and unifier of Georgia. His reign is acknowledged as the beginning of the golden age in the country which lasted till the beginning of the 13th century. Besides liberating the kingdom from foreign domination, e.g. external enemies, David managed to exterminate 'internal enemies' – feudal lords – and unified the Georgian Kingdom within borders even larger than those of contemporary Georgia. The 'Golden Age' is an integral part of Georgia's narrative template, which, as defined by Wertsch, is a cultural tool to mediate collective memory (Wertsch and Batiashvili 2008, Batiashvili 2012). Narrative templates are rigid frames containing key features and the main narratives on national identity. Batiashvili introduces three narrative templates of 'Georgianness':

a) Georgia's ceaseless effort to integrate its historic territories into a powerful state. The precedent for this existed during the golden age between the eleventh and thirteenth centuries. History is read here as a series of repeated attempts that are thwarted by the appearance of a 'new enemy'.

b) Georgian's ability to preserve national culture, namely language, religion (Orthodox Christianity) and national identity, despite the fact that external enemies persistently try to defeat and culturally assimilate Georgians. From this perspective, encounters with the external world endanger Georgian statehood and national traits constituting 'Georgianness'.
c) Georgians have been able to resist their enemies and preserve their culture because of their innate characteristics which make them irreconcilable to external domination. (Batiashvili 2012: 190)

Her study based on the analysis of different media sources, history textbooks and political discussions suggests that Georgian national narratives have not changed since the Soviet period (except contemporary narratives emphasize religion). As for 'official' discourses of Georgian nationalism Jones distinguishes three models of post-Soviet Georgian nationalism: a model of cultural assimilation advocated by president Gamsakhurdia (1991–92) who saw cultural and ethnical distinctiveness as threats to national unity, Shevardnadze's (1995–2003) policy of reconciliation between different ethnic and cultural groups and inclusive citizenship, and Saakashvili's (2004–2013) 'mix of his predecessors' (Jones 2013: 216). Going back to Saakashvili's pilgrimage I sketched above and the program introduced by his government, two points are notable: unification of the country and Eurointegration. The former is a part of the existing narrative template – Georgia's eternal struggle for reintegration – and the latter a continuation of relatively new narrative introduced by Shevardnadze. Following his direction towards Eurointegration, Saakashvili's government initiated liberal reforms. These affected the Georgian Constitution, police, tax and customs, privatization and education systems.

New start for old museums

In the context of my research two reforms are most significant: privatization and education. According to the new laws there were no restrictions for privatization including so-called 'strategic property'. There was no restriction also for transferring property to offshore companies and companies owned by another state/country. 4,280 objects were privatized in 2003–2010 (European Initiative Liberal Academy Tbilisi, 2012). Several laws for education were introduced (On General Education, On Higher Education – 2005 and On Professional Education – 2007; Legislative Herald of Georgia 2005, 2007). Privatization of national/state property including hospitals, railway and some monuments of cultural heritage and changes in the national curriculum, especially of Georgian History and Literature, caused public dissatisfaction. This was partly for socioeconomic reasons – people were fired in large numbers from newly privatized companies, hospitals and educational institutions, but mostly because it was perceived as an attack to 'Georgianness' (kartveloba) – the aggregate of values attributed to Georgian ethnical identity. Acts of protest started in the capital city. Reforms were emotionally debated in media as well

56   *Alisa Datunashvili*

as at public spaces – streets, backyards, transport. Even family gatherings and parties would end up with fervent discussion of ongoing reforms. Privatization of 'Strategic Objects' and heritage monuments, which often were destroyed or reconstructed, created fear that 'everything will be sold'. On the other hand, the introduction of the new history textbook and changes in the school curriculum were perceived as a threat to 'essential components of Georgianness' – language and history (Batiashvili 2012: 185). There was anxiety about 'being deprived' of national identity. But the 'Rose Government' was not going to retreat. One of its projects was museum reform. After the years of wars and financial crisis museums were barely functioning. Poor salaries, outdated equipment and amortized buildings, almost no visitors and no new exhibitions were the obvious problems to be solved. But the main goal of the reform was to entirely change museum management and its concept.

With a special presidential decree (No. 626, December 30, 2004) a new legal entity of public law – the Georgian National Museum – was established, which was considered to be the

> [B]eginning of structural, institutional and legislative reforms in country's cultural heritage management. Reforms include introducing new public management practices; elaboration and establishment of museum policies and an integrated administrative system; improvement of museum collection safety standards; increase of educational activities; collaboration between museums and academia. (Georgian National Museum 2012)

In fact, it was unification of the five leading museums of Georgia which house the largest collections of art, history, archaeology and natural history. In the following years more museums from all over the country were incorporated into the Georgian National Museum. Now it unifies ten leading museums, two research centres, the National Gallery, four house-museums, fourteen archaeological sites and repositories in the capital and different regions.

Establishment of the 'Museum of Soviet Occupation' (2006) and the massive renovation of Sighnaghi Museum (2007) – both under the umbrella of the GNM – were funded from the special Presidential reserve and initiated and supervised by high-ranking government officials personally (minsters of Culture and of Internal Affairs and the Prosecutor-General). GNM was subordinated to the Ministry of Culture and Monuments Protection. Internal elections of the Director were abolished. The General Director was appointed directly by the President instead.

Being 'Museumeli': self-reflection and methodology

I started to work in the Georgian National Museum in April 2005, three months after its establishment. Our offices were placed in the Simon Janashia

Museums as loci of nation building 57

Museum of Georgia, the oldest and largest museum in the country. As the assistant to the General Director I became part of the new management team, which consisted of the General, Executive and Financial Directors, a lawyer, a PR manager, an HR manager, Head of Chancellery, two managers and a Scientific Secretary.

Despite no experience or educational background in museum management (apart from the General Director who has worked in the Simon Janashia Museum since 1997) and relatively young age (most of us were between 25–40, the General Director himself was 41) we were unified by the idea of a new, modern museum. We easily became friends. Moreover, the lawyer and the Head of Chancellery were my classmates. I not only had free access to all documents, but was involved in their preparation. Managing the General Director's mail, organizing meetings and preparing reports, I had full information on ongoing projects and plans. After several training periods and an internship in the National Gallery of Art Palazzo Barberini (one of Italy's most prominent museums), I was promoted as Head of the newly established Collections Registration and Management Division. In my new position I met every registrar, curator, manager and assisting staff involved in the collection management process. I studied their biographies, the history of different museums and their collections. Discussing problems and working together on different projects opened a new perspective from below – visions and thoughts of museum workers, including their perception of new policy and changes. In private talks they would share their concerns and fears, and recall stories from the past. The more I talked to my elder colleagues, the clearer I saw the gap between the new management and 'old staff', old in both senses – age and time spent working in the museum. I discovered the museum as an entirely different world with its established rules, informal authorities (people not possessing high position but respected because of their knowledge/experience or personal features) and complex relationships. Most of the staff had worked here since their student days. During the ten years of my work in the museum I learned about the concept of 'museumeli' – a person who is not just working in the museum, but has a deep attachment to it. The suffix '-eli' indicates belonging to a certain group or place, 'Kartveli' for instance means Georgian. For most museum professionals there is a strong, not to say intimate connection to the museum as an important part of their identity and as a means to literally practice their nationalism. I observed the pride of belonging to the museum community (being 'museumeli') in almost all museums within the Georgian National Museum and also during my stay in the Baltic states, where I visited occupation museums and conducted interviews with colleagues. Starting from the 'wards' – staff monitoring the exhibitions, and ending with the deputy directors – all are proud to work in the museum. Some of them even compare the museum with the family – 'one big family', 'we are family'; in some departments younger colleagues refer to their elder co-workers as 'aunt' and 'uncle'. It is no wonder that in such a community the sensibility towards the 'other' is very high and

58 *Alisa Datunashvili*

museum staff as a community facing changes and defending the museum from 'others' demonstrate ignorance and fear. It explains also the alienation and even rejection my newcomer colleagues and I felt during our first years in the museum.

Getting to know the older colleagues they would typically welcome me with the words, 'You know what the museum is? Once you come here, it poisons you and you'll never be able to quit!'; one has to 'swallow the dust of the museum' to become a true member of the community. So museumeli is attached not only to the people one works with, but with the building and collection/objects in it: 'my objects', 'my collections' is how they mention in everyday conversation the objects under their curatorship. 'It is a feeling that you are doing something for your country' was the answer to my direct question, 'What is "museumeli"?' After ten years of working in the museum I am still not sure whether I became museumeli. At least my colleagues never address me as such. I assume this is an honour which depends on the years of experience and amount of museum dust swallowed, e.g. being directly in touch with the objects and collections. Nonetheless I developed a strong attachment to my job.

As for my research, being an insider in my field was an advantage and challenge at the same time. Unlimited access to all the data as well as personal relations with the informants and my personal experience gave me the full context and ability to choose the 'right' informants. But on the other hand it became more and more difficult for me to narrow the focus of my research and detach myself from the museum and develop a detached view. This was one of the reasons for me to focus on the Museum of Soviet Occupation. I was not directly involved in the implementation of the project and it was not an idea from within the museum but the government's initiative. All the museums united under the GNM umbrella were established institutions, but the Museum of Soviet Occupation was a completely new initiative presenting part of the hidden history of the country. Research data are based on regular observation in the exhibition hall during a six-month period (October 2015– March 2016) two or three times a week, talks with colleagues, research in the museum archive and interviews with exhibition managers, guides, the warden and the museum architect. Transcribing semi-structured interviews caused curiosity ('Why are you typewriting?' 'What is your paper about?'). One key informant refused to give me an interview when he discovered I was going to record it. Two colleagues hesitated but agreed because of their personal relation to me. They were all quite open in their opinions, even when negative. In some cases (one of the examples I will discuss below) the behaviour of the guides is unprofessional. Indicating their names would put them in danger of losing their job. Some stories are told in an informal talk or chat with the colleague by lunch 'just between us' or 'Don't tell anyone *I* told you that'. Thus, I decided to anonymize my informants partly for reasons of their safety, but also to comfort myself and not to feel like 'a spy at the rear of the enemy'.

Museums in Georgia: a brief history

Although the GNM was established at the end of 2004 its history goes back to the 19th century, when the Russian Royal Geographic Society's Museum of the Caucasian Department was founded in Tbilisi. Later on a group of Georgian intellectuals known as 'Tergdaleulebi' established the Museum of the Society of Spreading Literacy among Georgians, which was followed by the Georgian Museum founded by the decree of the government of the Georgian Independent Republic in 1919. The successor of the above-mentioned museums is considered to be the oldest and largest museum, today called the Simon Janashia Museum of Georgia (Figure 3.1). It is located in the very heart of the centre of the capital city, on its main street – Rustaveli Avenue. The building for exhibition spaces was built in 1929 based on a project of the Russian architect N. Severov. It houses nearly two million objects of Georgian and Caucasian natural and cultural heritage including hominid remains dated back to 1.8 million years; endemic, relict and rare specimens; goldsmithery and metalwork collections from the second half of the third millennia to the late Middle Ages; epigraphic monuments of Georgian, Aramaic, Greek, Jewish and Arabic scripts and Urartian cuneiform; and collections of the vernacular life of people living in Caucasia. In 1935 it was given the status of a state museum. Like most museums in the USSR the museum was managed by the Academy of Science. To get a position in the museum, one had to be either an acknowledged researcher or have an 'influential relative' – 'oh, one needed to arrange

Figure 3.1 Façade of the Simon Janashia Museum of Georgia: first banner on the right side advertises 'Museum of Soviet Occupation'. Museum archive.

60 *Alisa Datunashvili*

things in Central Committee', one of my informants noted. He got his job with the help of his aunt, who was an accountant in the Academy of Sciences. Wives and daughters-in-law of prominent scientists or members of the Central Committee were often hired. Another informant told me he was proposed for an internship in the Hermitage, but he refused, because it was for a long period and he would lose his job in the Simon Janashia Museum. Although salaries were not high (technical staff under 100 rubles, PhDs 250 rubles), it was a very prestigious, 'exclusive', not to say elitist institution with its own internal hierarchy (archaeologists were the most honoured) and connections/relations. 'This was a [good] time! We would have lots of feasts here'. 'We would have birthday parties [in the department]', I was often told by my elder colleagues in private talks or informal gatherings in the museum. The Head of one of the departments would even throw parties with traditional live music.

So, the Janashia Museum was an established community which had its vision of what a museum is: a 'museum is its objects'. Objects make collections and museums keep collections for future generations: 'to know who we were, where we come from'.

Re-presenting history: Museum of Soviet Occupation

Founded by a presidential decree, the Museum of Soviet Occupation was officially opened on the anniversary of Georgian independence, 26 May 2006. It occupies two large halls in the Simon Janashia Museum (app. 600m^2). As explained on the museum's webpage, 'Documental, photo and video material on the Occupation of Georgia by Bolshevik Russia (February–March 1921) and the seventy-year Soviet occupational regime (1921–1991) are presented here'. The exhibition starts with the list of victims of Soviet occupation. A huge picture of Georgian cadets shot by Russian soldiers lies on the floor. A reproduction of a wagon where Georgian noblemen were shot is mounted on the entrance to the second hall. On the left wall of the second hall there is a map of the 'Georgian Democratic Republic recognized by the League of Nations'. Actual storytelling starts with the Act of Independence of Georgia and the speech of its leader – Noe Zhordania. The guide's text highlights the excerpt:

> What do we have to offer to the cultural treasure of the European nations? A two-thousand-year old national culture, democratic system and natural wealth. Soviet Russia offered us a military alliance which we rejected. … They are heading for the East, We, for the West. … We would like to yell at Russian Bolsheviks: turn to the West to make a contemporary European nation. (Noe Zhordania, Head of the Government of the Democratic Republic of Georgia. Excerpt of the Speech made at the Extraordinary Session of the Constituent Assembly on January 27, 1921, on exhibition display)

Pictures of foreign diplomats – from Great Britain and Germany – alternate with photographs of Georgian leaders and commanders of the Democratic

Museums as loci of nation building 61

Republic. In an exhibit case the money and postal marks of independent Georgia are presented. The story goes on chronologically until 1991: declaration of Georgian independence on May 26, and ends with a map of Georgia depicting occupied territories by Russia. It can be divided into the following parts: independent Georgian Democratic Republic (1918–21); Russian 'subversive activities' and Russian invasion in 1921, followed by repressions and extermination of Georgian clergy and intellectual elite; revolt of 1922; repressions of 1920–30s; the Khrushchev period which is presented very cursorily, and the Georgian National Movement (1960–80). This division is very formal; narration is not strictly linear, and sometimes even chaotic – the revolt of 1922 is followed by the Soviet annexation. The letter of Georgian highlanders, Khevsurs, addressed to the US government is shown next to the portrait of Beria, Voroshilov and Mikoyan. To find out the causes of the lapses and some glaring mistakes (for instance, there is no evidence that the League of Nations ever acknowledged Georgia in the borders depicted on the map starting the exhibition), I started to ask colleagues about the author of the concept and content. The project was curated by a Member of Parliament of Georgia, not the employee of the museum, and fully implemented by an outside company belonging to an art historian and photographer who later became deputy Minister of Culture. In informal talks I was told the idea belonged to the then President of Georgia, Mikheil Saakashvili, and also a parliamentarian Nikoloz Rurua, who later became Minister of Culture. Having free access to the archives, it took me several hours to find the official document about the establishment of the museum. Surprisingly, the special presidential decree issued on 21 February 2006 is 'About the installation of the exhibit representing Georgian History, "History of the Occupation of Georgia"'. There is no mention of the 'Museum of Soviet Occupation', although the name on the banner at the museum entrance and museum website mentions a 'museum'. It was harder to find out who from the museum staff was involved in the process. One of my informants, an exhibition manager, Mr. G., was to formally supervise the installation process. He said in an interview: 'I have not seen anyone [from the museum] there', 'only **they** were coming. That [man] … what is his name … who later became deputy minister and **them**…'.

'He was only opening and closing the door [of the exhibition hall] for **them**, nothing more' – Mr. K., another colleague, talks about G., stressing that although formally supervising the installation, Mr. G. was not involved in the process.

Except for two parliamentarians, a photographer and an architect who are mentioned as 'their (MPs') friends', the city Mayor personally supervised the installation process. All the above mentioned, and the fact that the project was financed from special presidential reserve funds and implemented in three months, shows the keen interest of the political elite in creating a 'History of the Occupation of Georgia'.

I remember a colleague, a historian who studied Soviet history and led a department in the Simon Janashia Museum waiting at the door of the

62　*Alisa Datunashvili*

General Director, whom I was then assisting. He was outraged and frightened at the same time: 'How is it possible?' he was asking his colleagues. Later I heard a discussion between him and other colleagues expressing concerns about the 'truth' or 'authenticity' of the objects. Unfortunately, he and another colleague, who trained the newly hired guide for the Occupation exhibition, later passed away. From other colleagues I could only learn that no museum staff were involved in the development of the concept. With the help of a co-worker and close friend of mine I found the only internal document referring to the Exhibition of Soviet Occupation. It is a meeting report of the then Museum Director, his deputies, Head of the history department, four researchers from the same department, a senior researcher from the department of medieval history, a software engineer, a human resource manager and the Head of the administration chancellery. The report is dated but not signed nor registered in the archive. It contains very little information, but clearly demonstrates that the top management just informs, not gives orders to the employees to support the installation of the exhibit. From the two pages of the report, the speech of the Director occupies almost an entire page:

> You are well aware that upon the order of the highest government the exhibition of Soviet Occupation is being prepared in the museum. ... Organizers of the exhibition have their own thoughts and goals. The Concept and program is developed. ... Our museum is obliged to give them the material. ... We just have to give them the objects and that's it, this will be only contribution of the museum in the development of the exhibition. (Record of a Meeting in the Georgian National Museum Simon Janashia Museum of Georgia 'On organizing an exhibition of occupation of Georgia', 2 May, 2006)

In private talks with one of the representatives of top management (which he asked not to record) he explained that exhibition organizers did not share their vision (with him or his colleagues); they did not even ask for advice, although they were not historians: 'just random people'. It was a humiliation. 'We would not beg to involve us.' Paraphrasing his words, museum staff could not openly oppose the government because the museum is a state institution. But they decided to silently protest and let the organizers do what they wanted. 'See, what they did?! Just wasted money!'

Other colleagues directly or indirectly involved in the organization process or maintaining the exhibition now have different remarks, but all agree that the exhibition is poor. From the in-depth interviews and talks, and also by listening and observing the guided tours, I have identified two main claims of the museum professionals: (1) there are very few 'real' objects on display, mostly copies of the documents and photographs; and (2) the history is not complete: it depicts only the Soviet Occupation although Georgia was occupied by Russia long before the Bolsheviks. It shows only the negative side of Soviet rule. It ignores the everyday life of ordinary people.

Figure 3.2 On the left wall is the list of people shot by Communists; there is a also cannon and Wagon (imitation), where occupation victims were shot. A picture of Georgian Cadets shot during Russian invasion is on the floor, and there is a red spotlight – 'blood' – on the wagon with holes – 'shooting marks'. Altogether this creates an immediate emotional effect and creates unequivocally negative associations that are continued in the main exhibition hall. Museum archive.

Figure 3.3 Main exhibition hall, divided by the prison cell doors and massive pillars covered with concrete; together with the dimmed lights and dominant black and grey colours the exhibit makes an oppressive impression. Image from the museum archive.

Telling the 'real history': nationalism in action

To 'correct' the mistakes and fill out the gaps, guides have their own 'methodology'. In spite of having a standardized guide text, they often make their own interpretations of the narrative. Moreover, their nationalistic sentiments strongly influence the tour and sometimes create confusion as was the case with two Russian speaking tourists – a Russian woman and an Ukrainian man both about 40 years old. Ms. N., a lady in her late fifties, a guide with thirty years of experience, who usually does not guide Russian-speaking visitors, was starting the tour when I noticed them during one of my visits in the exhibition hall. Before I asked permission to record, she informed me in Georgian that she 'did not want them at all'. She was exhausted, she said, had a headache and, after all, she is not supposed to guide Russian-speaking tourists, but as there was no other guide available, she could not refuse. From the very beginning I felt tension. Soon I realized it was her 'patriotism' rather than her headache that made her anxious and even aggressive to some degree. Not following the official narrative, she started to recall her experience from the eighties, when she surprised a foreign tourist group by telling them an 'unofficial text': 'the KGB people were not there and I was saying the hell knows what, I mean, I said how it **really** was. "Is this the official text?" they asked. I said, "It is not official, but the **real** text"' she said proudly. 'Now they (organisers of the Occupation Exhibition) made this. There are only copies.' She invited visitors into the hall and expressed her discontent: 'Why only Soviet Occupation? When talking about the occupation, one should start with the 18th century.' The trouble began when the visiting lady asked whether Georgia joined Russia voluntarily. 'Voluntarily?' N. asked with her eyes screwed up. 'Did Crimea volunteer [to join Russia]?' The rest of the narration was more like a squabble. Ms. N. was irritated with the questions of the visitor, which sometimes were very naïve or appeared to N. as silly. At some point she thought the visitors were trying to deride her, especially when the lady asked whether woman were allowed to take part in the parliamentary/government elections in contemporary Georgia.

Although the standard full tour takes no longer than 45–50 minutes, this one took an hour and a half. During my observation I noticed that the guides with less experience follow the official text more strictly. The more experience the guide has, the more interpretation, but this particular tour, or to be more precise, emotionally very charged dialogue, was the most obvious demonstration of the emotional nature of nationalism. In her narration N. has clearly demonstrated not just an attachment or bond to her nation, but aggression and disgust towards an outgroup. Her comments in Georgian often referred to me as her group member who, she was sure, shared the same feelings: '[Why] Did I want them here?' 'They are insane.' At some points she even lost control and humiliated the visitors with cynical questions: 'Did you

Museums as loci of nation building 65

Figure 3.4 (Left) 'Sir John Oliver Wardrop. The UK's first Chief Commissioner in Transcaucasia, Active supporter of Georgia's independence and sovereignty'. (Right) 'Friedrich Werner von Schulenburg. Consul of Germany in Georgia. Co-author of the text of founding charter of Democratic Republic of Georgia'. This shows the Georgian–European relationship to emphasize Georgia's desire to be part of Europe. Museum archive.

attend elementary school?' 'Do you know what a democratic republic is?' 'Is Ural near to your home?' (being from Ural, a town in Russia, was synonymous to being an uneducated redneck in Soviet Russia). However, in the middle of the tour she tried to excuse herself: 'I am so tired, I've had an exam this morning and students knew nothing...', 'I have a terrible headache.' To explain her hatred at least partly it is important to mention that her family was victim of Stalin's repressions which she breifly mentioned in her narration, and she personally took part in the so called national-liberation movement of Georgia in the end of 80s, the culmination of which was on 9 April 1989, when Russian military troops attacked a civilian demonstration demanding the independence of Georgia from the USSR on the main street of Tbilisi.

This example demonstrates nationalistic sentiments as physiological bond (Connor 1994): how it influences human behaviour in spite of one's experience, education level and professionalism.

Figure 3.5 Georgian national costume, 'chokha', presented as belonging to Kakutsa Cholokashvili, the leader of the first Georgian Republic government. One of the stumbling blocks between museumelis and exhibition authors: the chokha did not belong to Cholokashvili. To present it as such means to lie to visitors, which is unacceptable for the museum. Museum archive.

Conclusion

The Museum of Soviet Occupation is a place for the renegotiation of Georgian national identity where the actors are the political elite – as initiators and organizers of the project; and the museum community – as mediators between the elite and society (Georgian and Non-Georgian), which can accept or reject the proposed narrative. The latter cannot be explored, because there is no instrument to differentiate visitors of the Soviet Occupation exhibition from other visitors of the Georgian National Museum, the Simon Janashia Museum where there are three other permanent exhibitions. There are also temporary exhibitions and just one ticket is sold to each visitor for all exhibitions in the Museum. There is no data or even simple statistics of how many people visit the Exhibition of Soviet Occupation yearly. This also indicates that in spite of its initial interest the political elite of Georgia did not have a clear strategy or mechanisms to evaluate the results of the project. They also underestimate the importance of the museum professionals, which led to the poor quality of the exhibition. The outcome: an incomplete narrative and representation of this important part of Georgian collective memory without any preliminary negotiation with the museum or Georgian society, leaving gaps which museum professionals feel obliged to fill, which in some cases can turn the exhibition into a battlefield between their professionalism and nationalistic sentiments, sometimes to the advantage of the latter.

Although the narrative represented by the political elite in the new exhibit fits well in the template of Georgia's eternal struggle to return to its Golden Age, thwarted by an enemy (in this case – Russia), two factors underpin the dissatisfaction of museum professionals: (1) external actors making changes, which is perceived as if an uninvited stranger came to clean up in their home; and (2) ignorance of their authority and knowledge.

As mentioned above, being Museumeli 'is a feeling that you are doing something for your country'. It is patriotism practiced daily. In contrast to Connor, who distinguishes patriotism and nationalism, Michael Billig sees these two terms as different perspectives of one sentiment – nationalism – and puts it thus: 'Our Patriotism and Their Nationalism', explaining that in spite of patriotism having positive meanings as it is defined as love of one's own nation, no one can really distinguish between them, because 'Even the most extreme of nationalists will claim the patriotic motivation for themselves. ... Hitler, for example, imagined that he was defending Germany against the Jews' (Billig 1995: 57). Different expressions of nationalism can be explained using Wetherell's concept of 'discursive psychology'. Discourse is 'the practical realm of language in action – talk and texts, words, utterances, conversations, stories, speeches, lectures ... ' (Wetherell 2012: 52). Discourse is constructed in a social environment, and forms certain patterns which become organized systematic practices for an individual. It is constructed and taught through socialization and turns into a unique 'personal order and identity' (ibid.). So too are individual practices also unique. Ideas and concepts of patriotism might be shared in a society, but it is individual discourse which translates one's nationalistic feelings and thoughts into emotions. Returning to Georgian nationalism, there is no conflict of narratives between the government and museum professionals, but instead a conflict of discourses. In other words, conflict between the ways different groups of society 'talk' about nationalism.

68   *Alisa Datunashvili*

Moreover, the museum is a place where its workers' discourse is constructed and maintained. Any change in its space, content, order or structure is perceived as an attack on a fundamental pillar of Museumeli identity. A feeling of Museumeli is 'nationalism in action', which is expressed in daily practices – guiding tours, selling tickets, watching over exhibits, curating collections, restoring and managing objects, writing scientific articles and cataloguing/registering objects. Museumeli is not just a transmitter of certain knowledge, but a bearer of individual discourse which influences one's practice of nationalism.

References

Anderson, B. 1983. *Imagined communities. Reflections on the origin and spread of nationalism.* London: Verso.

Antonsich, M. 2015. Nations and nationalism, in *The Wiley Blackwell companion to political geography*, edited by J. A. Agnew, et al. Malden, MA: Wiley-Blackwell, 297–310.

Ashworth, G., Larkham, P. eds. 2013. *Building a new heritage (RLE Tourism).* London and New York: Routledge.

Batiashvili, N. 2012. The 'myth' of the self: The Georgian national narrative and the quest for 'Georgianness', in *Memory and political change*, edited by A. Assmann and L. Shortt. London: Palgrave Macmillan, 186–200.

Bendix, R. F., Eggert, A. and Peselmann, A. (eds) 2012. Heritage regimes and the state. Göttingen. *Göttingen studies on cultural property*, Vol. 6. Universitätsverlag Göttingen.

Billig, M. 1995. *Banal nationalism.* London. Sage Publications.

Brown, R. H., Davis–Brown, B. 1998. The making of memory: The politics of archives, libraries and museums in the construction of national consciousness. *History of the Human Sciences* 11(4), 17–32.

Coombes, A. E. 1988. Museums and the formation of national and cultural identities. *Oxford Art Journal* 11(2), 57–68.

Cummins, A. 2004. Caribbean museums and national identity. *History Workshop Journal* 58(1), 224–245.

Connor, W. 1994. *Ethnonationalism. The quest for understanding.* Princeton, NJ: Princeton University Press.

Dianina K. 2010. The return of history: Museum, heritage, and national identity in Imperial Russia. *Journal of Eurasian Studies* 1, 111–118.

Graham B., Howard P. 2008. *The Ashgate Research Companion to heritage and identity.* Farnham: Ashgate.

Handler R. 1988. *Nationalism and the politics of culture in Quebec.* Madison, WI: University of Wisconsin Press.

Hein, H. S. 2000. *The museum in transition.* Washington, D.C.: Smithsonian Books.

Herzfeld M. 2005. *Cultural intimacy. Social poetics in the nation-state.* London and New York: Routledge.

Howard, P. 2003. *Heritage: Management, interpretation, identity.* London and New York: Continuum.

Isaacs, R., Polese, A. eds. 2016. *Nation building and identity in the post-Soviet space: New tools and approaches.* London: Routledge.

Isaacs, R., Polese, A. 2015. Between "imagined" and "real" nation-building: identities and nationhood in post-Soviet Central Asia. *Nationalities Papers* 43(3), 371–382.

Jones, S. 2013. *Georgia, a political history since independence.* London and New York: I.B. Tauris.

Kaeppler, A. L. 1994. Paradise regained: The role of Pacific museums in forging national identity. In *Museums and the making of ourselves: The role of objects in national identity*, edited by F. E. Kaplan, 19–44. London and New York: Leicester University Press.

Karp, I., Kreamer, C. M., Lavine, S. D. (eds) 1992. *Museums and communities. The politics of public culture*. Washington, D.C. and London: Smithsonian Institution Press.

Khinchagashvili, S. 2005. *Post-Soviet Georgian nationalism in the context of social memory and collective trauma theories*. MA Dissertation, Ilia State University.

Nora, P. *1989*. History: Les lieux de memoire. *Representations* 26, 7–24.

Pawłusz, E. 2016. The Estonian song celebration (Laulupidu) as an instrument of language policy. *Journal of Baltic Studies*, DOI: 10.1080/01629778.2016.1164203

Pawłusz, E., Seliverstova, O. 2016. Everyday nation-building in the post-Soviet space. Methodological reflections. *Studies for Transition States and Societies* 8(1), 6–86.

Pollock G., Zemans J. 2007. *Museums after modernism. Strategies of engagement*. Malden, MA and Oxford, Carlton: Blackwell Publishing.

Polese A., Horak S. 2015. A tale of two presidents: Personality cult and symbolic nation-building in Turkmenistan. *Nationalities Papers* 43(3), 457–478.

Skey, M. 2011. *National belonging and everyday life. The significance of nationhood in an uncertain world*. Basingstoke: Palgrave Macmillan.

Smith, L. 2006. *The uses of heritage*. London, New York: Routledge.

De Waal, T. 2011. *Georgia's choice*. Washington: Carnegie Endowment for International Piece.

Westerwinter M. 2008. *Museen Erzählen. Sammeln, Ordnen und Reprasentieren in literarischen Texten des 20. Jahrhunderts*. Bielefeld: Transcript Verlag.

Wertsch, J. V., Batiashvili N. 2008. *Mnemonic communities and conflict: Georgia's national narrative template*. Washington: University of St. Louis Press.

Wetherell, M. 2012. *Affect and emotion*. London: Sage.

Archival material

Policy of the Georgian National Museum (approved by the Minister of Culture, Monuments Protection and Sports of Georgia, January 13, 2005, No. 3/4)

Decree of the President of Georgia, December 30, 2004 ('On Establishing Legal Entity of Public Law – Georgian National Museum')

Decree of the President of Georgia, February 21, 2006 ('Regarding the Opening of the Exhibition of the History of Soviet Occupation in Georgia')

Georgian National Museum, Simon Janashia Museum of Georgia. Guided Tour Text (summarized by Nino Gogolashvili)

'Importance of the Museum of Soviet Occupation'. Exhibition Concept. Author unknown.

European Initiative Liberal Academy Tbilisi. 2012. *Economic Transformation of Georgia in Its 20 years of Independence, Interim Report*. Available from www.ei-lat .ge/images/doc/the%20economic%20transformation%20of%20georgia%20-%20 20%20years%20of%20independence%20eng.pdf [27 June 2014]

Web sources

Georgian National Museum. 2012. About GNM. Available from http://museum.ge/ index.php?lang_id=ENG&sec_id=87, [25 June 2016]

LEPL Legislative Herald of Georgia 2010–2017, Law of Georgia on General Education 08.04.2005; Law of Georgia on Higher Education 10.01.2005, Law of Georgia on Professional Education 23.04.2007 Available from: www.matsne.gov.ge/ka

Part II
Consumer practices

4 Made in Ukraine

Consumer citizenship during EuroMaidan transformations

Tetiana Bulakh

In the early 2000s, the Ukrainian government launched a major advertising campaign to support Ukrainian producers.[1] As a part of this program, huge posters stating 'Buy Ukrainian!' were placed in Ukrainian cities. Passing by one of them, a taxi driver who gave me a ride commented, 'Shame on them for wasting all this money on posters! They'd be better off using it to communicate to producers how to make quality products.' The colloquial wisdom of taxi drivers is well known in Ukraine and beyond, specifically for their ability to grasp public attitudes toward political and social nuances. In 2014, another taxi driver kindly offered me a piece of candy with change. 'Take it, it is Ukrainian and we need to support Ukraine in these times of need,' was his invitation. Like many Ukrainians after EuroMaidan, he approached the consumption of Ukrainian goods as one of the strategies of political participation. Russia's annexation of Crimea and the conflict in Eastern Ukraine transformed consumers' skeptical attitudes toward the 'Made in Ukraine' label, rendering the consumption of Ukrainian goods as practices of national belonging and citizenship. Support for Ukrainian producers along with the boycott of Russian produce enabled an explicit everyday articulation of national identity, a highly contested and ambiguous concept in the post-Soviet Ukrainian milieu.

The hybrid war in Ukraine (Dunn and Bobick 2014) encompasses economic relationships as the locus of citizenship production, nation building, and the manifestation of political stances. The economy became a battlefield, where trade sanctions, import bans, and market agreements leverage political decisions. Armed conflict with Russia politicized consumption in Ukraine, turning the boycott of Russian goods into a way for citizens to voice concerns and articulate their national belonging. 'Russian [produce] kills!' and 'Buy Ukrainian [goods]!' were among the immediate responses that actualized alternative forms of resistance on a micro level. Analysis of these consumer tendencies as practices of non-violent civil engagement highlights citizens' empowerment practices through the 'right to choose' and marks consumption as a form of political participation.

The focus of this chapter is on politically-charged consumer movements as a field of explicit and engaged production of a national identity. I approach

74 *Tetiana Bulakh*

consumer practices as a site where ideas about the state, nation and citizenship are actively shaped and reproduced from below. These practices generate a unifying effect for the nation and contribute to the formation of a national community, which is particularly important considering the internal identity conflicts and confrontations in Ukraine. To explore these processes, I interrogate the conceptualizations of the state and national belonging through consumer choices and, accordingly, discuss the conjuncture of the citizens' and consumers' roles. Analyzing the boycott of Russian products and patriotic consumption, which aims to rediscover and support local Ukrainian producers, I argue that a new interpretation of national identity is shaped among middle-class Ukrainians. This interpretation reveals more intimate and approachable relationships between citizens as a national community, as well as between citizens and their state.

My observations are based on three summers of fieldwork in Ukraine (2013–2015). During the course of this research, I interviewed Ukrainian middle-class representatives, with a particular focus on small entrepreneurs, consumer and social activists who organize and educate consumers about the larger implications of their everyday purchasing choices, and marketing professionals, who specialize in working with Ukrainian brands. The interviews were focused on informants' expert opinion about the consumer patterns that developed in Ukraine in the aftermath of EuroMaidan. At the same time, the conversations also covered respondents' personal experiences in transformations of consumer practices under the growing socio-political tensions in Ukraine. This data helped me to grasp the dynamics of social changes occurring at this time among middle-class consumers. In addition to 17 in-depth interviews in 2013, 12 follow-up discussions on consumer practices were held in 2014 and 2015. The sample of informants was selected through a purposive sampling by snowball technique. Respondents represented different genders, all of them have a college education, and their age varies between 22–35 years old.[2] The research took place in Kyiv and Odessa, which are dynamic urban centers. For a comprehensive analysis, I also examined media coverage and data from social media communities that are focused on social consumer movements.

The chapter starts with an exploration of the theoretical terrain, outlining my approach to the notions of state, nation, and consumer citizenship. It then moves to an overview of some recent socio-political changes in Ukraine, and particularly the revolutions of 2004 and 2013/2014, to contextualize the arguments and highlight the relationships between state-building processes and the development of national identity. Further, drawing from the idea that national identity is a phenomenon dependent on contextual changes (Isaacs and Polese 2015), I explore the recent Ukrainian tendency to heighten their European self-identification that can be captured through consumer preferences. The final section introduces a focused discussion on politicized consumer practices and explores how boycotts and consumer nationalism are forms of political engagement and national identification.

Theoretical perspectives

Several theoretical frameworks inform my arguments. Drawing from Michael Billing's ideas about 'banal nationalism' (Billig 1995), I approach consumer practices as hidden and explicit manifestations of national sentiments that, contrary to radical movements, constitute an implicit form of endemic nationalism. Though consumer choices are everyday routines, at the same time they carry high symbolic meaning. Consumption in general can be seen as a way to establish communities between people who do not know each other, but share similar experiences and/or loyalty to certain brands. Politicized consumer practices unite people who have common political stances and express them through consumer choices (Gurova 2018). This type of consumption can be seen as one of the tools through which a nation is conceived as an 'imagined community' (Anderson 1983). At the same time, political consumerism expresses citizens' understanding of the state, or, more precisely, their fantasy for the state as a political entity that provides a framework for the nation's existence. To scrutinize this idea, I draw from the theorizations of Philip Abrams (1988), who separates the state-idea from the state-system and highlights the conceptual mode of the state existence. According to Abrams, the state is the 'mask' that acquires symbolic identity and shields political reality. Thus, one of the modes of state existence is its functioning as a socially-constructed idea. However, as Abrams emphasizes the state to be an illusion, he seems to overlook the role of this illusion in structuring social processes. The way consumers transform their everyday lives, driven by the imaginary state as a strong national community, illustrates that the state-idea has repercussions and reifications in social life.

To investigate the interrelation between consumerism, nation and the state, the focus of the study is on the notion of citizenship and more precisely, *consumer citizenship*. Traditionally, citizenship is associated with a formal legal connection between individuals and the state.[3] In the context of a nation-state, citizenship also often refers to the politics of belonging to a national community. In fact, the rise of the nation-state as a dominant state formation in the 20th century turned the idea of a nation into an important unifying element of state building. Under the Westphalian model, a nation-state unites people, territory and the state entity into a singular polity. The concept of a nation in this model scenario[4] works as a structuring force. It creates a collective subjectivity of citizens, a 'horizontal comradeship' that bridges people with no personal connections (Anderson 1983). On the other hand, the dyad of a nation-state blurs boundaries between its two components. While typically the state is deemed as a form of political organization, the nation refers to a socio-cultural construct, rooted in shared experiences. The affiliation with a nation evokes emotional feelings of belonging (Connor 1978). Critically exploring this phenomenon, scholars argue that loyalty to the nation should be separated from loyalty to the state (Connor 1978, Hutchinson and Smith 2000). However, an inquiry into politicized consumer movements

76 *Tetiana Bulakh*

showcases that a threat to the state's integrity and sovereignty, such as conflict in Ukraine, evokes strong national sentiments. Consequently, the notions of the state and nation are diffused and mutually constructive, which correspond to a more complex nation-building process in the former Soviet counties.

The fall of the Soviet Union resulted in the rise of independent states, which necessitated the development of national identities, distinct from generalized Soviet identity. This process is often seen as a strategized, top-down elaboration of national ideology that promotes and represents a titular national majority. State actors implement this ideology through cultural policies related to language, education, national symbols and others. These nation-building processes were conceptualized in the term 'nationalizing states', coined by Rogers Brubaker (2011). Critically nuancing Brubaker's arguments, Taras Kuzio also posits that the nation-building process is a part of the state's policy, embedded in political decisions related to the cultural politics and rights of ethnic minorities (2002). Generally, studies of Ukrainian nationalism have largely focused on the political aspects of the nation-building process, which portrays the role of elites and institutions in it.

A recent wealth of research acknowledges nationalism as a top-down strategy in construction of national belonging. However, scholars also point out that this approach can be one-sided and overlook bottom-up factors, particularly the role and agency of non-state actors and ordinary citizens (Fox and Miller-Idriss 2008; Isaacs and Polese 2015; Seliverstova 2017 and in this volume). In this context, anthropological analyzes of everyday practices as an inquiry into the conceptualizations of state and nation serve as a useful lens to highlight the influences from below (Navaro-Yashyn 2002, Klumbyte 2010, Wilk 2004). The examination of consumption and how individuals make their consumer choices positions citizens as proactive actors and, thus, explicates how they understand and actually experience the state and belonging to a nation. Moreover, this approach elucidates that notions of the state and nation exist in modes of powerful ideas that are cultivated and reproduced on an everyday basis. From this perspective, consumer practices present a prolific area for investigation, where consumer decisions and their rationalizations both shape and communicate identities.

The political underpinning of consumerism and consumption as a possibility for citizens to be involved in political life is crystallized in the concept of consumer citizenship (Cohen 2003; Foster 2002; Gurova 2015, 2018; Seliverstova 2017). Historian Lizabeth Cohen (2003) elaborates the notion of consumer citizenship in her study on the political and social implications of consumerism during the Great Depression and after World War II. She analyzes consumerism as a way for citizens to participate in state building in times of crisis and as an arena for the negotiation of belonging, where often-separated identities of citizens (community-oriented) and consumers (self-oriented) overlap (Cohen 2003; Collins 2011). At the same time, politicized consumption is often approached as a two-folded process and regarded simultaneously 'as a manipulation tool the government uses to influence people's perception of nationhood and as a "politically charged arena" for people's expression of positive or negative nationalism' (Seliverstova 2017). Olga Gurova, in her exploration of political consumerism in Russia, emphasizes the role of the state (Gurova 2018). Gurova analyzes both governmental regulations of consumption, such as import bans and sanctions, and the production of a patriotic subject at the state level, such as the state's support of patriotic fashion and national producers. In contrast to the Russian case, political consumerism in Ukraine is represented through initiatives from below. Consumers turned consumption into a politicized arena with no direct intervention from the state. Moreover, in light of the war crisis, consumption became a field where citizens do not confront the state, but rather align with it. By boycotting the aggressor and/or supporting national produce they are turning their shopping carts into symbolic front lines. In this way, the consumer community of citizens unites in their efforts to contribute to the state's sustainability through everyday economic actions.

Importantly, consumption in post-Soviet countries is historically tied to the notion of the state. It is not surprising that a body of academic research has focused on consumerism, its relationship to the state and postsocialist crises (Verdery 1996; Humphrey 2002; Patico 2008; Fehérváry 2009). Anthropologist Melissa Caldwell, exploring everyday survival strategies in Russia from the late 1990s, argues that there is still a strong expectation for the state to act as a provider of material goods and social benefits (Caldwell 2004: 10). On the other hand, Olga Shevchenko observes that post-Soviet citizens tend to alienate themselves from the state by creating their 'zone of autonomy' through the consumption of durable goods (2009: 123). Contrary to these interpretations, consumption in Ukraine in the light of the EuroMaidan revolution of 2014 became an area for civil activism and proactive interactions with state. These interactions took various forms – from patriotic support of local entrepreneurs to crowdfunding for the Ukrainian army. These phenomena not only differentiate Ukraine in the larger post-Soviet context, they outline new directions of post-socialist state transformations and democratization. The changing understanding of the mutual interconnections between the state and citizens might have important implications for the further structuring of democratic processes in Ukraine. Politicized consumption also outlines avenues for the consolidation of the national community and offers nation-building tools, particularly for the production and material reification of national identity.

EuroMaidan and the European dimension of Ukrainian identity

To grasp the discourse of consumer citizenship in present-day Ukraine, it is important to acknowledge the impact of two historical events: the Orange Revolution and EuroMaidan. Both precedents of revolutionary transformations challenged the existing political status quo in Ukraine, demonstrated citizens' ability to exercise their democratic rights and freedoms, and highlighted the role of civil initiatives for nation-building processes. Even though

78 Tetiana Bulakh

the outcome of these public protests can be questioned in terms of changing the political system and addressing complex structural problems, such as corruption, they had significant value for reshaping the understanding of citizens' involvement in state affairs and the crafting of national identity. Both revolutions represented the interests of only a part of Ukrainian citizens, but at the same time, its proponents deem them as 'victories over regimes'. In this way, democratic rallies partially justified the idea of the state that responds to citizens' claims and demands. In the tradition of post-Soviet countries, this alternative optimistic image of the state is particularly significant, as the state is perceived predominately as an alienated and corrupt entity.

At the same time, EuroMaidan significantly differs from the Orange Revolution not only because of the escalation of violence as part of the protests, but also because of a broader agenda that protestors addressed and a growth of ethnic nationalism (Kuzio 2015). The Orange Revolution can be seen primarily as a protest against the falsification of the presidential elections, where participants aligned with one of the competing political forces, namely Viktor Yushchenko and his allies. In contrast, EuroMaidan initially started as a rally for a pro-European geopolitical choice, though later it developed into a massive demonstration against the state corruption and social injustice.[5] EuroMaidan articulated new features of Ukrainian identity, such as pro-European orientation, which is juxtaposed to the Soviet legacy. The widespread taking down of Lenin statues around Ukraine illustrated this moment of identity renegotiations. In this way, EuroMaidan can be seen as a protest situated outside the internal struggles between political establishments.[6] Thus, during the first days of protests, demonstrators called for the removal of all political parties' symbols and flags from the central protest venue, shifting the rally into a discourse of national interests. On a symbolic level, this pro-national spirit was captured in a collective singing of the Ukrainian national anthem that became a unifying musical ritual throughout the protests. The lasting repercussions of EuroMaidan are yet to be determined by researchers. However, EuroMaidan was marked in public discourse as the 'rebirth of the Ukrainian nation'[7] and was a powerful experience that mobilized the national community (Kuzio 2015).

One of the outcomes of EuroMaidan was the development of grassroots civil initiatives that reacted to the emergencies of the protest. Volunteers organized to provide assistance with medical care, security and legal help to the victims of violence. The state of emergency and shared political agenda redrew social boundaries between the protesters and created a unifying experience of what Victor Turner refers to as communitas (Turner 1969). In this unification, the dissatisfaction about the state institutional responses to the protests, such as police violence, were fused with the self-responsibility for the future of the state-idea. This tendency was highlighted in widely circulated messages and slogans 'Who if not me?' and 'I am making the future'.

Proactive stances of citizens and transformations of national identity were accompanied by the changing vision of the state. One of the reappearing narratives in my interviews with activists was the idea of the prosperous European Ukraine and that they all contribute to it:

> They [state authorities and decision makers – T.B.] realized that they need now to give some space for us [volunteers]. We do not want to live in the Soviet past and be dependent on Russia. Our future is in Europe and we are strong enough to prove this. (Masha 30 y. o.)

> [During EuroMaidan] we showed that we are not just a mass of people. We proved that we can organize and be responsible for our own country and for our future. We are capable to build a European country that the next generations will live in. This idea drives me to continue [my activities as a volunteer]. It is my everyday fight for the future Ukraine. (Roman, 29 y. o.)

The idea of a European Ukraine was one of the focal points of EuroMaidan and a referential point in the construction of the desire for the state. Similar to what Yale Navaro-Yashin calls a 'fantasy for the state' (Navaro-Yashin 2002: 178), the idea of a European Ukraine became a driving force that helped keep the notion of the state relevant. In this way, the EuroMaidan movement was producing and elaborating what Phillip Abrams refers to as an *idea* of the state, the illusion that is supposed to transform the functioning of the state (Abrams 1988). It also fostered a new understanding of what it means to be Ukrainian, introducing new understandings of national identity. 'We are the generation of European Ukrainians', commented one of my informants, adding 'and I have never been so proud to be Ukrainian'.

The adjective, 'European', in this sense does not necessarily refer to a political entity of the European Union. It signifies a qualitative dimension of understanding Europe as a more progressive polity with higher standards of life and politico-economic stability. This nuance is built into a larger framework, where 'European' takes a qualitative connotation in the Ukrainian language and becomes a synonym for words like 'better' and 'modern'.[8]

This qualitative understanding of 'European' is largely embedded in mediated experiences of Europe. According to a sociological poll, conducted a few years before EuroMaidan, more than 77% of Ukrainians have never travelled abroad.[9] Despite travel to Russia and neighboring countries, less than 4% of Ukrainians have visited Western Europe. Thus, Europe exists for the majority of Ukrainians as a place of non-direct knowledge, largely facilitated through media and consumer experiences. It also can be seen as a continuation of the Imaginary West, a concept coined by Alexei Yurchak to explain the illusive nature of the West in Soviet times. According to Yurchak, in times of late socialism 'abroad' (*zagranitsa*) was:

> [S]ignifying an imaginary place that was simultaneously knowable and unattainable, tangible and abstract, mundane and exotic […] *zagranitsa* as a Soviet imaginary 'elsewhere' […] was not necessarily about any

80 *Tetiana Bulakh*

real place. The 'West' (*zapad*) was its archetypal manifestation. It was produced locally and existed only at the time when the real West could not be encountered. We will call this version of the elsewhere, the Imaginary West. (Yurchak 2006: 159)

In a similar way, Imaginary Europe became a narrower epitome of 'elsewhere'. With the end of the Soviet propaganda against the capitalist West and the growing accessibility of media and material goods that represented the every-day experiences of European people, the Imaginary Europe acquired a popular image of a prosperous El Dorado – the land of wealth and social justice. Accordingly, it shaped a desire for the future of the Ukrainian nation and the state.

The European Ukraine is envisioned in constant dialogue with the concept of Imaginary Europe, obtaining utopian and idealistic qualities. While the generalization of 'European values' was often declared as an objective for revolutionary aspirations, everyday well-being, including access to consumer goods, can be seen as an important component that reinforced political changes. Practical interests that are often overlooked in the discussion on EuroMaidan were entrenched into its political agenda. From this perspective, consumer practices obtain significance, merging personal interests and national political agendas.

The state in the eyes of consumers

The idea of permeability of consumer and political demands can be traced in the words of my informant, who passionately stated: 'Ukraine will be a European country when we have IKEA and H&M here!' In his statement, well-known European brand names are indicators for state prosperity and European belonging. Consumers link their experiences to the state's responsibility to ensure favourable market conditions. This speaks to the understanding of the state's role as a provider, which is informed by the socialist experience of the state, or a so-called 'parent-state' as Katherine Verdery argues (Verdery 1996:61). The centrally coordinated distribution of goods and commodities grounded the experiences of the state through consumerism. As Verdery notes, '[the] socialist system legitimized themselves with the claim that they redistributed the social product in the interest of general welfare' (1996: 68). In post-Soviet Ukraine, the expectation for the state as a provider remains relevant. though the state polity is seen not only as a key actor for securing social rights, but also a guarantor of favourable economic conditions that can facilitate access to material goods.

In this light, consumer struggles to have brands like H&M and IKEA in Ukraine obtain almost symbolic meaning. These brands are markers of political ambitions for the pro-European state-building project. Both brands can also be seen as what Sigrid Rausing refers to as 'signs of the new nation' in post-Soviet Estonia (1998). H&M and IKEA represent the European identity for Ukrainians in the tangible domain of the material world. A few years ago, IKEA was named as the most desirable European brand in Ukraine and almost 50% of middle-class Ukrainian consumers stated that IKEA was anticipated in Ukraine more than any other global brand.[10] However, because of the unfavorable politico-economic situation, the agreement between the Swedish company and Ukraine has never been finalized. In 2012, Petro Poroshenko, at that time the Minister of Economic Development, defined IKEA's presence in Ukraine as a benchmark of the state's success in fighting corruption and achieving economic stability.[11] In other words, the absence of recognizable signifiers, such as well-known European brand names, identifies Ukrainian exclusion from the global consumer milieu and makes Ukraine 'less European', as one of my respondents framed it.

This backward status of Ukraine questions the legitimacy of the state, as the government is not able to provide its citizens with 'the right to buy' (Berdahl 2010: 89; see also Wilk 2006). The existing consumer challenges became even more complicated when Yanukovych's government announced that it had suspended the signing of the Association Agreement with the European Union in November 2013, which led to EuroMaidan.[12] The unexpected decision to cease the pro-European political course was seen (inter alia) as a threat to perspective consumer freedoms, the availability of the European goods, and the European identity of Ukrainians.

The relationship between citizens as consumers and the state as a guarantor of consumer rights renders consumerism as a part of the national agenda. Unlike more abstract discussions on national belonging, they present a tangible, material domain of interactions and practices. Consumer experiences in this way present a 'grey zone', where we can trace alternative narratives of the state, nation, and identity that lay between the normative, state-led discourses and their on-the-ground appropriations (Isaacs and Polese 2015). From this perspective, grassroots projects like boycotts and patriotic consumption present a rich area for investigation.

Politicized consumer practices: from street protest to economic actions

Talking about 'everyday nationhood', Jon Fox and Cynthia Miller-Idriss define four modalities of everyday nationalism, such as the discursive formation of the nation ('talking the nation'), making national decisions and choices ('choosing the nation'), making consumer choices and utilizing products that have symbolic national meanings ('consuming the nation'), and ritual performances ('performing the nation') (Fox and Miller-Idriss 2015). Unlike implicit everyday consumer behavior, boycotts and patriotic consumption present a mixture of all these four modalities. They elucidate national sentiments in a highly-visible, intensified, emotionally and politically-charged way. Both types of consumer practices contribute to the construction of national identity through conscious consumer choices

82 *Tetiana Bulakh*

that are performative and rationalized. They are actively discussed and explained between consumers, contributing to the discursive production of the nation-state.

During the EuroMaidan revolution, consumer manifestations such as the boycott of goods and the rise of consumer patriotism became important elements for consolidating the national community and creating forms of civil responses to the conflicting situations. These two processes often go hand-in-hand and are referred as 'boycott' and '*buy*cott' (Neilson 2010; Kneip 2012; Gurova 2018). They are often triggered simultaneously, especially when it comes to conflicts of national interests, where the rejection of antagonist products coincides with the support of national producers. This was the case of the Indian boycott of British commodities (Bayly 1986) and the Palestinian boycott of Israeli goods (Jean-Klein 2001). Both consumer activities illustrate how citizens employ consumption as a way to manifest their political stances. They also illustrate how material objects have the capacity to construe the identities of people (Douglas and Isherwood 1996; Miller 2008), which renders these consumer movements into a communal action of nation-building.

Both boycotts and patriotic consumption represent the practices of vernacular variation of conspicuous 'banal' nationalism (Billig 1995). It can be contrasted to the Russian state-led initiatives to ban European goods, which resulted in cases of smuggling and the emergence of black markets for European foods. By contrast, in Ukraine commodities became heavily loaded with emotional and moral meanings, which put additional barriers for consumer choices. Moreover, commodities are perceived as physical continuations of the state and nation (Ukraine) and/or embody the enemy state (Russia). From this perspective, Russian commodities represent taboo objects, in contrast to fetish objects – a new connotation that Ukrainian commodities acquired.

Case study: boycott as consumer activism

Analyzing the boycott in Ukraine during and after EuroMaidan, I define two distinct waves. The first one represents a confrontation with the politicians from the *Party of Regions*, which was in power, and targeted their business interests. The second wave emerged after the Crimean crisis and unfolding conflict in Eastern Ukraine, and aimed to protest against Russian goods. As the boycott originated from the EuroMaidan activism movement, its grassroots nature is accentuated. The first wave of the boycott offered tools for actions, but at the same time intensified a tension between local Ukrainian identities, divided by electoral choices into pro-*Party of Regions* supporters and their antagonists. Later, the boycott of Russian goods facilitated the unification of consumers as members of one nation in the face of a common threat. This, as Oleksandra Seliverstrova notes, depicts the construction of civic national identity (2017).

Made in Ukraine 83

As a form of civil engagement, a boycott is a non-violent strategy that has symbolic meaning, yet strives for long-term economic repercussions to influence political decisions and/or express political will. Akin to James Scott's interpretation of forms of everyday disobedience (Scott 1985), a boycott is an invisible form of resistance, quite difficult to control and regulate. Specifically, it creates a 'safe' area for confrontation at the edge of public and private spheres, a non-violent form of action (Sharp 1973, Friedman 1991). It allows consumers to turn their purchasing power into a political instrument, but, at the same time, protects their anonymity. As a form of everyday practice, a boycott is accessible to different populations. As one Ukrainian slogan claimed, 'Every housewife can now become a revolutionary!'

'You are buying, he is stealing!'

The first wave of the boycott was initiated at the end of 2013, after the first occurrences of police violence in Kyiv. Its strategy was to economically disempower politicians of the *Party of Regions*, whose members were seen as directly responsible for police brutality either through their inactions, silent endorsement or public support. This consumer protest elucidated the overlap of political and business interests, characteristic for the post-socialist political milieu (Humphrey 2002). Any profit that a politician possibly gets from retail marketplaces was interpreted as a direct 'investment' in the *Party*'s power usurpation, financial frauds and anti-Maidan measures, such as media propaganda and/or provocations by sponsored thugs (*titushky*).

Consumer activists employed various tactics to highlight the ideology of the boycott and to communicate the details of the movement. For this, they used informational flyers, stickers, flashmobs in stores and social media communities. A special mobile application, named explicitly 'Boycott to the Party of Regions', was released to provide a comprehensive list of boycotted brands along with a barcode scanner to identify them. Its description stated, 'Yanukovych and the *Party of Regions* have no morals. For long they have been replaced with a thirst for power and money. Now they harm innocent people and revoke our European future. Hit the most vital [thing] for them – their money.' The description reflected the larger philosophy of the consumer protest, which was captured in the following slogans: 'You are earning, he [Member of the Party of Regions – *T.B.*] is stealing', 'Not even a coin to the Party of Regions!', 'Boycott to those who finance bloody slaughter!' In these narratives politicians were indirect sponsors of EuroMaidan violence, while citizens' role was envisioned as indirect 'sponsors' of politicians.

The vernacular knowledge about business-political affairs linked consumer activities to the well-being of politicians and protection of their interests. Consequently, the complex relationships between producers/sellers/consumers were simplified and reinterpreted. Many stages and processes of actual production and market activities were omitted and ignored, assuming the immediate connection between the commodity price and a politician's profit.

84   *Tetiana Bulakh*

Even though the understanding of the market was oversimplified, citizens demonstrated their popular knowledge about the mechanisms of power and awareness about tacit business and political interconnections. In this way, the boycott enabled citizens to indicate their place in the nexus of power as consumers and to unite into a consumer community with alternative visions of politics, divergent from the pro-governmental program.

One of the crucial questions about the boycott is whether it had any real economic repercussions. In the case of the first wave of EuroMaidan boycotts, it is difficult to estimate the actual effects. First of all, the data on sales is not accessible. Besides this, it is almost impossible to separate the impact of boycott from other influential factors, such as the overall decline in expenditures during unstable political and economic situations. As experts argue, the ultimate goal of the boycott – to financially ruin the Party of Regions – was almost impossible to achieve. The business of politicians is diversified and the major sources of their income are industrial production, export and import operations, as well as contracts based on the state budget.[13] Thus, one can argue that the boycott held more power as a symbolic and performative form of citizens' protest rather than as a financial sanction. As a part of everyday practices, the first wave of the boycott addressed the internal political conflict and became a unifying factor for protest participants.[14]

'Beware of the armed matryoshka!'

The agenda of the boycott shifted in February-March 2014, when Russian and pro-Russian forces overtook control in Crimea, and when the conflict started to unfold in Eastern Ukraine. One of the public reactions to the threat to Ukrainian sovereignty was to protest against Russian goods. 'Do not buy Russian!', 'Russian [produce] kills!', 'Stop Russia! Stop buying Russian goods' – slogans and flashmobs with imitated blood imposed strong moral obligations upon consumers. They strengthened ethical considerations regarding consumer activities and altered the agenda of citizenship duties. This new danger 'zoomed out' the focus of the boycott from intra-Ukrainian political challenges to the confrontation between larger state entities.

Meticulous investigations about the origins of commodities became a part of shopping practices for those who supported the boycott resistance. According to TNS research, in April 2014, 52% of Ukrainians expressed their support for the boycott and almost 39% stated that they actively participated in the boycott, reducing the consumption of Russian goods.[15] Some of the major retail chains addressed the consumer movement by introducing national flags on price tags to mark the country-producer. In some stores, sales assistants became involved in the process as well.

The boycott required consumer awareness about features that usually do not matter or are obscure for purchasers. Specifically, it called for the rediscovery and reexamination of production stages. To some extent, it shifted what Marx describes as commodity fetishism in the capitalist model of

Made in Ukraine 85

economic relationships, where the producer is alienated from the product (Marx 2004 [1986]). The boycott stimulated the reintroduction of actors involved in the production of goods and reattached connections between them. Sometimes, it was complicated by the fact that Russian companies would have production facilities in Ukraine, or that international corporations use Russian raw materials and resources, but have production sites in Ukraine. These complex production-related issues enabled various degrees of involvement in the boycott by Ukrainian citizens – some would exclude all produce that is somehow related to Russia, some would stop buying just certain goods.

Similar to the first wave of consumer boycotts, protests against Russian produce became a unifying factor for consumers. The withdrawal from consumption offered an instrument for civic action and simultaneously a tool for consumer citizens to support the state in times of crisis. As one of the informants pointed out with regard to this ideological mission, 'The least thing that one can do for Ukraine is to stop buying Russian goods' (Roman, 29 y. o.). At the same time, a confrontation to Russian commodities established another point of reference for distinction from the Russian (and former Soviet) milieu. It introduced tangible markers of The Other (Russia), against which the narratives about Ukrainian-ness were built. From this point of view, the boycott became one of the 'ways of talking' about a nation (Billig 1995). Particularly, it conveyed Russian produce as foreign and hostile, which has an enduring effect on a larger scale.

Case study: *buy*cott and rediscovery of Ukraine

The unifying effect of the boycott was accompanied by patriotic consumption and support of national producers. This form of consumer activism – unlike regulated state campaigns aimed to encourage consumption of Ukrainian goods – evolved into a dynamic movement with strong positive connotations. Common efforts were put not only to find substitutions for boycotted items, but also to discover Ukrainian producers and 'invest in Ukraine' through the support of small businesses. As one of the activists of the movement 'Made in Ukraine!', Yulia Savostina, admitted, EuroMaidan and its consequent tragic events created a favourable business environment for Ukrainian producers.[16] One of the arguments is that Ukrainian entrepreneurs no longer need to use additional efforts to attract potential clients. Instead, loyal customers are actively looking for them, granting credibility based on producers' affiliation with Ukraine.

If boycotts aimed to weaken certain actors economically, patriotic consumption attempted to empower Ukrainian business for state's sustainability. This strategy is essentialized through the concept of *sviy*/*nash* (ours/us) that originates from earlier historical discourse. Catherine Wanner's interpretation of *sviy* states that it represents a Soviet identity produced by the 'shared experience with an oppressive state apparatus', in which '[we] bond together

86   *Tetiana Bulakh*

against "them", the enemy, the state and its institutions' (Wanner 1998: 9; Yurchak 2006: 102-108). Pro-Ukrainian consumerism appeals to this shared identity, confronting a common threat (e.g. Russia). The re-actualization of the slogan, '*Sviy do svogo po svoye*' (Ours (one of us) comes to us to get ours), highlights the idea of a self-sufficient national community with mutual support between producers and consumers, as well as between the citizens and their state. Under the new circumstances of war, the consumption of once boycotted goods (affiliated with the *Party of Regions* politicians) was justified in the face of a larger national threat.

Consumer patriotism frames consumption as an arena for the reification of national identity. Another tendency that appeared in accord with patriotic consumption was the massive replication of national symbols in commodities, such as the blue and yellow flag, Ukrainian trident, elements of traditional embroidery, and figures of national heroes. Consumption of these goods contributes to the shaping of national identity/nation building by creating material references and circulation of national symbols. It has a unifying effect for national community members who do not personally know each other, but share practices of consuming these goods. These practices illustrate how commodities embody abstract cultural phenomena and that consumption of goods are needed 'for making visible and stable the category of culture' (Douglas and Isherwood 1996: 38), an idea that was for a while on the margins of social sciences. Interestingly, the visual elements of national identity, such as national symbols or embroidery motives became traveling features, replicated or added in different commodities to increase their symbolic value. For instance, one of the popular examples is car stickers that 'Ukraine-ize' vehicles. On the one hand, cars in Ukraine are typically imported and often known for their origins as 'Japanese', 'German' or 'Korean'. But folk elements add Ukrainian touches to them and indicate the owners' patriotic belonging.

The commodification of national symbols required their modernization and renegotiation within a more-fashionable context. It encouraged producers to level their products to high consumer demands and European standards, embellishing them with Ukrainian specifics. The reappearing comments about the rediscovery of Ukrainian goods contained an element of surprise: 'It's so European', '[Ukrainian products are] not worse than European [ones]!' Thus, even in the rediscovery of Ukrainian goods, Europe serves as a strategic reference that defines nuances of the Ukrainian identity. Illustrative in this relation is the growing popularity of Ukrainian national dress, *vyshyvanka*. Soon after EuroMaidan, it was popularized as a fashion trend by international publications, such as *Vogue*. This success is often celebrated in Ukraine as an achievement of national culture and a form of cultural diplomacy. Before EuroMaidan, wearing *vyshyvanka* in everyday life was considered a *faux pas*. But with the political changes and the rise of positive national self-identification, this element of traditional costume was refined to be a part of fashion discourse. As Daria Shapovalova[17] mentioned to *Vogue*, 'I am proud to see people wearing [*vyshyvankas*] [...]. I think [traditional dress]

Made in Ukraine 87

is connected to the fact that Ukraine is experiencing this moment in politics.'[18] In a certain sense, this new, fashionable *vyshyvanka* symbolizes an aspired European-Ukrainian identity, crafted in EuroMaidan narratives. It shifts a familiar, traditional element into a new context of Western culture.

The use of folklore motifs in consumer goods, such as Ukrainian embroidery patterns, reinforced understandings of the nation as a community that shares historical roots. These elements served to point to the continuity of the nation, and its traditional background that was rediscovered under new circumstances. In lieu of the concept of 'invented traditions' (Hobsbawm and Ranger 1983) this new consumer tendency can be seen as a re-invented tradition. Historically, different parts of Ukraine belonged to various political formations, which resulted in a lack of understanding the Ukrainian nation as a homogeneous community. However, embroidery is commonly perceived as a part of nation's collective legacy, in which regional discrepancies are less apparent.

Conclusions

The conflict-driven tendencies in Ukrainian consumer culture reflect new interpretations of national identity among middle-class Ukrainians. 'I am Ukrainian. I am European' acquires a tangible domain. Within this new framework, self-imposed responsibility for the state gains value and becomes a feature that unifies the national community. Along with the rise of volunteer movements and civil initiatives, consumer activism represents how citizens manifest loyalty for the state, or, rather, a fantasy for the state. At the same time, reflecting on Daniel Miller's observations that 'objects create subjects much more than the other way around' (2008: 287), politicized consumption generates ideas about the state and nation. Accordingly, boycotts and patriotic consumption facilitate national belonging and present a domain where citizens take a patronizing role to contribute to the state's and national sustainability through everyday practices. The exploration of politicized consumer practices highlights how the notions of state and nation conflate and inform each other. While the larger economic impact of these processes is dispersed, it is hard to underestimate their symbolic value and contribution to the construction of national belonging.

There are questions that, so far, cannot be comprehensively addressed – will these practices survive post-revolutionary disillusion and will consumer movements transform into a lasting phenomenon? Since the conflict in Ukraine has shifted into a protracted phase and the post-revolution euphoria is fading away, these movements, most likely, will change as well. However, the importance of these experiences is significant. Boycotts and patriotic consumption showcased that practices of everyday consumption can become a battlefield for the desired state, a field for the production of ideas about the nation, and an area of active civil engagement. Communicated and represented in social media, consumer practices united and empowered citizens in a new way, solidifying an imagined online community through common actions.

Notes

1 I would like to thank the editors of this volume and anonymous reviewers for their insightful comments and productive critique that significantly helped to shape this contribution.
2 My particular interest was in the generation that was born in the mid 1980s–early 1990s in the USSR, but grew up and lived through the times of post-independence transformations in Ukraine. However, I did not intentionally limit the age criteria while selecting informants.
3 Anthropological tradition challenges this narrow understanding of citizenship through concepts like 'cultural citizenship' (Rosaldo 1994), 'flexible citizenship' (Ong), and 'post-political citizenship' (De Grazia 1996).
4 By referring to the 'nation-state' as a model scenario, I recognize wide academic critique that the nation-state rarely exists in its 'pure', essentially homogeneous form.
5 I acknowledge that these interpretations of both events are simplified to grasp the larger tendencies.
6 At the same time, I acknowledge that EuroMaidan as any drastic political change driven by massive protest opened opportunities for certain political forces to enter or to reinforce existing positions at the political arena.
7 A description used by EuroMaidan Press media initiative, http://euromaidan press.com
8 It can be seen in the notion of 'evroremont', which literally means 'European renovations' (see Seliverstrova 2017, Humphrey 2002)
9 The survey was conducted by Research and Branding Group in 2012 and published in *Korrespondent* as well as other media outlets. For the details of report, see http://korrespondent.net/ukraine/events/1355598-korrespondent-tri-chetverti-ukraincev-nikogda-ne-byli-za-granicej. Similar tendecies are reported in the statistical profile of Ukraine, released by the Ukrainian Migration Service. In 2013 – the year of EuroMaidan – the percentage of Ukrainians traveling abroad as tourists was lower than 2% of all exits from the country. At the same time, a leading destination for Ukrainians to travel abroad was the Russian Federation. Source: http://dmsu.gov.ua
10 According to the survey, conducted by Bloomberg in March 2014. For further details, see www.kyivpost.com/content/ukraine-abroad/bloomberg-dashed-ikea-dreams-in-ukraine-show-decades-lost-to-corruption-341463.html
11 As reported in the media, such as Korrespondent. For further details, see http://korrespondent.net/business/companies/1338617-poroshenko-obyasnil-bloomberg-nedoverie-investorov-k-ukraine-na-primere-ikea
12 Importantly, access to European markets and decreasing prices for European goods were named as one of the five key reasons to sign an Association Agreement with the EU (EU Delegation to Ukraine Bulletin 2014), http://euukrainecoop.net/2014/07/21/association/
13 An interview for the online portal 24tv.ua, January 2014. http://24tv.ua/news/showNews.do?vzhe_2_misyatsi_trivaye_ekonomichniy_boykot_partiyi_regioniv&objectId=404002
14 At the same time, the boycott of the first wave can be seen as a dividing factor. Those Ukrainians who supported the Party of Regions perceived it as a hostile move. Some media reported that AntiMaidan activists called for the support of boycotted goods. However, this initiative received less public and media attention.
15 TNS (Taylor Nelson Sofres) is an international custom market research company. Link to the research: https://tns-ua.com/news/chto-dumayut-ukraintsyi-ob-ubiystve-borisa-nemtsova-i-boykote-russkih-tovarov
16 Blog entry from January 12, 2015, www.savostina.com
17 Creative Director of Mercedes-Benz Kiev Fashion Days, fashion blogger and editor.
18 For further details, see www.vogue.com/13257041/ukrainian-traditional-costumes-in-fashion/

References

Abrams, P. 1988. Notes on the difficulty of studying the state. *Journal of Historical Sociology*, 1(1), 58–89.

Anderson, B. 1983. *Imagined communities. Reflections on the origin and spread of nationalism*. London and New York: Verso.

Bayly, C. A. 1986. The origins of swadeshi (home industry): cloth and Indian society. In *The social life of things: Commodities in cultural perspective*, edited by Arjun Appadurai, 285–322. Cambridge: Cambridge University Press.

Berdahl, D. 2010. *On the social life of postsocialism: Memory, consumption, Germany*. Bloomington: Indiana University Press.

Billig, M. 1995. *Banal nationalism*. London: Sage.

Brubaker, R. 2011. Nationalizing states revisited: Projects and processes of nationalization in post-Soviet states. *Ethnic and Racial Studies, 34*(11), 1785–1814.

Caldwell, ML. 2004. *Not by bread alone: Social support in the new Russia*. Berkeley: University of California Press.

Cohen, L. 2003. *A consumers' republic: the Politics of mass consumption in postwar America*. New York: Vintage Books.

Connor, W. 1978. A nation is a nation, is a state, is an ethnic group is a … *Ethnic and Racial Studies, 1*(4), 377–400.

Collins, J. 2011. Wal-Mart, American consumer citizenship, and the 2008 recession. *Focaal* (61), 107–116.

De Grazia, V. 1996. *The sex of things: Gender and consumption in historical perspective*. University of California Press.

Douglas, M., Isherwood, B.. 1996. *The world of goods: Towards an anthropology of consumption*. London: Routledge.

Dunn, E. C., Bobick, M. S. 2014. The empire strikes back: War without war and occupation without occupation in the Russian sphere of influence. *American Ethnologist, 41*(3), 405–413.

Fehérváry, K. 2009. Goods and states: The political logic of state-socialist material culture. *Comparative Studies in Society and History* 51(2), 426–459.

Foster, R. J. 2002. *Materializing the nation: Commodities, consumption, and media in Papua New Guinea*. Indiana University Press.

Fox, J. E., Miller-Idriss C. 2008. Everyday nationhood. *Ethnicities* 8(4), 536–563.

Friedman, M. 1991. Consumer boycotts: A conceptual framework and research agenda. *Journal of Social Issues* 47(1), 149–168.

Gurova, O. 2015. *Fashion and the consumer revolution in contemporary Russia*. Abingdon, Oxon: Routledge.

Gurova, O. 2018. Political consumerism in Russia after 2011. Forthcoming in *Cultural mechanisms of political protest in Russia*, edited by Beumers B., Etkind A., Gurova O. and Turoma S. London and New York: Routledge.

Jean-Klein, I., 2001. Nationalism and resistance: The two faces of everyday activism in Palestine during the Intifada. *Cultural Anthropology, 16*(1), 83–126.

Hobsbawm, E. J, Ranger, T. O.. 1983. *The invention of tradition*. Cambridge [Cambridgeshire]: Cambridge University Press.

Humphrey, C. 2002. *The unmaking of Soviet life: Everyday economies after socialism*. Ithaca: Cornell University Press, 2002.

Hutchinson, J., Smith, A.D. (eds). 2000. *Nationalism: Critical concepts in political science*. London: Routledge.

Isaacs, R., Polese, A. 2015. Between 'imagined' and 'real' nation-building: identities and nationhood in post-Soviet Central Asia. *Nationalities Papers, 43*(3), 371–382.

Klumbyte, N. 2010. The Soviet sausage renaissance. *American Anthropologist*. 112 (1), 22–37.

Kneip, V. 2012. Consumer citizenship soft governance in political market arenas. *Krisis*, Issue 1. www.krisis.eu

Kuzio, T. 2002. *Ukraine: State and nation building*. London: Routledge.

90   *Tetiana Bulakh*

Kuzio, T. 2015. 'Competing nationalisms, Euromaidan, and the Russian-Ukrainian conflict. *Studies in Ethnicity and Nationalism* 15(1), 157–169. Marx, K. 2004 [1986]. *Capital. Volume 1. A critique of political economy*. Digireads.com Publishing.

Miller, D. 2008. *The comfort of things*. Cambridge, UK: Polity.

Navaro-Yashin, Y. 2002. *Faces of the state: Secularism and public life in Turkey*. Princeton, NJ: Princeton University Press.

Neilson, L. A. 2010. Boycott or buycott? Understanding political consumerism. *Journal of Consumer Behaviour* 9(3), 214–227.

Ong, A. 1999. *Flexible citizenship: The cultural logics of transnationality*. Duke University Press.

Patico, J. 2008. *Consumption and social change in a post-Soviet middle class*. Washington, DC: Woodrow Wilson Center Press.

Rausing, S. 1998. Signs of new nation: gift exchange, consumption and aid on a former collective farm in north-west Estonia. In *Material cultures: Why some things matter*, edited by D. Miller. Chicago: University of Chicago Press, 189–213.

Rosaldo, R. 1994. Cultural citizenship and educational democracy. *Cultural Anthropology* 9(3), 402–411.

Scott, J. C. 1985. *Weapons of the weak: Everyday forms of peasant resistance*. Yale University Press.

Seliverstova, O. 2017. 'Consuming' national identity in Western Ukraine. *Nationalities Papers* 45(1), 61–79.

Sharp, G. 1973. *The politics of nonviolent action*. Boston: P. Sargent.

Shevchenko, O. 2009. *Crisis and the everyday in postsocialist Moscow*. Bloomington: Indiana University Press.

Turner, V. 1969. *The ritual process: Structure and anti-structure*. Chicago: Aidine Publishing.

Verdery, K. 1996. *What Was Socialism, and What Comes Next?* Princeton, NJ: Princeton University Press.

Wanner, C. 1998. *Burden of dreams. History and identity in post-Soviet Ukraine*. University Park, PA: Pennsylvania State University Press.

Wilk, R. 2004. Morals and metaphors: The meaning of consumption. *Elusive Consumption* 3, 11–26.

Wilk, R. 2006. *Home cooking in the global village: Caribbean food from buccaneers to ecotourists*. English ed. Oxford: Berg.

Yurchak, A. 2006. *Everything was forever, until it was no more: The last Soviet generation*. Princeton, NJ: Princeton University Press.

5 National food, belonging, and identity among Russian-speaking migrants in the UK

Anna Pechurina

Introduction

The connection between food, culture and identity has been well established in the research of diasporic and migrant communities. By focusing both on food types and practices related to their consumption – including cooking and sharing traditional meals on important ethnic/religious holidays (Burrell 2012), bringing national food from the home country (Petridou 2001) and buying national food from ethnic food shops (Rabikowska and Burrell 2009) – scholars explore complex and often contradictory relationships between choices of food, migrants' reflections on their identity and their perceptions of the receiving culture (Alfonso 2012, Chapman and Beagan 2013, Coakley 2012, Rabikowska 2010).

Russian food in immigration is a relatively new topic of research that has attracted more attention in recent years as part of the wider interest in Russian migration after 1991. In this context the socialist past is seen as an important cultural dimension that affects how the notion of Russian food is defined today and how the existing distinctions of Russian, post-Soviet, or Eastern European foods and foodways have been challenged in Russia and abroad. Some of the recent studies in this area explore the complex meanings of specific foods from the Soviet past that have become important points of reference within the production of national identity narrative and the expression of patriotism. At the same time, apart from dwelling on the cultural meanings of the past and maintaining nostalgic attachments to 'home' and 'home country' – the characteristics that can be specific to post-socialist cultures – some other practices of identity construction can be observed among recently established Russian diasporas. Thus, it can be argued that due to the transnational nature of Russian communities abroad it has been possible to redefine, reshape and challenge existing notions of foodways and to use them as a way of maintaining connections with a wide range of imagined communities both in Russia and in the receiving country.

The aim of this chapter is to explore relationships between food practices and the sense of national belonging within the context of recent Russian-speaking migration to the UK. More specifically, the chapter examines how attachments

92 *Anna Pechurina*

to familiar and national food are articulated by UK-based Russian-speaking migrants and migrant communities in a new cultural context. Drawing on themes that emerged during the study of Russian homes and complemented by the analysis of the recent Russian migrant food discourse, the chapter will discuss several culture-specific food practices that reveal complex connections between diasporic culture and the sense of Russianness in immigration.

Russian migration to the UK has risen significantly in recent decades. The 'new' groups of Russian/post-Soviet migrants of the late 1990s and 2000s, characterized by greater social and ethnic diversity,[1] reshaped the communities of Russian-speakers who arrived during the Soviet period. Although the statistical evidence is the subject of ongoing debate, the wide range of Russian-related cultural activities, business ventures, and initiatives – including mass festivals and celebrations as well as smaller and less formal get-togethers and events – point to the increased presence of an established and resourceful diaspora community (Byford 2012). These activities have provided an important context to a wide range of issues concerned with definition and distinction between categories of Russian and post-Soviet culture, traditions, identity and diasporic belonging. Specifically, the changing context of Russian diasporic activities in recent years has facilitated the development of the Russian ethnic food scene in the UK. The examples include a growing number of events and business initiatives that feature national food, such as cultural festivals, pop-up themed food events, Russian cookbooks written in English (e.g. Baldry 2010, Hercules 2015) and openings of Russian food restaurants that aim to cater for multi-ethnic customers. Interestingly (and in some way, expectedly), these 'new' Russian food venues and practices co-exist with the 'old' Soviet-style restaurants and nostalgic practices of consuming food associated with the Soviet era; the activities that distinguish ethnic cuisines from the generic Soviet label co-exist with reproductions of the iconic Soviet Book of Healthy and Tasty Food recipes (Syutkin and Syutkin 2015). The important question that follows is whether these practices mark new hybrid identities and senses of belonging among Russian-speaking migrants. And, if yes, what is the meaning and significance of migrants' food practices to their Russianness?

The argument in this chapter arises from my previous research that explored the connection between the material culture of Russian migrants' homes and their sense of identity.[2] Although that study focused mainly on the importance of home possessions and home décor, food was frequently mentioned by the Russian-speakers as one of the 'items' they brought from 'home', missed or cooked in their UK homes as a way of maintaining their Russian identity. The topic of food was also used to refer to and explain cultural traditions that characterize and signify Russianness and Russian identity (e.g. mushroom picking, celebrating important events at Russian restaurants or at home round a big 'tableful' with friends). The participants referred to specific foods they brought from home or bought in the UK, places and events where food is consumed and how some food items could or could not symbolize their Russian identity.

National food, belonging, and identity 93

This chapter will explore the processes highlighted above in more detail, starting with an overview of current debates on diasporic identity and senses of home/belonging through food practices, followed by the analysis of the role of food within the context of Russian migration to the UK. The analysis is based on 30 in-depth qualitative interviews with Russian migrants from mixed social and generational backgrounds whose ages range between 29 and 70 at the time of interview, who had moved to the UK from any part of the former USSR (including other parts of the Russian Federation) between 1939 and 2005, and who did not expect to go back to Russia. The majority of the interviews took place 2007 and 2008 in northwest England; a few were conducted in other areas including Scotland, Wales and the South of England. All of the interviewees identified themselves as Russians, although not all of them migrated to England from Russia itself. Eight participants had lived in other countries before coming to the UK, including Canada, Germany, Holland, UAE, Singapore and Israel. All Russians interviewed were born during the Soviet era in different parts of the former USSR. Most were born in Russian cities; three participants were born in Belarus, Moldova and Ukraine, and two were born in Bulgaria and France.

The diverse character of the sample, combined with the ethnographic nature of the study, helped to get closer to the everyday experiences and interactions of a relatively small and close-knit community. The shifted focus, from larger London-based diaspora life to smaller geographic regions, enabled exploration of the experiences of relatively under-studied and under-exposed community that was comparatively uninvolved in centralized and more organized community building initiatives promoted by Diaspora communities in London (Byford 2012).[3] The main focus of the interviews was to explore the relationships between tangible and intangible dimensions of Russianness and a feeling of being at home from the perspective of the participants themselves. In this, food and food-related practices appeared as strong reference points to illustrate and explain various manifestations of a sense of home country and culture identity. As the interviews were conducted at participants' homes, they often involved the element of hospitality: on some occasions participants offered me food or tea, and the choice of the room for the interview could also direct the conversation towards food. In fact, the kitchen was the room where the majority of the interviews were conducted.

The interview discussions facilitated further research interest in this topic that resulted in additional analysis of the more recent Russian diasporic activities around 'gastronomic nostalgia' ([*Russian Gap*] Nikitina et al. 2016). Consequently, the analysis of individual narratives was complemented by the selective media analysis of Russian diasporic media publications and events such as Olga Hercules' cookbook presentations (by Dash Arts in 2015), or the Dacha project (Dash Arts in 2015 www.dasharts.org.uk). The aim is to provide broader context to interview content and to explore more recent changes in performances of Russian diasporic identity within the UK.

94 *Anna Pechurina*

Diasporic homes and foodways in immigration

The subject of food and food cultures has been an important theme in studies of migrant and transnational communities in recent years. Within this body of research the concept of foodways is often used to emphasize the dynamic, changeable and constructed nature of food practices that are interlinked with broader contexts and processes of transnational migration and identity construction. Correspondingly, food and ways of consuming it simultaneously mark and shape multiple attachments to various cultures and identities. Overall, the recent studies of foodways offer several important arguments with regards to the meanings of food, migration and identity that are relevant to this chapter.

Firstly, researchers emphasize that national food cannot be fully understood in essentialist terms as a specific list or a 'Cookbook' (Alfonso 2012: 192, Chapman and Beagan 2013: 381), with a defined list of recipes. It is argued that in the context of global migration national food practices are not a result of the preservation of cultural traditions but rather of the reconstruction and rediscovery of cultural identity within the global cultural conditions that allow simultaneous attachments to several imagined communities. Foodways cannot be preserved or 'frozen' (Chapman and Beagan 2013: 381) because cultures that produce them keep changing, so even preserved food practices lose their authenticity with time. Additionally, other important dimensions such as class, gender and age affect what is perceived as 'traditional' or 'western' ways of cooking and eating.

The important point that follows is that the notion of 'traditional' food within the diaspora is highly varied and hence any stereotypical constructions of a national food, as in a uniform and stable collection of recipes and practices, should be avoided. Migrants' foodways are not static, but a lived experience; they can be disrupted, reconfigured and reinvented in new cultural contexts. As Wilk shows, using the example of Belizean food culture, some national cuisines emerge through the processes of globalization and transnational exchange as the notion of local food gets reinterpreted within the global context, making it possible to compare and (re)position the local cuisine as the national one (Wilk 1999). National identity and national cuisine are constructed through and as a result of the increased integration of Belize into the global context through migration, tourism and communication that brings higher exposure to foreign cultures and their traditions (Wilk 1999: 246). In other words, the definition of national (or 'our') food is constructed in relation to the 'Other', that is foreign foods from the West.

Furthermore, the global context and the access to the global media resources expose migrants to a variety of ethnic foods and ingredients as well as to vast online collections of recipes that were unknown to them before emigration. As a result, while searching for something familiar, people actually discover new ways of combining ingredients to cook familiar national dishes. In other words, the notion of national food 'is expanded in diaspora' (Alfonso 2012: 193), as well as the meanings of home and identity.

National food, belonging, and identity 95

These arguments point to the complex and ambivalent nature of migrants' food choices and their relationship to culture and identity. As Coakley (2012) states, the process of making connections to cultures through food and tastes is characterized as 'an ongoing negotiation of likes and dislikes, of traditions and new discoveries' (Coakley 2012: 323), and – like a migration journey itself – always involves 'both losses and gains' (Coakley 2012: 323). The important point here is that migrants' food cultures are not uniform and often involve a combination of opposing practices that can simultaneously mark a person's belonging to one community and distance them from another. In fact, the very act of reproducing existing cultural food practices within a diasporic context, be it buying food from a local ethnic food shop (Rabikowska and Burrell 2009), bringing it from home in a suitcase (Petridou 2001) or even 'growing food from home' in a local allotment (Gerodetti and Foster 2015), implies hybrid practices and complex meanings of identity construction. Thus, food can be defined as 'familiar' and/or 'national', which is not because it is different as such (e.g. potato mash powder or 'hamburger' are 'global' mass produced items) but because it is brought 'from home'. Correspondingly, the related qualities of food being 'cleaner', 'healthier', or 'more nourishing' are constructed and closely connected with invested emotions, memories and practical efforts of finding the ingredients for a meal or bringing it from a home country. The idea that foodways can mark identities and divide existing communities has been developed further within research of consumption and political resistance (Seliverstova 2017). Other research also shows the importance of patriotic consumption in the production of national identity that often reflects and shapes discourses and popular mythologies around existing identity categories, and thus show socio-cultural contexts in a new light that give food its meanings and significance (Gurova, 2018).

Migrants' foodways are an important tool in the construction of the sense of home. In this context foodways represent and embody one of the dimensions of the homemaking process maintained by migrants. Everyday practices such as bringing, buying, cooking and consuming food contribute to and constitute the 'feeling of being at home' and a related ethnic atmosphere; they are part of home-making, and essentially of culture building. Several studies have specifically focused on exploring relationships of food, identity and homemaking, including Petridou's study of Greek students in London (Petridou 2001) and several studies of Polish migrants in the UK (Coakley 2012, Rabikowska 2010, Rabikowska and Burrell 2009).

The presented conceptualizations of food and identity are reflected in the theoretical standpoint that has informed the analysis in this chapter. Thus, following constructivist approaches, food and identity are defined as constructed and mutually dependent. The process of identity construction is manifested through a wide set of diasporic practices that reveal migrants' multiple and flexible attachments to cultures and communities. In addition, identity is linked to 'home' (both physical and 'imagined'), which represents an important point of reference within the migration journey. In this I follow the argument that by studying migrants' homemaking practices it is possible

96   *Anna Pechurina*

to reveal the ways in which both cultural identity and the feeling of belonging to a homeland are created and maintained (Basu and Coleman 2008). The concept of foodways deployed in this research connects the changeable meanings of food products and ways of consuming together with broader processes and contexts of creating and representing diasporic identity. The experience of migration provides the important context in which identities and cultures are redefined and practiced.

Researching food in the Russian migrant context

Researching Russian food in immigration is a challenging task. On the one hand, the significant transformations of Russian culture and society, as well as the increased mobility of Russian-speakers since the 1990s, have changed both the types of food available for Russians and their ways of consuming it. On the other, these processes also exposed and revealed ongoing controversies and complexities related to shared memories and experiences of both socialist and post-socialist cultures (Caldwell 2009: 3-4).

Russian migrants represent an interesting case in this sense as their strategies often combine practices that draw on the preservation of the Soviet past as well as on processes of adaption to the changing and multiple contexts of the present. However, while the subject of the Soviet and post-Soviet food cultures has been receiving significant attention from academic researchers (Caldwell 2002, 2009; Gronow 2003, Glants and Toomre 1997), the study of Russian food in immigration is a relatively new area. Among the studies that give insight into Russian immigrants' food consumption it is important to mention Boym's (2001) work on nostalgia that considers nostalgic reconstruction of the past as a characteristic of post-Socialist diasporic communities in the USA. Importantly, the Soviet past is an important element of migrants' shared memory that potentially creates a sort of 'diasporic intimacy' (Boym 2001), or an elusive feeling of belonging to an imagined community, embodied through 'materiality of place, sensual perceptions, smells and sounds' (Boym 2001: 259). The taste of familiar food of the past evokes rich memories, but in an ironic way – the object is missed, but not because it was liked, only because it is not here anymore. This can explain migrants' desire to consume food from the past that was characterized by poor quality or was not easily available during the Soviet time. Boym uses the example of 'Poliustrovo' water which coloured her teeth grey after she drank it on her trip to Saint Petersburg. The taste and smell of food and sounds of cooking provide the context that enables images of the past, present and future to be reconstructed and remade in a desired (but never authentic) way (Boym 2001).

There are some interesting parallels that can be drawn between this discussion and the research conducted by Zborovsky and Shirokova (2003). These authors were particularly interested in the factors that influenced the development of the feeling of nostalgia among Russian migrants in Finland. According to researchers, Russian migrants' nostalgia is split between two feelings: on the one hand, migrants miss USSR/Russia 'back then', or a particular period of time and traditions associated with it; on the other hand, they miss the modern Russia which they visit a couple of times a year and their existing attachments and relationships in it (Zborovsky and Shirokova 2003: 78). As a result, some groups of migrants were more inclined to maintain their sense of Russianness through reconstruction of past experiences, by bringing more Russian things and food, furnishing their homes with Russian objects, keeping up Russian traditions and celebrating Russia holidays such as the 8th of March. Ironically, since they persuaded people to think about their home country, all these activities strengthened feelings of nostalgia even more.

In her more recent study Holak (2014) adds a transnational dimension to nostalgia when studying Russian food cultures both in Russia (where the cultural context 'moved') and the USA (the new cultural context into which Russians moved), paying particular attention to the discourses of nostalgia in cyberspace. Thus, nostalgia in Russian diasporas can be rooted either in Time (for Russians who remained in Russia following the breakup of the USSR), or in Time and Space (for Russians who migrated to the West) (Holak 2014: 190). Cyberspace is considered as a New Modality that enables nostalgic reconstructions of food for both groups of Russians. Overall, Holak shows that the interest in Russian/Soviet brands of the past is still high within diasporas and that so-called retro products continue to be stable reference points for the Soviet era and associated symbols, values, traditions and ideals. The Russian migrants' online food blogs and food communities specifically analyzed by Holak offer a slightly different experience for the consumer of national food. Usually presented from a first-person perspective and written in English by Russian female immigrants, the food blogs speak to a diverse global diasporic audience. The active conversations help to reconstruct cultural memory and expand the knowledge of Russian food and culture at the same time. The personalized and interactive style of the blogs with their commentaries and exchanges of opinions offer an active platform for shared community-based interactions that contribute to broadening of the 'national' content. In a sense, this practice bears out the earlier mentioned arguments of the hybridity of diasporic identity and its constantly changing and expanding nature. Thus, by communicating their personal memories and experiences to their readers, Russian-speaking food bloggers rediscover their own sense of Russianness and thereby maintain and share it with others.

Following on from the above, this chapter will expand presented arguments and explore the connection between the meanings of food and national belonging among Russian-speaking migrants in the UK. Several themes emerged during the research that will be discussed in the following sections: (1) the specific practices surrounding bringing food from Russia; (2) the 'exclusivity' of Russian food and its significance to migrants' Russianness; (3) the nostalgic longing and need for food, maintained by migrants as way of connection to Russian culture; and (4) the influences and relationships between 'Soviet', 'post-Soviet' and 'Russian' within migrants' shared mythology and cultural memory.

98 *Anna Pechurina*

The practices surrounding the bringing and consuming national food

AUTHOR: What do people bring from Russia to England?

ALLA: Well, initially people brought food, because there weren't any Russian shops around. They wanted herring, dumplings, sausages, cheaper vodka, cigarettes.... Now we have these all here, so ... we don't bring any food, just some nicely packaged sweets and that's all. One can buy really nice beautifully packaged sweets in Leningrad and Moscow, but other stuff such as cucumbers, cabbage, tomatoes, herring, sausages, dumplings, eggplants, dill, kvas, or rye bread we can get from the shop, which is only 10 minutes away from us. (52 female, works from home)[4]

Going back 'home' is an important part of the migration journey, in which national food is often revisited, tasted, brought back and nostalgically remembered (Burrell 2008, Boym 2001, Petridou 2001). The meaning of these experiences can be significant to migrants' identities and their relationships to their homeland and the receiving country (Rabikowska 2010). Food brings back memories and emotions (Boym 2001: 354-355); it signifies relationships, a sense of belonging, and attachments (Gabaccia 1998: 51).

The majority of my participants agreed that consuming Russian food was a meaningful experience for them and they could easily name typical products that constitute Russian food; the quotation above is a typical example of such a list. Most of them were able to visit Russia annually and confirmed they brought food on their way back. However, it is interesting to see the differences in meanings that the practice of bringing and consuming national food revealed. Thus, while bringing food was certainly a way of connecting to a home country for some, such as George, who compared his experience of going back from Russia to England to 'going to a famine land', there were others whose attachment to Russian food was integrated into their broad diasporic identity. For instance, Polina's cooking of national food focuses on the construction of family rituals which would be neither English nor Russian, but family-specific and personal. For New Year's she cooks special biscuits with her children that would be remembered as part of the family history. Easter too is celebrated as a social or family event rather than a religious holiday. She calls these activities 'pseudo-traditions' that do not have an original meaning and are not to be taken seriously. 'I am pleased that we have it, but I do not make any effort to get it', concludes Polina. The effortless nature and spontaneity of the experience is important; it is the actual practice of eating and drinking that marks Russianness in a person, not thought or imagination. The following quotation from the interview with 40-year-old university researcher Oleg illustrates this experience very well:

The story is the following: I do not visit Russia for a year and literally forget about it. But when I arrive in Russia ... Ooh! All these smells, native talks, tastes, views. It makes me so excited. How could I live without

National food, belonging, and identity 99

all these things? And friends, of course. But after ten days or so all the freshness of these emotions blows away. I eat pelmeni (meat dumplings), Russian bread, and herring. I drink and eat non-stop. Someone abuses me in a shop and I want to get out of Russia and go home. I fly, land in Britain, I see the fog, feel wet and green, it is so good. I feel that it is my cave here where I can relax.... At the beginning you lose a lot. But it is possible to live without all these things.

According to this informant, food cannot be considered a defining feature of Russianness and clearly there are many Russians who can live without Russian food. He is happy to eat English meals but can also cook something Russian 'to impress his friends' or to remember the particular tastes if he wants to. In a similar way, one of the women stated: 'Russian food is tastier but it does not mean that a Russian must drink tea from Russian cups, eat Russian sausages and drink vodka. This would not make me more Russian' (Olga, 28 year-old, works in marketing).

The presented examples follow a similar pattern to other transnational migrants who continuously balance different cultural identities and connections (Chapman and Beagan 2013). The attachments to national food reflect well the ambivalence of migrants' experiences in which loss is a constant element. The ties with the home country established through bringing and consuming national food require continuous effort, which is not possible to maintain and which can also give the opposite effect. The tastes and smells of food and the emotions that surround it may emphasize the difference between cultures even more and encourage nostalgic feelings (Boym 2001), or they may constantly remind a person about things that s/he cannot have. At the same time, it is possible to see that traditional food practices can change and become 'hybridised' (Chapman and Beagan 2013; Gerodetti and Foster 2015) when new meanings are added and mixed to reflect a different way of dealing with contradictory experiences of comparison and adaptation, integration and refusal.

Maintaining the exclusivity and authenticity of Russian food

In her research of London-based Polish migrants' food habits, Rabikowska (2010) gives an interesting example that reveals the controversy of characteristics assigned by migrants to Polish and British foods. Thus, one of Rabikowska's participants Ewa is strongly opposed to British food, which she describes as 'tasteless', 'unvaried' and unhealthy. Ewa prefers 'good food', i.e. Polish food, which is nutritious and healthy, made from fresh ingredients: 'I make my sandwich with ham, tomatoes and green salad. But rice, puree, chips and spaghetti are our basics. For lunch I eat hamburgers and chips as I know it from home and I can swallow it' (Rabikowska 2010: 380). Rabikowska uses the concept of habitus (Bourdieu 1984) to explain migrants' attitude to food: that is, a constituted order of tastes and preferences internalized by individuals to the point that they start to believe it to be a part of their identity. The constructed

100 *Anna Pechurina*

dichotomies between Polish and English food and their related practices and rituals of eating illustrate this point well: migrants appropriate and recognize certain foods as Polish due to the fact that they used to consume them repeatedly back in Poland. Thus, even the products that are not traditionally Polish (such as hamburgers and chips) are labelled as 'home foods' because they were first known at home.

As my research shows, Russians also actively comment on both Russian and English foods; in fact, the willingness to talk about food does not always represent actual involvement in buying or cooking Russian products. Whether participants ate Russian products recently or have not had them for a while, they expressed strong opinions towards food in their daily lives. The important theme that emerged during the interviews is how the Russianness of national food was constructed in relation to the local products available to them. Even if Russian products were of the same type as the British, they were labelled as different: more 'natural',[5] fresh, and even exclusive. Consider the following quotations by Nikolay and Dasha:

> The products are different here. You need to try ten types of flour to see which one fits best.... We make our own kefir and mushroom tea.[6] ... It's not easy to spot familiar products, because you wouldn't even know where to look. But gradually we found them, first, where to get rye bread, and then replicas of smetana and tvorog. (Nikolay, 36 years old, researcher)
>
> I do not eat it here. Bakery is different here. Dumplings are not on sale. I eat fish, but it is still different. So the names are the same: 'pastry', 'fish', but the actual thing turns out to be very different. (Dasha, 29 years old, project manager)

Thus, the Russianness of food is constructed in a similar way as Polishness in Rabikowska study: it is closely related to notions and performative rituals of 'home', culture and collective identity. It can be argued that by maintaining the exclusivity of Russian food and ways of cooking it, migrants reproduced the distinctions linked to so-called 'us' and 'them' identities. In other words, the cultural meanings of Russian and British food are constructed through the continuous antagonism between the two. 'I do not cook, but of course I love Russian food and of course I hate English food absolutely ...' says Maria (80 years old, retired), who later states that authentic Russian food can only be cooked by a Russian person. 'When a Russian person cooks, it's one thing; when another person cooks using a Russian recipe, it is totally different!' Thus, one cannot replicate Russian food through using local (i.e. 'fake') ingredients, even if they are sold through Russian shops, because the quality would never be the same. Food brought back from Russia is different: it is authentic, unique and exclusive; it is 'ours'.

Thinking of the relationships between food practices and cultural identity, it can further be argued that the strategy of withdrawing into products from the 'homeland', be they food or material objects, can be an indicator of the

National food, belonging, and identity 101

type of identity associated with an antagonistic attitude to British culture. The resulting 'cultural exile' becomes internalized within a person's identity and their way of life. In this, food and food practices both remind and connect one with Russia and through this enable them to maintain sense of home and of belonging to an imagined community:

> You can never get used to the local food even if you start cooking it well. We have a friend. Sometimes we take him with us on mushroom collecting trips. He does not drive and suffers from being alone all the time and because of that he really needs Russian products. (Nikolay, 36 years old, researcher)

Thus, for people like Nikolay and his friend it was almost as if they could not be Russian without eating and cooking Russian food or performing traditional food related rituals. However, it should be noted that not all participants supported this notion. Thus, there are people like Max (37 years old, works in sales) or the previously mentioned Oleg who try to separate themselves from those who constantly need to talk and think about products, as if they bring a 'piece of Russia with them and carry it everywhere' (Max). For this group, migration opens a possibility to expand and integrate different tastes and experiences in which Russianness is one of many dimensions. In other words, the acceptance of difference, rather than a refusal of it, becomes a way of practicing and maintaining one's identity and sense of belonging. This will be discussed in the next section.

Russian, Soviet, and post-Soviet diasporic foodways

In Summer 2016 the topic of 'Gastronostalgia' was featured in the Russian migrant magazine *Russian Gap* as part of a thematic issue 'Food and Cities'. The main material of the issue presents an overview of London cafes and restaurants that offer Russian and post-Soviet cuisine on the menu, ranging 'from expensive and traditional to democratic and very odd' ([*Russian Gap*] Nikitina et al 2016: 8). It appears that the terms 'Soviet', 'Russian' and 'post-Soviet' are used interchangeably and refer to a unified body of Russian-speakers (the targeted audience of the magazine) rather than to different distinct sub-communities. The restaurants reviewed by the Russian Gap seem to fit this concept too and cover several ethnic cuisines including Russian, Georgian, and Central Asian, among others. The editors also pay attention to the Russian-owned restaurants serving international and European food ([*Russian Gap*] Nikitina et al 2016: 16-20). as well as to the broader questions of cultural identity and Russian mentality in their interview with a well-known London restaurateur of Russian origin, Mikhail Zelman ([*Russian Gap*] Tikhonova 2016: 22-29).

This thematic issue of the *Russian Gap* is one of the many examples that mark growing interest to the national food coming from within the diaspora in recent years. The particular feature of this interest (which includes

102   *Anna Pechurina*

business initiatives such as ethnic restaurants and supper-clubs, publications in the global and ethnic/migrant media,[7] as well as a number of Russian and East-European cookbooks and web-resources)[8] is its diasporic nature, of which 'gastronostalgic' experiences and practices reveal a polysemy of cultural meanings and contexts. These processes certainly make Russian food more visible within the multicultural context of the UK, offering multiple opportunities for establishing a sense of community and belonging. At the same time, the diasporic identifications constructed through this growing migrant food culture are complex and contextual, reflecting the diversity of the migratory experiences of UK-based Russian-speakers. In this, the distinctions between Soviet and post-Soviet identities and practices are not definite and distinct, but rather interrelated and even blurred into one another. The shared cultural discourse reproduced through these diasporic practices simultaneously reconstructs and reinvents popular imaginations related to the Soviet past, integrating them within the overall deterritorialized post-Soviet migrant context.[9] The research literature on post-Socialist food practices also confirms the importance of Soviet food politics in shaping cultural meanings of the present (Burrell 2003, Caldwell 2009, Harper 2003). As a result, some of the themes and practices have become ingrained in the cultural memory and continuously 'travel' through various recollections of the past. Examples of the most recognizable themes are queuing for food (Burrell 2003); the limited choice of products and/or empty shelves (von Bremzen 2013); strategies around informal 'food-hunting' (Caldwell 2009); 'kitchen culture' (Boym 1994); and antagonistic relationships with the West (Caldwell 2002, Klumbyte 2009). These strategies have been recalled by my research participants too, in both nostalgic and ironic ways (Pechurina 2015: 119-131). For instance, arranging Russian-style get-togethers (zastolye), going out to Russian restaurants, or celebrating Russian holidays were often mentioned as activities that helped my research participants to feel at home and enabled them to keep the sense of continuity between past and present, even if only imagined. In this context the Russian restaurants play the role of diasporic places that enable migrants to 'transform their immediate spaces into places of familiar rituals, smells and tastes' (Rabikowska and Burell 2009: 358), ultimately helping them to re-create the feeling of being at home. Reiterating the words of my participants, people do not go there to eat, they go there to be Russians: 'I was very surprised when I first came here that a restaurant here is made for eating food. It is not associated with having fun. For us restaurant is not really about food, we went there to have fun, to dance and so on', says Larissa (40, social worker). Or, 'we celebrate all Russian holidays and only at the [Russian] restaurant. New Years and our Christmas – all there' (Lena, 40, bar manager).

At the same time, in recent years the diasporic food places and spaces began to reveal some other dimensions to their Russianness. New groups of Russian-speaking migrants of the late 1990s and early 2000s who mainly experienced the Soviet era during their childhood use the traditions of the past in a slightly different way. Thus, the deeply emotional nostalgia for the food habits of the

National food, belonging, and identity 103

Soviet era specific to the generations of migrants who came during the Soviet time (Boym 1994, 2001) has been replaced by a more positively engaging strategy of regeneration and rediscovery of authentic food traditions of the past that had been forgotten and/or suppressed by Soviet policies. The varied nature of nostalgia has been also discussed by Kannike (2011) in her research of postsocialist Estonia. As Kannike shows, nostalgic feelings for the past emerge and develop through variations of experiences and practices of the present. In the UK this trend is driven by a number of food bloggers and chefs who have been actively promoting Russian and Eastern European food in the UK, such as Ukranian chef Olga Hercules (2015), the Eastern-European duo 'Russian Revels' (who organize Russian and Soviet themed gastronomic pop-up dinners), and the cinema-supper club KinoVino, whose pop-up dinners are performed together with films that inspire the menu. The uniting theme of these gastronomic pop-up performances is their immersive and staged nature that interlinks cultural dimensions of the past and present within a deterritorialized migrant setting. The spontaneous and temporary character of suppers that are not attached to any permanent physical space (as opposed to a traditional restaurant) emphasize even more the flexible and changeable nature of cultural attachments and borders. Events vary and include anything from a Soviet-style pop-up to a Tolstoy-inspired dinner; they can be themed around a particular ethnic cuisine such as that of the Baltics, Ukraine or Georgia. The emphasis on the diversity of cultural roots helps to overcome the ambiguity of the post-Soviet identities that are represented by various combinations of attachments based on multi-ethnic family connections and life trajectories, not uncommon to the Soviet-born generation. For instance, chef Olga Hercules, who strongly identifies herself as southern Ukrainian, acknowledges many other cultural influences that stem from her family background: 'My paternal grandmother is Siberian, my mother has Jewish and Bessarabian (Moldovan) roots, my father was born in Uzbekistan and we have Armenian relatives and Ossetian friends' (Hercules 2015: 6). This complex mixture of attachments expresses very well the diasporic and multi-ethnic nature of the post-Soviet migrant body and enables more flexibility in self-identification.

Perhaps one of the ultimate examples of mixing cultural borders and identities is the festival of Russian culture called 'the Dacha' which has been held in London annually since 2014 and is organized by the British art group Dash Arts. The Dacha is a continuously changing immersive theatre performance that reproduces the atmosphere of a traditional Russian country house through elements of décor, food, music and acting. The space is in constant transformation to reflect changes in time that Dacha and its visitors travel through during the three-day performance: from Tsarist Russian through the Socialist era into the post-Soviet times of today. The audience, i.e. the Dacha visitors, are part of the performance and co-produce the unique and constantly changing cultural atmosphere through various multisensory practices of listening, eating, touching and interacting. The Dacha is not

104 *Anna Pechurina*

targeted at the Russian-speaking diaspora only, in this it aims to blur cultural borders and attachments. The experience it offers is multiple and diverse; cultural memorabilia and material objects, emotions and senses, tastes and sounds reconstruct past and present and mix the old and the new, enabling diasporic connections and experiences to creatively evolve.

Conclusion

This chapter has analyzed several aspects of the UK-based Russian migrants' food consumption practices and revealed a diverse repertoire of meanings related to home, identity and cultural memory. The Russian community is still a relatively new group in the UK and its active engagement in performances of identity reflects the demand for constructing a community narrative that would provide points of reference for a diverse group of Russian speakers. National foodways is one of the tools that capture cultural dynamics and reveals their essential characteristics, which helps 'to illustrate, analyse, and explain the most important and interesting issues facing modern societies' (Nestle 2009: x). Through an analysis of Russian immigrants' strategies related to engagement with national products, this chapter highlighted several important themes that ran through participants' narratives of self-identity and their everyday life experiences. Specifically, it was concerned with the role of nostalgic attitudes towards the Soviet past and their role in shaping food cultures of the post-Soviet generation of migrants who currently reside in the UK. Clearly, the symbolism and cultural forms of the Soviet period is an important point of reference that has its bearing on how migrants maintain and perform their identity. Nostalgia is still an important part of the process, but it is used as a tool to both rediscover one's culture and heritage and to connect one with wider communities of Russians and non-Russians. In this process, meanings related to 'Soviet' or Eastern European food and practices have merged with sensorial evocations of childhood. Careful explorations of the past and its rediscovery become an important part of the performances of identity and build connections within highly diverse diasporic settings. Family photographs, stories and personal memories as well as national recipes and products have been carefully collected, researched and presented by food enthusiasts in order to discover and share the essence of the national cuisine. For instance, Katrina Kollegaeva, a food writer and former blogger of The Gastronomical Me,[10] explores the childhood memories of living in Soviet Estonia that sparked her current curiosity about the food of her homeland.[11] She strongly believes that food is part of one's identity and connects one to personal roots, bringing with it the 'warmth and sensuality' associated with one's homeland. At the same time, as a long-time resident of London exposed to a variety of tastes and cultures, Katrina emphasizes the positive value of diversity and combinations of tastes, i.e.

National food, belonging, and identity   105

'a more cosmopolitan, accepting attitude towards national origins – and food' ([*The Calvert Journal*] Kollegaeva n.d.). Rye bread and homegrown tomatoes are still brought back carefully wrapped in paper, but food is not used as a way of escaping into the past, rather to help cultural exchange and integration.

Some of the questions that the analysis has generated have potential for future research. Certainly, a more detailed research into gender, class and generational differences among migrants would contribute to a better understanding of existing complexities within Russian diasporic communities. The analysis of the British food context and its own position within global food cultures would present an interesting study as to whether and to what extent migrants' withdrawal into national food is affected by the local food culture. Would Russians living in Italy or France show a more positive attitude towards food cultures of the receiving society? This question leads to another relevant topic of patriotic food consumption and the broader practices of exchange that involve not only food brought back from the home country, but also products that are sent home from the country of residence. The changing nature of the Russian diaspora, including its socio-demographic composition and cultural practices, could in itself be the basis for further research. Food, its meaning and the rich sensory experience that accompanies it is a constant reminder of home, imagined and missed or experienced and desired.

Notes

1 Researchers distinguish several migration waves from Russia to the UK, with the latest starting in 1991. During this period the number of Russian speakers increased within the overall East-West migration bloc; however, the precise number is unclear due to the diversity of a group that includes Russians who belong to different generations (Soviet-born, Russian-born and British-born Russians) and Russian speakers/ethnic Russians who came from the ex-Soviet Republics. The latest ONS Census data shows that in 2011 there were 66,366 people in England and Wales who considered Russian their main language. The statistics by country of birth and nationality shows that there is around 49,043 Russian-born migrants in the UK and 35,172 Russian nationals, which is not including those born in the USSR and other former Soviet republics, such as Ukraine – born (26,452), Belarus (6,303), Azerbaijan (6,202) and some others (ONS).
2 The PhD research 'Creating Home from Home: Russian Communities in the UK' was conducted in 2006–2010 at the University of Manchester. For more details see Pechurina (2015).
3 Certainly, the geography of the research also defined the available choices of Russian products and subsequent food consumption strategies expressed by research participants. However, although one can argue that there are more shops that sell Russian food in London, it does not necessarily mean easier access due to many other factors related to geography, class positions and involvement in local networks.
4 All original names have been changed.
5 See Caldwell (2007) for a discussion on natural food discourse in the post-Soviet Russia.

106 *Anna Pechurina*

6 Russian name for Kombucha.
7 Several publications about Eastern European, Soviet and Russian food have been featured in the *Calvert Journal*, e.g. 'Soviet Food Stories' (http://calvertjournal.com/features/show/4633); the articles by Nechepurenko (2014) and Kushelevich (2014) discuss socio-political dimensions of Russian food cultures. Omidi (2013) and Raspopina (2015) go back to foods of the Soviet past. *The Guardian* reviews a recent translation of the iconic Soviet Cookbook (15 October 2015) and questions Russia's obsession with dill (10 August 2015).
8 For example, *Russia on a Plate* by Baldry (2010); *Mamushka: Recipes from Ukraine and Beyond* by Olia Hercules (2015); *Mastering the Art of Soviet Cooking* by von Bremzen (2013). For an overview of the food-related web resources see Holak (2014).
9 Byford applies the term the 'last Soviet generation' to describe discoursive strategies and identity performances utilized by Russian migrants in the 1990s-2000s Britain (Byford 2009).
10 See Holak (2014) for detailed analysis of the blog.
11 There are interesting parallels to the research on nostalgia and homemaking in postsocialist Estonia by Kannike (2011) who also mentions the emergence of nostalgia/retro trend with a more 'relaxed' attitude towards the Soviet past among young generation (Kannike 2011: 67).

References

Alfonso, I. D. 2012. We are what we now eat: Food and identity in the Cuban diaspora. *Canadian Journal of Latin American and Caribbean Studies/Revue canadienne des études latino-américaines et caraïbes*, 37(74), 173–206.
Baldry, K. 2010. *Russia on a plate*. London: Stonewash DD&AG.
Basu, P., Coleman, S. 2008. Introduction. Migrant worlds, material cultures. *Mobilities*, 3(3), 313–330.
Bourdieu, P. 1984. *Distinction: a social critique of the judgement of taste*. London: Routledge.
Boym, S. 1994. *Common places: Mythologies of everyday life in Russia*. Cambridge, MA: Harvard University Press.
Boym, S. 2001. *The future of nostalgia*. New York: Basic Books.
Bremzen von, A. 2013. *Mastering the art of Soviet cooking. A memoir of food, family, and longing*. London: Black Swan.
Burell, K. 2003. The social and political life of food in socialist Poland. *Anthropology of East Europe Review* (special issue: Food and Foodways in Post-Socialist Eurasia) 21(1), 189–194.
Burrell, K. 2008. Materialising the border: Spaces of Mobility and material culture in migration from post-socialist Poland. *Mobilities* 3(3), 353–373.
Burell, K. 2012. The objects of Christmas: The politics of festive materiality in the lives of Polish immigrants. In Moving subjects, moving objects: migrant art, artefacts and emotional agency, edited by M. Svasek. Oxford: Berghahn, 55–74.
Byford, A. 2009. 'The last Soviet generation' in Britain. In *Diasporas: Critical and inter-disciplinary perspectives*, edited by Fernandez, J. The Inter-Disciplinary Press. Online. Available online at www.inter-disciplinary.net/publishing/id-press/ebooks/diasporas/ [accessed 13 Oct 2012].
Byford, A. 2012. The Russian diaspora in international relations: 'Compatriots' in Britain. *Europe Asia Studies* 64(4), 715–735.
Caldwell, M. 2002. The taste of nationalism: Food politics in postsocialist Moscow. *Ethos* 67(3), 295–319.
Caldwell, M. 2007. Feeding the body and nourishing the soul. *Food, Culture and Society* 10(1), 43–71.

National food, belonging, and identity   107

Caldwell, M. 2009. *Food and everyday life in the postsocialist world*. Bloomington, IN: Indiana University Press.

Chapman, G., Beagan, B. L. 2013. Food practices and transnational identities. *Food, Culture and Society* 16(3), 367–386.

Coakley, L. 2012. Polish encounters with the Irish foodscape: An examination of the losses and gains of migrant foodways. *Food and Foodways: Explorations in the History and Culture of Human Nourishment* 20(3-4), 307–325.

Gerodetti, N., Foster, S. 2016. 'Growing foods from home': Food production, migrants and the changing cultural landscapes of gardens and allotments. *Landscape Research* 41(7), 808–819. ISSN 0142–6397 DOI: 10.1080/01426397.2015.1074169.

Glants, M., Toomre, J. S. 1997. Food in Russian history and culture. Bloomington: Indiana University Press.

Gronow, J. 2003. Caviar with champagne. Common luxury and the ideals of the good life in Stalin's Russia. Oxford: Berg Publishers.

Gurova O. 2018. Political consumerism in Russia after 2011, forthcoming in *Cultural mechanisms of political protest in Russia*, edited by E. Etkind, B. Beumers, S. Turoma, and O. Gurova. London and New York: Routledge.

Harper, K. 2003. Green carnivores, mad cows, and gene tech: The politics of food in Hungarian environmentalism. *Anthropology of East Europe Review* 21(1), 103–108.

Hercules, O. 2015. *Mamushka: Recipes from Ukraine and beyond*. London: Mitchell Beazley.

Holak, S. L. 2014. From Brighton Beach to blogs: Exploring food related nostalgia in the Russian diaspora. *Consumption Markets and Culture* 17(2), 185–207.

Kannike, A. 2011. Refuge or resource: Home and nostalgia in postsocialist Estonia. *Journal of Ethnology and Folkloristics* 3(1), 57–72.

Klumbyte, N. 2009. The geopolitics of taste, the 'Euro' and 'Soviet' sausage – industries in Lithuania. In *Food and everyday life in the postsocialist world*, edited by M. L. Caldwell. Bloomington: Indiana University Press.

Kollegaeva, K. n.d. Taste of home – Searching for the real Estonia, one bite at a time, in *The Calvert Journal*. Available online at http://calvertjournal.com/features/show/4634 [accessed 20 April 2017].

Kushelevich, M. 2014. Taste of freedom, in *The Calvert Journal*. Available online at http://calvertjournal.com/articles/show/3046/mcdonalds-moscow-closure-russia-martin-parr [accessed 3 July 2016].

Nechepurenko, I. 2014. You are what you eat: Why food, culture and politics go hand in hand in Russia, in *The Calvert Journal*. Available online at http://calvertjournal.com/comment/show/3057/food-culture-politics-russia-sanctions [Accessed 3 July 2016].

Nestle, M. 2009. Foreword, in *Food and everyday life in the post–Socialist world*, edited by Melissa L. Caldwell. Bloomington and Indianapolis: Indiana University Press, IX–XII.

Nikitina, K., Basyrova, E., and Konurbaeva, D. Gastronostalgia. *Russian Gap. Mind the Russians*, (6), 8–19.

Omidi, M. 2013. Soviet kitchen: A culinary tour of Stalin's iconic cookbook, in *The Calvert Journal*. Available online at http://calvertjournal.com/articles/show/1746/soviet-kitchen-culinary-tour-of-stalins-iconic-cookbook [accessed 3 July 2016].

Pechurina, A. 2015. *Material cultures, migrations, and identities. What the eye cannot see*. London: Palgrave.

Petridou, E. 2001. The taste of home, in *Home possession: Material culture behind closed doors*, edited by D. Miller. Oxford: Berg, 87–107.

Rabikowska, M., Burrell, K. 2009. The material worlds of recent Polish migrants: Transnationalism, food, shops, and home, in *Polish migration to the UK in the 'new' European Union after 2004*, edited by K. Burrell. Aldershot: Ashgate, 211–232.

108 *Anna Pechurina*

Rabikowska, M. 2010. The ritualisation of food, home and national identity among Polish migrants in London. *Social Identities* 16(3), 377–398.

Raspopina, S. 2015. Unmodern dining: Why pre-Soviet cuisine is back on the menu in Russia. *The Calvert Journal*. Available online at http://calvertjournal.com/articles/show/3651/pre-Soviet-cuisine-traditional-Russian-recipes-LavkaLavka [accessed 3 July 2016].

Seliverstova. 2017. 'Consuming' national identity in western Ukraine. *Nationalities Papers*, 45(1), 61–79 DOI: http://dx.doi.org/10.1080/00905992.2016.1220363.

Syutkin, O., Syutkin, P. 2015. *CCCP cook book: True stories of Soviet cuisine*. London: Fuel Publishing.

Tikhonova A. Mikhail Zel'man, M. 2016. Ya v Moskve vse prodal i pereyekhal v London. *Russian Gap. Mind the Russians* (6), 22–29.

Wilk, R. R. 1999. 'Real Belizean food': Building local identity in the transnational Caribbean. *American Anthropologist* 101(2), 244–255.

Zborovsky, G., Shirokova, E. 2003. Nostalgia rossiyskih emigrantov: probny opros v finlandii. *Sociologicheskie Issledovaniya* 8, 75–79.

6 Consumer citizenship and reproduction of Estonianness

Oleksandra Seliverstova

Introduction

This work focuses on the context of post-Soviet countries, where apart from complex ethnic composition of newly established states, there was another condition, namely the introduction to market economy and the growth of consumer culture. This introduced new elements into how national identity construction was and is being interpreted and reproduced by the local population. This chapter explores the aspect of national identity formation that is still understudied: the construction of national identity originating at the bottom level, where ordinary people play a role.

The aim of this chapter is threefold. Theoretically it aspires to demonstrate that concepts of banal nationalism (Billig 1995) and consumer citizenship (Foster 2002), previously mostly applied to Western societies, are pertinent to national identity formation processes in the post-Soviet context. Methodologically it contributes to a still very small body of literature that promotes the more frequent use of political ethnography while addressing major socio-political processes of post-Soviet countries. Empirically, through the case study of food consumer culture in Estonia, it will show how ordinary people enact, renegotiate and express national belonging in everyday life. In particular it focuses on how citizens who identify themselves with groups of different ethnic/language background can all participate in formation of one collective identity.

This study addresses such goals through the case study of the Estonian capital – Tallinn. The case cannot be considered as representative of the Estonian society; it is rather used to illustrate the main argument of this work and to show how a small-scale study can provide additional details to (or in some cases challenge) an understanding of large socio-political processes, traditionally studied by political scientists through top-down approaches. This is done using the interpretative everyday approach (Finlayson et al. 2004, Schwartz-Shea and Yanow 2012), which only was recently applied to the post-Soviet context (Cheskin 2013, Knott 2015, Pawlusz 2016, Seliverstova 2017). Such a bottom-up approach implies a focus on the role of ordinary citizens and their everyday practices in the process of formation and renegotiation of a nationhood (Brubaker et al. 2006, Fox and Miller-Idriss 2008).

110 *Oleksandra Seliverstova*

The use of Estonia as a case study sheds light on another aspect of post-socialism, which is the presence of Russian speakers in former-Soviet states. Russian-speaking populations, while being citizens or just residents of former Soviet states other than Russia, very often tend to be perceived as a challenge to the successful formation of national policies and in some cases as a threat to national security (Kuus 2002, Pryce 2011). The official Estonian national narrative since 1991 has been built around the idea of ethno-cultural nationalism, giving preference to ethnic Estonian and ignoring a type of collective identity whose elements were and are usually shared by Russian speakers in Estonia. By discovering how both native Estonians and Estonian Russians participate in the everyday consumer culture, this chapter also explores aspects of inter-ethnic dynamics, and how different ethnic/language groups themselves relate to common national categories through consumer culture.

In particular, this work analyzes how national belonging is experienced in Estonia through the prism of food consumer culture. The interpretation of data, gathered through semi-structured interviews and observation of every-day consumption practices and sites, suggests that consumption itself represents a symbolic stage for the re-negotiation and performance of national belonging. It provides individuals with a variety of symbolic tools: to express their national sentiments; to support/reject official national discourse; and to generate new markers of national identity by embedding new objects and practices with national meanings. Previously I have illustrated the same processes with the help of the case study of Western Ukraine, where consumption related to home appeared to be the most representative of the main argument (Seliverstova 2017). In the case of Estonia where the data was collected in the same way, food consumption first was identified as the most contested sphere of consumption, as the official narrative of Estonianness is intensively promoted through food products and food habits (Vosu and Kannike 2011).[1] Second, discussions of food consumption were the most vivid and rich parts of interviews conducted in Tallinn. These two predispositions informed my choice to present ideas of this chapter through the prism of food consumption, which here is understood as a cultural practice (Caldwell 2002, Pechurina 2015).

In order to support theoretically the link between consumption and formation of national identity this study will first refer to works that elaborate the concept of banal nationalism and analyze the lived experience of identity through the lens of everyday life. Then it will draw from works that discussed the role of consumer as a citizen: a citizen that contributes to the performativity of a nation through consumption practices (Cronin 2005, Foster 2002). These two strands of literature follow Hobsbawm's (1990) advice to study national communities from both upper and bottom levels.

Empirically this chapter is informed by 25 informal semi-structured interviews, conducted in Tallinn in 2014–2015 with representatives of two language groups[2] – Estonian and Russian speakers. Snowball sampling was used for finding potential respondents, who could be defined as urban citizens, representatives of either the educated middle class or the lower middle class, born between 1950–1990. To complement the data derived from interviews, this work relies also on the results of intensive observation of consumption sites, such as markets and supermarkets in Tallinn. The analysis of printed and online materials promoting Estonian cuisine and various Estonian food events which took place in 2014–2015 serves as an additional source of data included in interpretations presented.

The rest of this chapter is structured in the following way. First, it presents a short literature overview that serves to frame the results of this research in both the worldwide and in particular post-Soviet debate on national identity formation. The following empirical part reveals what food consumption practices and some food products tell about how belonging to Estonia is expressed and re-negotiated. It shows different ways in which Russian speakers, though sometimes differently from the titular group, participate in these processes. The last section is a summary discussion of the advantages of using a bottom-up approach for the study of national identity.

From the worldwide to area literature

The use of a bottom-up approach in research on identity politics and nationalism is not novel (Brubaker et al. 2006, Edensor 2002, Fox and Miller-Idriss 2008, Foster 2002, Skey 2011). These scholars prompted interested in how ordinary people understand and experience ethnicity, nationality and citizenship in their everyday lives. Michael Billig's *Banal Nationalism* (1995) is emblematic. Billig discusses banal aspects of nationalism and in particular analyzes the mundane use of national symbols by ordinary citizens, showing that nation is built on a day-to-day basis. For instance, Edensor (2002) and Skey (2011) analyzed popular culture, popular discourses and symbolics of physical settings and material objects to reveal how nation is grounded in the everyday realm. The work of Foster (2002) is particularly relevant for this research. Through his study of elements of the mass media and commodity consumption in non-Western contexts Foster showed how different aspects and details of mundane life 'serve to anchor the nation in the everyday life' (Foster 2002: 64). When discussing the idea of 'consumer citizenship', Foster refers to it as to the 'production of national identity by way of shared consumption practices' (Foster and Özcan 2005: 5).

These types of studies advocate shifting the dominant focus on the role of political elite and institutions in nationalism studies, suggesting that nation also gets materialized in everyday life, in which ordinary citizens have an active role (Lofgren 1993). With the use of their empirical data they demonstrate that the formation of national identity and how it is experienced is a much more sophisticated and nuanced process than it appears if studied through traditional top-down approaches.

112 *Oleksandra Seliverstova*

Post-soviet context

In the context of Estonia, issues of nation building, national identity and integration processes were thus far mostly explored through top-down approaches, in particular, through the lenses of policy making (Linz and Stepan 1996, Pettai and Kreuzer 1998, Vetik and Helemäe 2011), use of language and national symbols (Jacobson 2002, 2006, Laitin 1998, Lohmus et al. 2009, Siiner 2006, Vihalemm 1999), citizenship (Aasland 2002, Hallik 2006, Smith 1991 Vetik and Helemäe, 2011), culture (Laitin 1998, Nimmerfeldt 2011, Vihalemm and Kalmus 2009) and ethnic tensions (Ehala 2009, Melberg 2002, Korts 2009). The most recent results of such studies show that Russian speakers are still considered poorly integrated into Estonian society (for instance, apart from cultural and social segregation, unemployment among Russian speakers remains high, compared to Estonians). However, these works are informed by the official narrative of the Estonian nation, which is based on ethno-cultural values of the ethnic majority group, and highlights the 'otherness' of the Russian-speaking community. According to this perspective, the term integration usually has a meaning more similar to assimilation: a complete acceptance of values shared by ethnic Estonians. Learning Estonian, development of loyalty towards Estonia, whitewashing of traces of life under the Soviet Union and rejection of values associated with Russian culture are the minimum 'requirements' for successful integration of Russian speakers (Wulf 2016). This one-sided account of integration, called by Meike Wulf (2016) *Estonianisation*, omits acculturation processes happening among Russians and therefore also excludes the possibility of constructing a culturally distinct, but common Estonian-Russian identity.

At the same time in the last decade a growing number of scholars started to show that moving beyond the perspective of official nationalistic discourse while analyzing national identity is useful, as it helps to reveal some discrepancies and implicit aspects of the sense of belonging in Estonia (Nimmerfeldt 2011, Pawlusz, 2016, Wulf 2016). Such studies demonstrate that the division along ethnic lines prevailing in Estonian official discourse does not always play the decisive role in how national identity is shaped and practiced after 1991. Nimmerfeldt (2011) observes that while measuring the level of integration of Russian speakers it is important to avoid labelling a national identity category as 'Estonian', as Russian-speaking informants could almost automatically associate it with Estonian ethnicity and as a result avoid identifying themselves with it. She suggests to rather focus on 'the formation of attachment to the host country and society' which can equally reveal the 'sense of belonging at the national level' (ibid: 204). Wulf (2016) through the analysis of collective memory of the past demonstrated that the way Estonian nation is imagined differs among different generations, and accordingly there are also shifts in the perceptions and position of Russian speaking population residing in Estonia. The conclusions informed by the analysis of Estonian home settings of Kannike (2006) also correspond to arguments provided by

Consumer citizenship and Estonianness 113

Wulf (2016). Kannike (2006, 2011) shows how national identity is negotiated through everyday creative practices and finds that whereas the dominating public discourse on proper *Estonianness* regards the recent Soviet past as a period of total rupture, the negation of it in the everyday life is indeed only partial, showing that Estonian society has cognitive and aesthetic continuity. Pawlusz's (2016) ethnographic study of the national song festival Laulupidu revealed that even festival organizers who act as representatives of the state might shift their views on what constitutes the Estonian nation and change their own national self identification depending on the context in which they would act. Such studies, though not engaging in a comparative analysis of how the sense of national belonging is shaped within different ethnic/language groups of Estonia, still suggest that there might be a large variety of identity features, shared by representatives of each group, but existing in parallel and therefore overlapping and even competing with each other.

Another strand of literature that helps to identify the gap that this work aims to address focuses on the role of consumption in the process of national identity formation within a post-Soviet context (Keller 2004, Klumbyte 2010, Gurova 2018, Seliverstova 2017, Vihalemm and Keller 2011). However, despite the growing role of consumption in socio-political processes worldwide it remains understudied particularly through the prism of everyday life of an average citizen. Kannike (2006, 2011) analyzes material culture and consumer practices related to the home in Estonia to reveal how transformation from Soviet everyday culture into Western consumer culture is conceptualized through ideas about the home and how this process forges formation of new collective identities. The work on how Estonian youth consumers establish symbolic boundaries among different ethnic/language group through consumer culture by Vihalemm and Keller (2011) inspired this research. It explores differences in consumer patterns among Estonian Russians and ethnic Estonians and suggests that some elements of collective ethnic identity are constructed through consumer culture. Kalmus, Keller and Kiise (2009) focus on consumer types appearing in Estonia, categorizing first their respondents according to their age and ethnic identification and then developing a typology of Estonian consumers. Their study shows that despite differences in consumer preferences among different ethnic groups, this difference decreases with age of respondents. In addition, becoming a 'good' consumer, according to the ethnic Estonian perspective, can allow Russian speakers to better integrate into Estonian society.

All of these works contribute to the understanding of how Estonians reacted to changes brought about by the dissolution of the Soviet Union, such as introduction of a market economy and openness to the Western world. They are informative of how such reactions and adaptation to new conditions affected identity formation processes. However while introducing very rich empirical data and useful insights about everyday life of transition societies, the above-mentioned studies still do not focus fully on the interrelation of two processes – formation of national identity and formation of consumer identity.

114   *Oleksandra Seliverstova*

Coming from disciplines like sociology or anthropology they rarely fully address questions in which political scientists might be interested and which regard connection of those identity formation processes to the major political and economic transformations.

The current research takes into consideration the contribution made by the above-mentioned studies, and explores further, through the bottom-up approach, how the sense of national belonging in Estonia is developed or renegotiated through consumer culture. The following section will illustrate how residents of the Estonian capital, where around 40% of population is Russian speaking,[3] create, negate or re-negotiate non-official national symbols originating in the domain of food consumption.

National identity at the dinner table

There is an impressive body of literature that discusses the symbolic power of food. Those who so far have been assigning to food the role of a symbolic tool in the formation processes of individual and collective identities have demonstrated that such a tool can be used for both expression and creation of identity (Bell and Valentine 1997, Pechurina 2015, Wilk 1999). As a way to express identity, either individual or collective, food offers us a variety of instruments, such as products, dishes and practices connected to them, which we then use as markers of our self-portraits (Barthes 1967, Douglas 2002, 2014). At the same time, food conceptualizes the 'us' and the 'them'. Thus from one side it is one of the ways to establish distinctions and group boundaries, and from another it is a type of social 'glue' that brings people together (Goody 1982). Also food constitutes a universal and easy to understand language or a 'system of signs' through which one can express his/her social position (Levi-Strauss 1978 [2013]) or send messages to masses (Barthes 1967). This feature has always made food a powerful instrument in the hands of political leaders. Historians regularly provide examples of how problems connected to food were among the main reasons for war outbreaks or how they evoked and continue to evoke social, economic and political crises worldwide (Pilcher 2008). Political elites tend to use food as a tool also in nation-building processes (Caldwell 2002, Cusack 2000, Cwiertka 2006, Gronow 2003, Wilk, 1999, 2004). Promoting national products, reinventing national cuisines, banning foreign products or ignoring food traditions of ethnic minorities are all examples of how food could be used in nationalism politics.

In Estonia food is deeply rooted in the current official national ideology. After the collapse of the Soviet Union when there was a need to re-negotiate or develop a concept of a new national identity, the Estonian government needed to decide what to include and what to exclude in the official narrative of it. Food became one of the sources of cultural material, necessary for construction of a new national discourse. One of the main characteristics of such discourse is a total rupture with the Soviet past, discrediting the impact of Russian culture with the re-discovery and return to pre-Soviet roots and traditions of ethnic Estonians. Such ideas are also reflected in modern Estonian

Consumer citizenship and Estonianness 115

cuisine and how Estonian food products and food habits are promoted in official national media sources and incorporated in Estonian nation branding as a Nordic nation (Jordan 2014). Although the political elites' ideas on Estonian nation dictate national food ingredients, symbols and practices with which Estonian citizens might associate themselves and through which the imagination of Estonian nation might be facilitated, it is not the only actor that defines how the sense of national belonging is shaped and experienced through the food. Ordinary people, as consumers, also play an important role in embedding food products and practices with symbolic national meanings (Cusack 2000). In the bottom-up perspective taken in this chapter, Estonian citizens are viewed as those who through their food practices, choices or attitudes contribute to or challenge the creation of common national identity, which can however often deviate from or challenge the official national rhetoric.

In the following paragraphs I show how some basic food products and practices associated with them can have different symbolic meanings in different contexts for Estonian citizens with different ethnic/language background. In particular I reveal meanings which could be connected to the sense of national belonging or in other worlds those food products or practices connected to them which could complement national self-portraits of Estonian citizens. The ways people 'use' food consumption as an arena for re-creation and expression of their national sense of belonging are split into three behavioural categories: denial, acceptance and competition. These categories are not deterministic, but still illustrate some behavioural patterns in relation to the dominant discourse on national identity in Estonia. They are not mutually exclusive, as different consumer practices and preferences of one respondent could apply to different categories depending on the context. For instance, one respondent could express an attitude as refuser in one situation and as acceptor or competitor in another: identity is a fluid process that changes according to the context in which it is being evoked (Brubaker et al. 2006).

Acceptance

Different studies have provided analyzes of the relations between ethnic Estonians and Estonian Russian speakers since 1991. The majority agree that Estonia has 'two parallel societies with minimal interaction both in the structural and cultural domains' (Vetik and Helemäe 2011: 15), and that a lot remains to be done in order to make the Estonian society more united and harmonious. However, other literature on everyday life presents more optimistic accounts on Russian speaker integration and the development of a more inclusive collective identity. Thus Laitin (1998) argued that already at the end of the 1990s Russian speakers showed signs of cultural 'accommodation' (ibid: 335) for pragmatic reasons. While they might reject the official ethnocentric discourse that they find discriminating, everyday Estonian culture elements are more easily accepted. Consumer culture is one domain of everyday

116   *Oleksandra Seliverstova*

life that offers both tools to establish distinctions and to unite through the sharing of consumer practices (Belk 1988, Dunn 2008, Foster 2002). Basic food products represent the category of products that are consumed regularly and in volume. Moreover in Estonia the majority of basic food products like bread, milk and meat are locally produced, potentially creating material representations of Estonia. Indeed the local food industry very often promotes its products through national symbolics, traditional Estonian-patterned packaging, or puts an accent on traditional recipes used at the stage of production. Thus one can easily visually identify some Estonian products in sites of consumption without even reading the information on their packaging. Accordingly the exposure to variety of such products, their advertising in media space and their actual consumption impacts consumer habits of all those who reside in Estonia and potentially creates a symbolic union of citizens-consumers.

One Russian-speaking respondent noticed that with every year the variety of dishes on her family's festive table for New Year's Eve is subtly changing. She acknowledged that their table has more and more common features with ethnic Estonian families, according to her imagination:

> National cuisine experiences its boom during Christmas and New Year's holidays, supermarkets are full of these typically Estonian things and they look actually very attractive. So in the end my family and, as I see also my friends' families, starts to consume these products and cook with them some of our festive dishes. Now in Russian homes blood sausage and other kind of sausages for New Year is something more normal than it used to be in the past. (Ekaterina,[4] 35)

Foster (2002) notes that if people are exposed to the same variety of products and same advertisements it stimulates the development of the sense of belonging and facilitates the imagination of the nation.

In my data, while being asked about national cuisine, the majority of my informants would instead of national dishes mention some particular products that they associate with Estonia. Food products, like bread, meat, milk or other dairy products produced in Estonia more often generated feelings like pride or admiration, both among ethnic Estonians and Estonian Russian speakers, than national dishes. This was because national dishes 'classified' as national are 'not very attractive, too simple, coming from poor peasant past and are not impressive' (Eva, 65). Some Russian speakers would express even more scepticism and would say that they rarely turn to Estonian cuisine as its variety is poor compared with Russian or some Western cuisines. However, if one takes some basic products, which are perceived as those that have national characteristics, then Russian speakers would praise them and consume with enthusiasm.

> After travelling a lot outside of Estonia, for me Estonia started to be associated with local dairy products. There is a big choice of them, plus they

Consumer citizenship and Estonianness 117

are very fresh and tasty. This is what is purely Estonian for me and what makes me feel proud. (Sergey, 39)

The same respondent earlier confessed that he did not manage to become '*Estonian*', meaning cultural assimilation (despite acquiring Estonian citizenship and speaking fluent Estonian) and that there were a lot of mainly political factors that were pushing him away from this process. However, while describing his consumer practices he demonstrates his attachment to Estonia and acknowledges that simple little things can make him feel proud to be from Estonia. This type of pride for things that are produced and consumed daily in Estonia was expressed by other Russian speakers. In particular among such informants there was a strong belief that food products produced in Estonia are special because of their 'purity, authenticity and high standards of quality' (Hendrik, 25). Estonians prefer to live in proximity with a wild nature and value rural landscape over an urban one and thus the symbolic attachment to nature through food is particularly important for them. The reflection of such recognition of Estonian products could be found also in some official accounts. In the Estonian TV show '*Kasaetsya vsekh*' (Russian language: '*Concerns Everyone*'),[5] Estonian minister of Rural Affairs Ivari Padar characterized Estonian products as those that in 'a sustainable way take the best from local nature, implying a minimum use of chemicals, colorants and additives'. Also during the Expo 2015 in which Estonia was presented in a modern wooden pavilion with a pop-up forest on its roof, food was a central theme. Among slogans present there were those like 'We do not produce GM foods' or 'Up to half of our population can be considered food-gatherers' (meaning hand-gathering of berries, mushrooms and wild herbs in a traditional way).

I believe that this sharing of pride in, and loyalty to local consumer products by ethnic Estonians and Estonian Russian speakers, can be considered as a sign of acceptance by both categories of my respondents of at least some aspects of the way Estonian nation is promoted and supported by official and public discourses. In particular, such acceptance is crucial while analyzing national portraits of Estonian Russian speakers, since it points to some positive dynamics in their acculturation and in the same time indicates to some potential controversies in their identities. While in some cases they might not express their loyalty to the Estonian government, for instance, by not sharing official national symbols, they still associate themselves with some elements of Estonian material and consumer cultures: locally produced dairy products, sausages and candies might not have been endowed with any symbolic meaning at their point of creation, but they become markers of collective identity at the stage of their consumption. These observations, in my view, can be seen as echoing a very powerful argument by Fox and Miller-Idriss (2008): 'Consumers do not simply buy national commodities; they constitute national sensibilities, embody national pride, negotiate national meanings, thus making nationhood a salient feature of their everyday lives' (p. 551).

118   *Oleksandra Seliverstova*

Denial

Foods are being re-imagined, repeated and re-invented across the world. Thus the black rye bread which is one of the symbols and is considered to be 'unique' in Estonia might be equally 'unique' in Latvia, Lithuania or Russia. What is important is not which food belongs to which nation, but a concept which unites a group of people around that food (Bell and Valentine 1997). Some Estonian food products, depending on how they are promoted and what type of packaging and qualities they have, might be more associated with the native Estonians' culture. Usually more sophisticated food products, like Estonian delicatessen or local organic products, could fall into such category. Such non-official symbols associated with Estonian ethos might be contested by those Russian speakers who do not accept 'the reversal of power relations between ethnic Estonians and the Russian-speaking population following Estonia's independence from the Soviet Union, and the ensuing citizenship and language politics of the new elites' (Korts 2009: 121). As any symbol, national or ethnic symbols are interpreted differently in different moments by different segments of the nation (Kolstø 2006), because they 'are inherently multivocal and multivalent' (Fox and Miller-Idriss 2008: 546). Accordingly, experiences of not buying (boycotting) Estonian products among Estonian Russian speakers, which were mentioned in my interviews, could be interpreted as signs of protest against some ideas associated with the ethnic majority or their elites' policies. Such interpretation does not come from explicit answers of my respondents regarding what they do not buy and for which reasons. Indeed their practices of not buying were usually explained by more pragmatic reasons, like 'those things are unjustifiably overpriced' (Oksana, 40) or 'the combination of ingredients seems weird to me' (Sergey, 39). This is shown by the juxtaposition of consumer practices to talk about identity, the perception of place in Estonian society (themes also addressed in my interviews). Alexey (35), who admired the quality of Estonian chocolate and milk, but was sceptical about Estonian products with a 'Nordic twist', expressed his feelings of belonging to Estonia as follows:

> Estonia is my country of habitation, to which I am grateful for opportunities it gives me. I love my city, I love my work, I love Estonia's nature, but all this did not become my motherland. I am afraid to acknowledge this, but I do not have any patriotic feelings for Estonia. It is just a useful citizenship for me. The Estonian government does not respect Russians even though we work, live and raise our children here. This humiliates people like me, our identity, our honour and because of this we cannot share so many things with Estonians. We cannot be fond of their festivals, traditional costumes and flags.

Among the concepts that are materialized through particular products, there are those that promote a relatively new framework of the Estonian nation as

Consumer citizenship and Estonianness 119

a Nordic one. Since the late 1990s, the Estonian political elite have started to develop the image of Estonia as a Nordic state, which would re-frame collective identification in Estonia and reposition the country in the eyes of international community, as a country which is a part of Northern Europe and not of the Soviet bloc (Jordan 2014). As Pryce (2011) states, 'the Nordicization of Estonia seems to be more a rejection of Russian cultural influences exerted upon the country' and rather emphasizes Estonian connection to Scandinavian countries, in particular Finland. However, the discourse of the Nordic state is present mainly in official speeches and as rhetoric of the Brand Estonia campaign (ibid). Identity markers that are provided by this framework still did not find major support among Estonian population.

> The state tries to promote this idea of Nordic cuisine as a local Estonian, but it differs from the everyday reality because in everyday life people did not and cannot change their habits from one day to another. There are many discrepancies between what they impose and what we have. For instance, Estonians cannot get proper fish, affordable and local. So how can they promote it as a main ingredient [meaning the ingredient of modern Estonian Nordic cuisine]?! I do not know, probably it will take time. (Kadri, 40, specialist in food sector analytics)

Still, ethnic Estonians have much more ground to associate themselves and accept ideas of Nordicization than the Estonian Russian-speaking population. The materialization of Nordicness, which partially happens through the creation of modern Estonian cuisine, gets promoted in particular through the network of modern Estonian restaurants. Among my informants, only a few ethnic Estonians, who were young professionals working in international companies, mentioned their experience of visiting such kind of places. All other respondents either did not know about them or considered them too expensive. Among Russian speakers there were those who expressed the idea that restaurants with modern Estonian cuisine were invented by the Estonian elite specifically to please themselves and draw another line between them and other 'normal' people.

The patterns of denial through food consumption practices were not demonstrated only by Russian speakers. According to my data, ethnic Estonians defined the borders of their identity through the denial of consumption practices, associated with the 'other' group, even more often than Russian speakers did. Asking questions about where people buy their groceries and what they look for when selecting products I tried to understand whether in some cases it was a place of consumption and not commodities which could appear as an identity marker. In the interviews with some ethnic Estonians such questions evoked a series of stereotypes. Though stereotypes are extremely over-generalizing and subjective, one cannot negate their potential impact on the relationship of two opposite groups, using those stereotypes against each other (Elias and Scotson, 1994). Here I would like to provide several

120   *Oleksandra Seliverstova*

examples of how stereotypes might impact consumer practices, which in the end establish or visualize boundaries of a collective identity.

> When I am choosing things for myself or my family, sometimes I rely on judgment: 'You cannot buy it, it looks Russian.' It is a sort of criteria for describing or evaluating things. Like it is not acceptable for myself. (Gerli, 39)

Maxima supermarkets, as well as some markets in Tallinn, namely *Keskturg* and *Baltijaam turg*, have a cliché of being sites of consumption for the Russian-speaking population.

> I go to *Comarket, Rimi* or *Stockman* if I need something special. *Maxima*?! No, we actually call it *Mahima*, as Russians sometimes pronounce it and we make fun of it. So about this stereotypical connotation about Russian supermarket, a little bit yes, but not too much. (Kerli, 31)

One Russian speaker also confirmed such a stereotype by sharing her experience as a consumer and provided an opinion of her Estonian colleague.

> I go to *Prisma* or *Rimi*, because they are the closest ones. *Maxima* is a cheap brand, the quality is low and service is not good. Once my colleague said: 'I am Estonian, I do not go to Maxima, how could I?!' ... and still one can see Estonians there because of low prices. (Oksana, 42)

One of my respondents complained about the 'plastic' quality of fruits and berries in the supermarkets even in the summer season and while her house was situated just in front of the *Keskturg* – an open-air market in the city centre of Tallinn – she never went there. When I came to our interview with a basket of fresh blueberries, just bought at that market, she was very surprised that I went there:

> Which market?! Oh this one ... I see, I actually never went there, it is such a Russian place and I am a little bit scared to go there. I heard that actually people are friendly there, but still something prevents me from going there. (Eva, 31)

The *Viimsiturg* and *Nommeturg* markets, on the contrary, have a cliché of being 'expensive Estonian markets', however when I visited *Nommeturg* several times during the winter in 2015, I noticed differences mainly in their look and structure (if compared to *Baltijaam turg* and *Keskturg*), but not that much in the variety of products sold.

> I think Estonian market goers are a bit snobbish and I suppose none goes to the Russian market! There are Estonian markets which are cleaner, nicer and more expensive, snobbish people go there. The market does

Consumer citizenship and Estonianness 121

not mean organic, for organic there are other systems to buy. It is just for local food, not from Spain or whatever. (Gerli, 39)

In such a context, denial does not mean only boycotting some products, it is rather a denial of the concept that stands behind those products. By saying 'no' to some products or services consumers communicate their desire of not being associated with another culture whose representatives would in their imagination choose to acquire those things. A choice of not consuming is a protest against the undesired model of society or undesired culture with which people do not want to be associated (Douglas and Isherwood, 1996). As discussed here, denial is not only about the protest, but it also represents an area where through consumption or non-consumption one can see the expression of fear, a fear of being associated with and dominated by the 'other' group. Ethnic Estonians might deny some consumer practices or products, which they associate with Russian and Soviet cultures, as part of a general fear of being again dominated by Russian culture and power. This fear might be conscious or subconscious, but it continues to nourish stereotypes about Russians speakers and defines some practices of ethnic Estonians and in some cases also of Russian speakers willing to assimilate.

Competition

The denial discussed above can take also the form of competition. Ethnic Estonians and Estonian Russian speakers might have different consumer habits and might buy different things, shop in different places and even attach different symbolic meanings to their practices, but they still act first of all as Estonian citizens. As a result, one can see a sort of competition in *Estonianness* with an idea of being 'Estonian' being interpreted in different ways but supported by both groups. Russian speakers who acknowledge and keep their belonging to Russian culture might be including their Russian features into the national identity of Estonia through their everyday practices. Russians also use a richer variety of references for construction of their collective identity (Masso 2010) and are more open for cosmopolitan values than Estonians, favouring a more inclusive, multicultural type of national identity (Toots & Idnurm 2012).

The evidence from the festive tables of some Russian-speaking families, whose members considered themselves as successfully integrated members of Estonian society, continues to display many traditions from Soviet times. One can observe a cultural continuity (Kannike 2006). There is no evidence of rupture with Soviet times, as is demanded by the official discourse of Estonian identity, which views the Soviet period as a period of colonization and occupation that should not leave any traces in the minds of modern Estonians (Wulf 2016). People continue to make *Oliv'ye*[6] and *Vinegret* (typical salads prepared for New Year's Eve), which became popular during the Soviet times, and consider those dishes as elements of Estonian culture.

122 *Oleksandra Seliverstova*

Soviet New Year's traditions do live in our family, but we do not perceive them as Soviet anymore. Currently they continue to be practiced widely used, even by young generations who mix them with elements of other cultures. I believe that if we live in Estonia and practice them, then they are current Estonian traditions. It is kind of natural continuation of traditions and nobody is against it, even Estonians, I believe, in the end they do the same. (Andrey, 40)

One of my young Estonian-speaking respondents Eva also told me about her family cooking traditions during the Christmas and New Year's holidays. She started with a description of *Kartulisalat*:

Our potato salad is special, it is so tasty. It is not like a German one, where you have just potatoes, mayonnaise and onions. In Estonian potato salad every ingredient is cut into cubes, and it has pickles, ham, carrots, peas, eggs and of course potatoes. We usually have it for Christmas, New Year or any other special occasion. Even though it is just a salad, it is very central in Estonian cuisine. Then we have another potato salad, which is more like Russian style, because it has beetroot [talking about *Vinegret*].

Though Eva's description of Estonian traditional potato salad completely corresponded to the traditional recipe of Russian *Oliv'ye*, she was completely unaware that it might be also a dish which is typical of Russian culture. Moreover, both her family and a family of a Russian-speaking respondent mentioned the same type of salad as a traditional central element present at their festive tables during the same type of holiday. Accordingly, both respondents believed that their version of salad represented an indispensable part of Estonian culture and both were talking about the same dish.

At the same time, despite official accounts of the Estonian nation as based on the values of ethnic Estonians and a considerable amount of previous studies displaying acceptance of such discourse by ethnic Estonians, not only Russian speakers adopt a more multicultural perspective on collective identity in Estonia.

Sometimes Russians are more anti-Russians than Estonians. Me and my friends we fancy these old cafés from Soviet times with very simple interiors, or even Armenian or Georgian taverns with their 1990s Russian pop music. Russians of my age would find such places kitschy and something to avoid, but I think they are those places which make Estonia look much less ethnocentric. (Eva, 31)

In everyday life there are myriad examples where people mix different cultures and refer to this mix when constructing their self-portraits. The desire to maintain and establish links with both Russian and Estonian culture sometimes creates new markers of identity which represent a mix of

Consumer citizenship and Estonianness   123

two cultures. One of my respondents identified herself as someone who stays in 'between-ness', talking about her sense of national belonging.

> My parents are Russians, but culturewise I am more into Estonian culture than Russian. At the same time Russian culture is still important to me, I am kind of mediating between the two of them. (Anna, 35)

Also, when listening to her experience of cooking and sharing of food with her guests, one could possibly observe how she was mediating between two cultures, including elements of both of them and incorporating also some exotic or cosmopolitan cuisine trends.

Patterns of competition of what is *Estonianness* produce most of the non-official markers of collective identity. As Fox and Miller-Idriss (2008) note 'people are not just consumers of national meanings; they are simultaneously their contingent producers'. (p. 546). Insights on everyday life show that in reality people share a large number of things together, as a German historian Meike Wulf (2016) also observed 'many aspects of identities of Russian speakers and Estonians are overlapping and competing with each other' (p. 170). What they lack is rather the ability to recognize that they have something in common with each other.

Conclusions

This chapter provided empirical evidence of the connection of consumer culture to the process of national identity formation. National identity that traditionally is studied through top-down approaches, focusing on the role of political elites, here is approached from the perspective of everyday life. Ordinary citizens are not only important actors in terms of how national discourse is interpreted, accepted or contested, but also as producers of the nation. Through the exploration of symbolic meanings of food products and food consumption practices this study showed how ordinary urban citizens of a relatively recently (re)born nation participate in the construction of their national self-portraits. The behavioural patterns of acceptance, denial and competition of symbolic meanings of food are understood as acceptance, denial and competition of different national or ethnic concepts, which are attached to particular food products or food consumption practices.

Food consumption, as an indispensable part of everyday life, has been presented first as a field for practice and support of a rather exclusive narrative of Estonian nationhood, then as a field for expression of protest against this narrative and a fear of cultural and political domination and finally as a field in which people's choices shape from the bottom level a less mono-culturally based and more shared type of national identity.

This study contributes to the body of literature that uses a bottom-up approach for exploring identity politics issues, which however remains thin particularly in the post-Soviet context. Such an approach is useful when trying

124 *Oleksandra Seliverstova*

to understand how often taken-for-granted notions of ethnicity, nationality and citizenship are interpreted and experienced at the level of mundane life. The insights on everyday use of such concepts show discrepancies which exist between official discourses and what people perceive and experience in their daily life.

In the post-Soviet area, where there is still a legacy of distrust towards official discourses and official instruments of inquiry about national surveys (Knott 2015) everyday practices and material objects represent a much more nuanced and sophisticated source for learning of how people construct their collective identities. As Foster (2002) argues everyday consumption practices serve to 'anchor the nation', to move the concept of nation from the ideological to the tangible.

In particular thorough the case study presented here, I suggest that there exists a multitude of ways to shape and express a common identity category. While ethnic Estonians are considered to have greater national capital than Estonian Russian speakers, when defining which elements are to be included in their national identity, both groups participate in the creation of new identity markers and perceive their behaviour as that of Estonian citizens. However, because of different factors representatives of each group fail to recognize that they have already a large amount of identity markers that are overlapping. This failure of recognition of similarities and lack of openness to a more multicultural view of the nation, in particular from the ethnic Estonians, is one of the factors that possibly slows down of the formation of a *national* identity in Estonia.

Notes

1   For examples of promotion of national narrative through food products and food practices the website of the Estonian Ministry of Rural affairs is illustrative (http://estonianfood.eu/en) as well as some other official sources that are part of the Brand Estonia campaign www.visitestonia.com/en/why-estonia/introduction-to-estonian-cuisine

2   I prefer not to categorize my respondents according to ethnicity, but to shape my categories according to the natively spoken language as in Estonia Russian speakers are represented by several ethnic groups.

3   Information provided in the report *Statistics Estonia 2015*, available at: http://pub.stat.ee/px-web.2001/Dialog/varval.asp?ma=PO0222&ti=POPULATIO N+BY+SEX2C+ETHNIC+NATIONALITY+AND+COUNTY%2C+1+JANUARY&path=../I_Databas/Population/01Population_indicators_and_composition/04Population_figure_and_composition/&lang=1 [last accessed on 20.05.2016].

4   In order to provide anonymity to my respondents, all names are pseudonyms.

5   A TV show that appeared in the end of 2015 on a recently launched TV channel ETV+, which is oriented to the Russian-speaking population of Estonia. The TV show from 10.02.2016 about GM foods in Estonia is available under: http://etvpluss.err.ee/v/ac6bb70f-8cbc-4ba7-8557-fdc0460cd810 [last accessed on 12.05.2016].

6   A salad invented in by a French chef Lucien Olivier around 1860, while he was working in one of the restaurants of the Russian Empire. In many countries outside of the former Soviet Union, this salad is commonly referred to as a Russian salad. During Soviet times *Oliv'ye* became very popular among ordinary people; in particular it is considered to be an indispensable dish for the New Year's festive table.

References

Aasland, A. 2002. Citizenship status and social exclusion in Estonia and Latvia. *Journal of Baltic Studies*, 33(1), 57–77.

Barthes, R. 1967. *Elements of semiology 1964*. New York : Hill and Wang, 58–60.

Belk, R. 1988. *Possessions and self*. Hoboken, NJ: John Wiley and Sons, Ltd.

Bell, D. and Valentine, G. 1997. *Consuming geographies: We are where we eat*. New York: Psychology Press .

Billig, M. 1995. *Banal nationalism*. London : Sage.

Brubaker, R., Feischmidt, M., Fox, J. and Grancea, L. 2006. *Nationalist politics and everyday ethnicity in a Transylvanian town*. Princeton, NJ: Princeton University Press.

Caldwell, M. 2002. The taste of nationalism: Food politics in postsocialist Moscow. *Ethnos* 67(3), 295–319.

Cheskin, A. 2013. Exploring Russian-speaking identity from below: The case of Latvia. *Journal of Baltic Studies* 44(3), 287–312.

Cronin, A. M. 2005. *Advertising and consumer citizenship: Gender, images and rights*. Vol.8. New York: Routledge.

Cusack, I. 2000. African cuisines: Recipes for nationbuilding? *Journal of African Cultural Studies* 13(2), 207–225.

Cwiertka, K. J. 2006. *Modern Japanese cuisine: Food, power and national identity*. London: Reaktion Books.

Douglas, M. 2002. *The world of goods: Towards an anthropology of consumption*. London: Psychology Press, vol. 6.

Douglas, M. 2014. *Food in the social order*. Routledge.

Douglas, M. and Isherwood, B.C. 1996. *The world of goods: Towards an anthropology of consumption*. New York: Routledge.

Dunn, R. 2008. *Identifying consumption. Subjects and objects in consumer society*. Philadelphia : Temple University Press.

Edensor, T. 2002. *National identity, popular culture and everyday life*. London: Bloomsbury Academic.

Ehala, M. 2009. The bronze soldier: Identity threat and maintenance in Estonia. *Journal of Baltic Studies* 40(1), 139–158.

Elias, N. and Scotson, J. L. 1994. *The established and the outsiders*. London: Sage, vol.32.

Finlayson, A., Bevir, Rhodes, R. A. W., Dowding, K. and Hay, C. 2004. The interpretive approach in political science: a symposium. *The British Journal of Politics and International Relations* 6(2), 129–164.

Foster, R. J. 2002. *Materializing the nation: Commodities, consumption, and media in Papua New Guinea*. Bloomington, IN: Indiana University Press.

Foster, R. J. and Özcan, D. 2005. Consumer citizenship, nationalism, and neoliberal globalization in Turkey: The advertising launch of Cola Turka. *Advertising and Society Review*, 6(3).

Fox, J. E. and Miller-Idriss, C. 2008. Everyday nationhood. *Ethnicities* 8(4), 536–563.

Goody, J. 1982. *Cooking, cuisine and class: A study in comparative sociology*. Cambridge: Cambridge University Press.

Gronow, J. 2003. *Caviar with champagne: Common luxury and the ideals of the good life in Stalin's Russia*. Berg.

Gurova, O. 2018. Political consumerism in Russia after 2011. Forthcoming in *Cultural mechanisms of political protest in Russia*, edited by Beumers, B., Etkind, A., Gurova, O. and Turoma, S. London and New York: Routledge.

Hallik, K. 2006. *Citizenship and perspectives of equal political participation in Estonia. Media against intolerance and discrimination: Estonian situation and international experience*. Tallinn.

Hobsbawm, E. 1990. *Nations and nationalism since 1780*. Cambridge: Cambridge University Press.

126   *Oleksandra Seliverstova*

Jakobson, V. 2002. The Role of the Russian-Language Media in Estonian Society. *Role of the Estonian Russian-language Media in the Integration of the Russian-speaking Minority into Estonian Society: 79.*

Jacobson, V. 2006. Русскоязычные как часть населения Эстонии: 15 лет спустя (Russian speakers as part of Estonian population: 15 years after). *Мир России. Социология. Этнология*, 15(4).

Jordan, P. 2014. *The modern fairy tale: Nation branding, national identity and the Eurovision song contest in Estonia.* Tartu, Estonia: University of Tartu Press.

Kalmus, V., Keller, M. and Kiise, M. 2009. Emerging consumer types in transition culture: Consumption patterns of generational and ethnic groups in Estonia. *Journal of Baltic Studies* 40(1), 53–74.

Kannike, A. 2006. Creating cultural continuity in the domestic realm: The case of Soviet Estonia. *Acta Historica Tallinnensia*, 10, 212–229.

Kannike, A. 2011. Refuge or resource: Home and nostalgia in postsocialist Estonia. *Journal of Ethnology and Folkloristics*, 3(1), 57–72.

Kannike, A. and Vosu, E. 2011. My home is my stage: Restaurant experiences in two Estonian lifestyle enterprises. *Journal of Ethnology and Folkloristics*, (2), 19–47.

Keller, M. 2004. *Representations of consumer culture in post-soviet Estonia: Transformations and tensions*, vol. 3. Tartu: Tartu University Press.

Klumbytė, N. 2010. The Soviet sausage renaissance. *American Anthropologist*, 112(1): 22–37.

Knott, E. 2015. Generating data studying identity politics from a bottom–up approach in Crimea and Moldova. *East European Politics and Societies*, 29(2), 467–486.

Kolstø, P. 2006. The sustainability and future of unrecognized quasi-states. *Journal of Peace Research*, 43(6), 723–740.

Korts, K. 2009. Inter-ethnic attitudes and contacts between ethnic groups in Estonia. *Journal of Baltic Studies*, 40(1), 121–137.

Kuus, M. 2002. European integration in identity narratives in Estonia: A quest for security. *Journal of Peace Research*, 39(1), 91–108.

Laitin, D. 1998. *Identity in formation: The Russian-speaking populations in the new abroad.* Ithaca, New York: Cornell University Press.

Lévi-Strauss C. 1978/2013. *Myth and meaning.* London: Routledge.

Linz J. J., and Stepan A. 1996. *Problems of democratic transition and consolidation: Southern Europe, South America, and post-communist Europe.* Baltimore, MD: JHU Press.

Löfgren O. 1993. Materializing the nation in Sweden and America. *Ethnos* 58(3–4), 161–196.

Masso, A. 2010. Geographical perspective on identity construction: Identification strategies of Russian youth in Estonia. *International Journal of Interdisciplinary Social Sciences* 5(6), 51–62.

Melberg, H. O. 2002. Integration, alienation, and conflict in Estonia and Moldova at the societal level: A comparison. In *National integration and violent conflict in post-Soviet societies: The cases of Estonia and Moldova*, edited by Kolstø, P. Lanham, MD: P. Rowman & Littlefield Publishers.

Nimmerfeldt, G. 2011. Sense of belonging to Estonia. *The Russian second generation in Tallinn and Kohtla-Järve: The TIES study in Estonia.* Amsterdam: Amsterdam University Press, 203–224.

Pawłusz, E. 2016. The Estonian song celebration (Laulupidu) as an instrument of language policy. *Journal of Baltic Studies*, 1–21.

Pechurina, A. 2015. *Material cultures, migrations, and identities: What the eye cannot see.* London: Palgrave Macmillan.

Pettai, V. and Kreuzer, M. 1998. Party politics in the Baltic states: Social bases and institutional context. *East European Politics and Societies* 13(1), 148–189.

Pilcher, J. M. 2008. *Food in world history*. New York: Routledge.

Pryce, P. 2011. The civic solution to the Estonian identity crisis. *Romanian Review of European Governance Studies*, 3(6), 5–23.

Schwartz-Shea, P. and Yanow D. 2012. *Interpretive research design: Concepts and processes*. London: Routledge.

Seliverstova, O. 2017. 'Consuming' national identity in Western Ukraine. Nationalities Papers 45(1), 61–79.

Siiner, M. 2006. Planning language practice: A sociolinguistic analysis of language policy in post-communist Estonia. *Language Policy* 5(2), 161–186.

Skey, M. 2011. *National belonging and everyday life*. Houndsmill Basingstoke: Palgrave Macmillan .

Smith D. A. 1991. *National identity*. London: Penguin.

Toots A. and Idnurm T. 2012. Does the context matter? Attitudes towards cosmopolitanism among Russian-speaking students in Estonia, Latvia and the Russian Federation. *Journal of Baltic Studies* 43(1), 117–134.

Vetik R. and Helemäe J. 2011. *The Russian second generation in Tallinn and Kohtla-Järve: the TIES study in Estonia*. Amsterdam: Amsterdam University Press.

Vihalemm, T. 1999. *Formation of collective identity among Russophone population of Estonia*, vol. 2. Tartu: Tartu University Press.

Vihalemm, T. and Keller, M. 2011. Looking Russian or Estonian: Young consumers constructing the ethnic 'self' and 'other'. *Consumption Markets & Culture* 14(3), 293–309.

Vihalemm, T. and Kalmus, V. 2009. Cultural differentiation of the Russian minority. *Journal of Baltic Studies* 40(1), 95–119.

Wilk, R. 1999. 'Real Belizean food': Building local identity in the transnational Caribbean. *American Anthropologist* 101(2), 244–255.

Wilk, R. 2004. Morals and metaphors: the meaning of consumption. In *Elusive consumption*, edited by Ekström, K. M. and Brembeck, H. Oxford: Berg, 11–26.

Wulf, M. 2016. *Shadowlands: Memory and history in Post-Soviet Estonia*. Oxford: Berghahn Books.

Part III

National discourses in everyday life

7 How to pronounce 'Belarusian'? Negotiating identity through naming

Anastasiya Astapova

Introduction

In this chapter, I aim to show how a young country which gained independence only recently struggles in widening its symbolic sovereignty, through the means of naming. I will concentrate on the vernacular discourse rather than the official stance, since, as the reader will observe, these positions are divergent, if not opposing. Starting with the history of naming of the Belarusian territories, I will proceed to the methodology of this research and present other examples of post-colonial countries debating on self-naming as well as the main arenas of the arguments over it. Finally, I will show how the Russian factor and the authoritative official Belarusian discourse made the Belarusian naming case different from other countries' debates. To illustrate the Belarusian disputes, I start with presenting one of the typical situations in which it takes place – a situation which also initiated this research.

It should be clear from the very beginning that the debates on how to spell and pronounce *Belarus* and the derivatives from it in different languages are not a matter of conscious choice or reflection for the majority of the population. My own example of being a Belarusian without knowing that the ethnonyms for my country are subject to arguments is quite telling. It was only in 2011 when I became aware of this issue visiting the Belarusian diaspora living in New York. This was a trip of discoveries for me, a Belarusian who had lived the major part of her life in Belarus. Not only did I hear the Belarusian language spoken as a mother tongue for the first time, but I was also informed that I have been mispronouncing an important aspect of the language. My interlocutor, a notable activist of the Belarusian diaspora who has been living in the US from her early childhood, noticed that I pronounce the adjective deriving from the name of the country incorrectly, saying [ˌbelə'rʌʃən] in English, as I had been taught in the Belarusian school. She insisted that the right form of pronunciation was [ˌbelə'ruːsən] and immediately supported her argument with several authoritative sources available in her huge home Belarusian library.

First, according to the English-Belarusian dictionary published in 2006 (among other resources at her library), the two possible forms of the adjective,

132   *Anastasiya Astapova*

Belarusian and *Belarusan,* are pronounced correspondingly as [ˌbelə'ruːsiən] and [ˌbelə'ruːsən] (Pashkevich et al. 2006). The dictionary did not make any distinction between the two forms; however, a predisposition to the form Belarusan [ˌbelə'ruːsən] was underlined in the leaflet that members of the Belarusian diaspora had to create and spread in order to stay in control of the right pronunciation. This leaflet has been published in one of the Belarusian newspapers and bulletins appearing in the USA. According to the author of the leaflet, Alla Orso-Romano, once she had an argument with her friend on how to derive the English adjective from Belarus. To her point of view, the right form is *Belarusan* ([ˌbelə'ruːsən], also suggested and used by the New York Belarusians). The leaflet provides the reader with a solid argument for this form: three columns of words – the first one is the name of the country, the second is the adjective deriving from this name and the third one is a potentially wrong form, if it had been formed in the same way as *Belarusian* rather than *Belarusan.*

Alla Orso-Romano also suggests that the second possibility is to use the adjective *Belarus,* the homonym form of the noun, and it is possible to say either *Belarus language* or *Belarusan language.* In the leaflet, she uncovers the utilitarian reason for using these adjectives: they prevent the speakers from confusing Belarus with Russia and Belarusians with Russians.

In the oral conversation my interlocutor also argued for pushing other countries to use the noun *Belarus* rather than the calque translations of Belarus as 'White Russia' in different languages (e.g. *Vitryssland* in Swedish, *Valgevene* in Estonian, *Weißrussland* in German, *Valko-Venäjä* in Finnish, etc.).

Research methodology

It was after this conversation and reading that I decided to explore the question and the attitude toward it among the Belarusians living in Belarus and abroad in a series of interviews on Belarusian political and ethnic identity. The interviews were, of course, broader: they included topics such as interviewees' ethnic belonging, their relationship with Russian/Polish/Lithuanian identities, and their stance towards the current Belarusian political trajectories. My concrete questions were on Belarusian political and ethnic jokes, rumours about Alexander Lukashenko and window-dressing in Belarus, the preference for different national symbols or beliefs related to various aspects of the Belarusian official and oppositional ideologies. The interviews were recorded in Belarus, in Vitebsk and Minsk; others were recorded among the Belarusians living in Russia, the United Kingdom, the United States, Poland, Lithuania and China. Since 2011, in total, I collected more than 50 full interviews in addition to many shorter recorded comments upon different issues. The majority of interviewees were mostly urban educated males[1] 25 to 45 years old found through snowball sampling. Judging by their own willingness to be interviewed, I suggest that this sample is representative of politically-engaged Belarusian society. My research thus cannot boast of a thorough study of different Belarusian social groups,

How to pronounce 'Belarusian'? 133

and I am sure that the results of the interviews based on the research done, for instance, in the rural areas, would have been quite different. Through analyzing the current group sample I rather aim to identify a certain discourse that exists within Belarusian society – the people who care about constructing a certain ethnic identity. I concentrated on the group for whom the problem is not only familiar, but also essential to solve.

In addition, I base my research on constant observation of the Belarusian political situation through the official (pro-state) and alternative (oppositionist) press and the comments made to their publications on the internet. The split between the officially approved and the oppositionist mass media is crucial in Belarus, supporting completely different ideologies and influencing the division of the Belarusian society. As much as the former may be accused of propaganda, the latter is often quite radical too, since in many cases the headquarters of oppositionist mass media are led by Belarusian political refugees or political migrants living abroad.

The history of searching for the name

Linguistic explorations, as well as a need to understand Belarus and Russia as two separate entities, have increased in relevance rather recently with the independence of Belarus (1991). This is reflected in the toponyms: other sources, including those in the same library of my interlocutor, but published before 1991 argued for completely different forms. For instance, the English-Byelorussian-Russian dictionary published in 1989 provided the form *Byelorussian* ([ˌbjeləˈrʌʃn]) as the only possible one (Susha and Shchuka 1989). The bulletin *Facts on Byelorussia* published in 1974 in the US by one of the leading researchers on Belarus, Jan Zaprudnik, suggests a quote from the Soviet historian Jazep Jucho regarding the naming of Belarus on the title page: 'Confusion in terminology leads to distortion of the whole historical process of development of the Belarusian people' (1968: 182). The quote is not used randomly, as the major article of the bulletin is dedicated to *The Name of Bielaruś (Byelorussia)* by Jan Zaprudnik too (1974: 86-91). The author gives an overview of the names which existed throughout Belarusian history for different parts of the Belarusian territories: the Northwestern Region (*Severo-Zapadnyi Krai*), the Western Region (*Zapadnyi Krai*), the Western gubernias, Belaya Ruś, Western Russia, Russia, Whiteruthenia, Lithuania (*Litva*), Byelorussia, etc. In addition to the confusion between these terms, he states, none of them incorporated what is current Belarusian territory now compared to what it was in various periods of history. The multiplicity of names also reflects how the borders fluctuated, making what is today's Belarus a part of Kievan Rus', the Great Duchy of Lithuania, and the Polish-Lithuanian Commonwealth. At the end of the 18th century, a prolonged era of Russification within the Russian Empire with its culmination in Soviet rule followed for the Belarusian territories, from which many names derived (e.g. the Western gubernias).

134 *Anastasiya Astapova*

The first questionable independence gave rise to extremely brief and mostly unacknowledged Belarusian People's Republic (1918), giving way to Soviet rule. The name *Byelorussia* was officially accepted by the Belarusian Soviet government then. Other names used in English at the time of the writing Zaprudniuk's article (1974) were White Russia, Whiteruthenia (or White Ruthenia), and Byeloruthenia. Zaprudnik complained that many American and British encyclopaedias and dictionaries still used the term *White Russia*. Using the names *Byelorussia* and *Bielaruś* throughout the article, Zaprudnik himself did not provide the reader with a reason for his choice. However, similar to the leaflet mentioned above, his article expresses the following concern: the confusion between the names 'adds to the confusion and to the tendency to consider that both terms [Byelorussian and Russian] connote the same historico-ethnical entity'. This concern, important for the Belarusian dissidents who emigrated to the US fleeing from the Soviet regime, has been recently reinforced by Belarusian independence, which was followed by the de facto cultural and economic dependence on Russia and the presupposed failure in constructing the own Belarusian nation.

Place names and post-colonialism

Ethnonyms gain increasing importance when the long-dependant territories face sovereignty. Often, different names project opposing ideologies: that of independence and colony-nostalgic attitudes, as has happened in Belarus too.

Becoming independent in 1991, after the Soviet Union's collapse, Belarus found itself at the crossroads of two competing constructs of identity: pro-European and pro-Russian (or pro-Soviet) (Gapova 2008). Initially, at least on the official level, the pro-European inclination as an opposite of the Soviet doctrine dominated, with a reference to originally being part of Europe – the Great Duchy of Lithuania (rather than Russia) – and expressing the need to return to this imagined European homeland. The pro-European discourse grouped around several symbols and arguments: in addition to the Great Duchy of Lithuania past, Belarusians were sometimes considered Balts (Europeans) rather than Slavs. The Soviet past was labelled colonization, and this ideology started to force out Russian language for the sake of using only Belarusian. On September 19, 1992, during this early stage of Belarusian independence, the Belarusian Soviet Socialist Republic (traditionally shortened as *Byelorussia*) was renamed to the Republic of Belarus (*Respublika Belarus'*).

Similar processes were taking place in the other former Soviet countries which also chose to reconsider the usage of self-naming toponyms – native versions versus Russified/Soviet variants. *Moldavia* became *Moldova*, *Kyrgyzia* turned into *Kyrgyzstan*, and *Turkmeniya* to *Turkmenistan*. The process of the quest for the right name, which often had its inert start in the Soviet times, is still up in the air for many. One of the most famous cases is the usage of the preposition before *Ukraine* as either *na Ukraine* (literally – 'on Ukraine') or *v Ukraine* ('in Ukraine'). The latter form *v Ukraine* was officially

How to pronounce 'Belarusian'? 135

introduced in 1993 by the demand of the Ukrainian government. The more habitual form *na Ukraine* had always had a connotation of 'being in the outskirts' (*na okraine*), whereas the new collocation allowed for getting rid of this pejorative submeaning. By introducing the norm *v Ukraine,* Ukraine also received a symbolic linguistic proof of being a sovereign state, since the names of states (rather than regions) are more frequently used with the preposition *v* (in) in Russian language (Graudina et al. 2001: 69). Yet, the majority of Russian speakers, including those of Ukrainian origin are used to the form *na Ukraine*: the language norm being very difficult to suddenly change on a broad vernacular level due to political changes. The *v/na Ukraine* linguistic and political conflict received a new development recently, after the 2013–2014 Euromaidan demonstration and the following annexation of Crimea by Russia. Using either *na Ukraine* or *v Ukraine* has become the conscious marker of supporting either Russian intervention or Ukrainian sovereignty.

Even though the linguistic questions and forms of toponyms are different, most of them carry the connotation of a particular attitude towards the Soviet past and the current independence of this or that country. The choice of name is discussed not only for the Russian language. It is curious, for instance, that another post-Soviet country, Estonia, which has developed strong cultural ties with Georgia,[2] is now actively discussing how to name Georgia in Estonian. It is often stated that the country's self-nomination *Sakartvelo* or the European name *Georgia* should be preferred to the transliteration of the Russian variant *Gruusia* (Kaalep 2005). To resolve the discussions the Estonian Language Institute had to publish its recommendation upon the usage of the name for Georgia, advising to use either *Gruusia* or *Georgia*, yet acknowledging that the Estonian Native Language Council prefers *Gruusia* as a toponym with a longer tradition of usage (Päll 2008).

Interestingly, the change of the names of the cities seems to be less politicized than the names of the states. There is rarely a political attitude expressed through naming *Saint-Petersburg* instead of *Leningrad, Bishkek* instead of *Frunze, Almaty* instead of *Alma-Ata*. The preference towards the usage of this or that city name is often the matter of generational habits (the older generation prefers the older name) rather than of ideological attitudes. Yet, there are exceptions. In 1988, still in Estonian SSR, it was officially decided to write Таллинн (*Tallinn*) with two -*nn*- in Russian in accordance with the Estonian version, which also has two -*nn*-. Due to the subsequent confusion, the Institute of Language and Literature of the Estonian Soviet Socialist Republic had to publish a letter explaining the need to change the form. According to their reasoning, -*linn* in *Tallinn* means 'city' and it would be unnatural to cut the last letter from it as it would be, for instance, from Leningrad, where *grad* means the 'city' too. Moreover, according to the letter, the form *Tallin* (with one -*n*-) appeared due to the widespread incorrect opinion that combinations of letters unusual for the Russian language should be eliminated in Russian transliterations. Such an approach, however, prevents from conveying the original name and related information (Päll 1989). As a

136 Anastasiya Astapova

result, in the current Russian language as used outside of Estonia the form Таллин (*Tallin*) is standard (Rosreestr 2011), while the Russian-language mass media in Estonia mainly uses the double -*nn*-Таллинн form in accordance with the demands of the Estonian Language Inspectorate. This has become a matter of multiple debates as much in Estonia as abroad: Russian speakers often argue against the imposition of foreign language rules, while some Estonian public figures try to convince Russia to use *Tallinn* with double -*nn*- too (Delfi 2004). As in the case of Belarus, for Estonia, the problem started to be publically discussed on the threshold of independence.

The debates mentioned above are typical for post-colonial developments far beyond the Soviet Union. One of the most famous examples is the choice between the names Burma and Myanmar, since these names, their derivatives, and other related country ethnonyms (e.g. Rangoon vs. Yangon for the capital) carry their own semantic luggage and symbolize two divergent national identity trajectories for the country (Dittmer 2010: 1). The term *Burma* links to the country's colonial past, since it was actively used by the British. The ruling military junta changed the name to *Myanmar* in 1989, a year after thousands were killed in the suppression of a popular uprising. Since then, *Myanmar* is strongly associated with junta, while the rejection of *Burma* becomes an attempt to break from the colonial past. In many ways, there is an ideology under the choice of *Burma/Myanmar* name, similar to the situation with *na/v Ukraine*: the choice of the term often provides the listener with the information on his or her interlocutor's knowledge and ideological choice. Similar debates, although including different connotations, surround the post-colonial choices between *Burkina Faso/Upper Volta*, *Cambodia/Kampuchea*, *Ivory Coast/Republic of Côte d'Ivoire*, etc.

The choice of the name not only becomes the tool for negotiating the identity, but also serves to eliminate any reference to the right of the previous dominators to this territory. For instance, when Mexico gained its independence from the Spanish Empire in 1821, numerous place names across the country changed to become uniquely Mexican, highlighting the country's Amerindian past (Tucker 2001). A similar (although ongoing) process of pulling the territory towards this or that identity through the use of opposite toponyms takes place in the long disputed territory of Nagorny Karabakh, where naming becomes instrumental for the construction of either Armenian or Azerbaijani domination and ownership (Foster 2009). Finally, in many countries, such as in Israel, the naming of landscape becomes a conscious political project implemented for the sake of ethnic unity and nation-building (Azaryahu and Golan 2001).

Belarus and *Belorussia*: arguments and main arenas for the debate

To choose in between the major forms of the country name, *Belorussia* and *Belarus*, their proponents draw several groups of arguments. Most of them

How to pronounce 'Belarusian'? 137

are listed in the excellent research of Somin and Poliy (2016) who analyzed the opinions expressed by Belarusians on how to name their country on the internet, yet the oral discourse analysis from my interviews adds to this data. Unlike my encounters in the United States described above, these arguments mostly focus on Russian and Belarusian pronunciation and spelling: both languages have equal state status in Belarus.

The first group of reasonings concerns the need and the choice of source language for **transliteration**. The adherents of the *Belorussia* name in Russian argue that they do not have to follow the *Belarus* version from Belarusian, since the name of many other countries and cities (e.g. *Deutschland, France* or *Roma*) are not transliterated into Russian, and Russian uses its own place names (e.g. *Germania, Frantsiya, Rim*). The proponents of *Belarus* object: Russian is a state language of Belarus and the name *Belarus* is consolidated by the Russian-language version of the Belarusian constitution, while the countries the names of which are not transliterated (Germany, etc.) do not have Russian as a state language. Similarly, the *Belorussia* proponents argue that the post-Soviet changes in the countries' names (*Moldova, Kyrgyzstan,* etc.) do not have to correspond to actual Russian language, and one state cannot dictate how to name itself to the other state. In response, the defenders of *Belarus* appeal to the Belarusian law: the name should be transliterated to all the languages of the world in accordance with the Belarusian pronunciation. The similarity of Belarusian and Russian as well as the usage of Cyrillic by both only enhances the debates.

The second group of reasoning draws on **competing linguistic norms**. The proponents of *Belarussia* argue against *Belarus* since this form does not correspond to the rules of Russian language: the copulative vowel connecting two roots (*bel* and *rus* – 'white' and 'Russian') should be either *-o-* or *-e-*. Their opponents reply that *Belarus* is used by the Russian speakers living in the country and the status of Russian as a state language of Belarus legitimizes their right to influence the Russian language norms.

The third group concerns the examples of how the name is used in the **official discourse and what such a usage symbolizes**. The pro-*Belarussia* activists emphasize that *Belorussia* is sometimes used by the president of the country, Alexander Lukashenko, on the nameboards at the official international meetings. Their opponents, being often counter-Lukashenko and his neo-Soviet politics, argue that *Belorussia* is the name for the Soviet republic, whereas *Belarus* is the name for the independent state.

Finally, the adversaries often refer to various **authoritative sources** as competent enough to solve the argument. The first side argues that Wikipedia uses the name *Belorussia* rather than *Belarus* for the title page about the country. The second side strikes back with the Institute of Russian Language, the Institute of Geography, All-Russian Classifier of Countries of the World, and some other official sources arguing for the form *Belarus* (Somin and Poliy 2016: 655-656). In addition, the activists sent so many letters demanding to use the form *Belarus* to Wikipedia that the latter had to launch the page *The*

138   *Anastasiya Astapova*

Naming of the Belarusian State in Russian Language about these arguments and the reasons Wikipedia chooses to use *Belorussia* (Imenovanie n.d).

The argument for the norm *Belarus* often goes together with a number of other statements and symbols, in particular, the white-red-white flag and the Pahonia coat-of-arms used in the Great Duchy of Lithuania (as opposed to the current symbols invented in the Soviet time), the argument for Belarusians being of Baltic rather than Slavic origin, labelling the Soviet and Russian Empires colonialist, and seeing the right future in integration with Europe rather than Russia.

The arguments about how to name the country arise in **various cases**. In oral communication, one Belarusian corrects another Belarusian (or mainly Russian) explaining why he or she has to use the form *Belarus*. Similar debates rise on internet social media, forums, Belarusian non-state mass media and comments to online news on them. The rarer cases include official letters, usually from Belarusians to the Russian mass media (or Wikipedia, as mentioned above) and the court claims of an individual against the Russian press. For instance, since 2014, a citizen of Belarus, Kirill Laninsky, has sued Russian mass media sources Lenta.ru, RBK and Russia Today for using the incorrect form *Belorussia* three times (Regnum 2014). As it is obvious from this list, the debates over the naming of the country remain on the vernacular level, since the country's elites seem to be completely uninterested in this question. This is a situation which makes the Belarusian case quite unusual compared to other post-Soviet countries.

Official naming vs. vernacular usage

The choice between the colonial and traditional/novel names is usually accompanied with what Alena Gapova calls 'a pack of complaints' put forward to the colonizers by the former dominated. In this sense, Gapova mainly mentions the complaints related to the socialist oppression of ethnic groups: the Soviet occupation in the Baltic states, the Chernobyl catastrophe in Ukraine, and Stalin's crimes against peoples and their cultures everywhere (Gapova 2008: 42). The ideology of many of the post-Soviet countries came through not only actual, but also symbolic liberation from Soviet influence – the acknowledgement of the cost of the Soviet period and building new identities. Yet, unlike other post-Soviet countries, Belarus did not have its fully-fledged period of pushing complaints: after a short period of nationalism approved by the state in the early 1990s, the official ideology soon returned to the pro-Soviet moods. The nationalism imposed by the state in the early 1990s was too unfamiliar for the majority of its people who could not speak their supposedly native Belarusian language, were yearning for the golden age of the Soviet Union, and had a strong Russian identity.

That is why when Alexander Lukashenko appeared in the political arena and contested the nationalist moods by promising Soviet-like stability and values, Belarusians voted for him in 1994. After another election, Lukashenko changed the constitution through a referendum allowing him to remain the president for more than two terms, or 22 years to date. Even though there are many rumors about the frauds at the Belarusian presidential election carried out for the sake of Lukashenko's victory, according to the independent opinion polls, at every election he remains the most popular candidate (Astapova n.d.). Lukashenko's Belarus is a characteristic case of civic nationalism, deriving its political legitimacy from the active participation of the citizenry, who re-creates the system, representing the 'general will', built on the civil ideals appealing to the majority (Leshchenko 2004). Yet, there remains the minority, whose nationalist discourse grew popular in early 1990s and who would prefer a completely different trajectory of development – ethnic nationalism. It is for them that the question of how to name their country is extremely important and decisive for the country's symbolic and factual independence.

The following excerpt from my interview exemplifies the life story of an individual for whom the question of naming remains as crucial as the dissent was once.

> When I was young, I was looking for the signs of dictatorship in my country ... [Being a student] I started to get interested in politics, since if you are not interested in politics, the politics will get interested in you. I started to grow intellectually, to read different books, dystopias, George Orwell turned the world upside down for me, and then I read Max Stirner ... In about five years I calmed down and decided to concentrate on making my own business. I understand that waving my fists and stamping I will do less than if I publish an encyclopaedia or perform in the European concert tour. And I do my small business playing music in the European tours. They ask me: 'Are you from Russia?' – 'I am from Belarus.' – 'You mean from Belorussia?' – 'No, from Belarus.' Every time this small discussion takes place. But I always make sure that they know that I am from Belarus, not Belorussia.
>
> (Minsk 2012, male (30))

This interview is representative of the typical personal development of my average interviewee: well-educated, interested and active in the dissent in his early youth, disappointed in the open protest afterwards, nowadays dealing with some aspect of the Belarusian social/political life without openly defying the Belarusian government. Even though the interviewee acknowledged that he gave up active participation in politics, the correct name of the country where he comes from is important to deliver to his international interlocutors. This is one of the many interviews with those who question Lukashenko's hegemony and civic nationalism society. In a way, the debates over naming Belarus remain a milder dissent for those who grew tired of open protests.

Unlike this minority, the official Belarus represented by Lukashenko and his government, to my knowledge, has never opened the floor for an official

140   *Anastasiya Astapova*

debate on the right name for Belarus. Neither has it made a solid statement upon the matter. The avoidance of expressing an official position may have several reasons. First, the name Republic of Belarus (*Respublika Belarus'*) as opposed to *Belorussia* was given to the country in 1992, when the nationalist currents as opposed to the Soviet or pro-Russian trajectories in the Belarusian government started to prevail. In this sense, the current name opposes the neo-Soviet politics of Lukashenko and it is safer not to raise this contradictory question. Second, another contradiction lies in the country's collective identity, mixed with Russian. The name *Belarussia* is very much associated with the Soviet and Russian past; moreover, it is mostly used in the Russian press. Yet, such a discrepancy does not challenge directly the collective consciousness of the majority whose identity does not oppose the Russian one. This links to the contradictions lying in basic theoretical constructions about nationalism.

As Isaacs and Polese rightfully argue, research on nationalism has mainly concentrated on the efforts of the political elites to popularize the idea of the nation and the national community. Yet, in reality, nation building often refers to the agency of non-state actors – the people (Isaacs and Polese 2015: 372). This idea corresponds to Michael Billig's concept of banal nationalism, which shifts the focus from official politics of nation building to everyday vernacular practices that materialize the nation. Yet, Billig only looks for banal nationalism in what he calls established states – Western countries, underlying that it is essential to study them to see that nationalism is not only a matter of the peripheries (Billig 1995). This rather elitist and colonial constraint side of Billig's approach puts limitations on his otherwise overall useful theory.

The constant negotiation between the official norm and the real everyday practice is well exemplified by Belarus, which would have been ignored by Billig as a periphery with not yet established nationalist practices. The Belarusian case represents an active clash of official representation and spontaneous, informal usage. Interestingly, the opponents on the different sides of the clash also exemplify two different types of nationalism: civic, or nationalism of consent, as represented by the official discourse, and ethnic nationalism represented by the (opposing) minority. Between these groups, there are multiple average language users who choose this or that form to name their country, yet always have a different set of reasons for this. The persistence of forcing others to use the name *Belarus* is habitually reenacted, sometimes unconsciously, but often becomes the subject of surveillance from the community members (Edensor 2002: 19). As shown above, despite being an official name for the country, *Belarus* stands in line with the number of other symbols (alternative flag, coat-of-arms, etc.) emerging within the alternative narrative with national meaning opposing the official storyline. Both positions also have a Russian factor at the core of their reasoning and arguments.

Belarusian ethnic identity and the Russian factor

From the very first interviews many respondents pointed to the Russian constituent as fundamental for the problem of Belarusian self-naming. The attitude towards this Russian factor varied as well:

> I decided for myself [how to write *Belarus*]. *Belorussia* is a wrong form, while many Muscovites and Russians think this is right. They are wrong, this form is wrong.
>
> (Minsk 2013, male (29))

> Many Russians try to write *Belorussia*, as it was before. I use the *Belarus* form in everyday life. If they respect our country, they must use our constitutional form of the word too.
>
> (Minsk 2013, male (35))

> When Russians write *Belorussia*, I see no problem: they have historical traditions and we cannot impose our name. We cannot order other countries to use this or that name.
>
> (Minsk 2012, female (25))

The contradiction of Russian and Belarusian attitudes towards naming Belarus is uncovered by Somin and Poliy (2016) who held opinion polls with Russians (living in Russia) and Belarusians on how to name Belarus. 73.2% of Belarusians expressed negative attitude to the variant *Belorussia*. Meanwhile, 67% of Russians were for the variant *Belorussia*, while only 32% were for *Belarus* (pp. 651-653). This discloses the essence of the conflict: these are mainly Russians who use the Soviet form rather than the name for the independent country. When Russians do not make the distinction and say *Belorussia* (which sounds so close to *Russia*), this is seen as a continuous colonial attitude as if to a current district of Russia.

This relates to another reason for why the Belarusian official discourse avoids specifications and public statements on how to name Belarus. Despite official independence, Belarus is highly dependent on Russia not only culturally (the folk traditions are similar, the language used in Belarus is mainly Russian, the major mass media read and watched are Russian, etc.), but also economically. Belarus heavily relies on Russian resources, gas and oil, the Eurasian Customs Union, Russian investments and tourists. Taking an official stance against Russia by arguing that Russian mass media and officials who have insistently used the form *Belorussia* must change their habits would mean risking the loss of some of the current benefits from the Russian state.

142   *Anastasiya Astapova*

It is in this constant balancing between the need for its own identity and solving economic difficulties that the Belarusian leader, Alexander Lukashenko, chooses to manipulate his identity too, depending on the political climate. In 1994 the official Belarusian newspaper *Sovetskaya Belorussia* (most representative and supportive of current political directions) published excerpts from an interview with Lukashenko in which he states that he was born in a 'godforsaken half-Belarusian half-Russian village bordering with the Smolensk region' (1994: 2). This and many other publications were to confirm his and Belarusian brotherhood with Russians. Ironically, Lukashenko does not speak either Russian or Belarusian purely, and is often reported as using *trasyanka* – a dialect containing lexical and phonetic features of both languages. Another telling angle is the differences of the president's name's spelling – Aliaksandr Lukashenka and Alexander Lukashenko (similar variations emerge in the majority of the Belarusian proper names). Both versions are used interchangeably in the foreign press and research papers. This results from bilinguism and the consequent dualism of Romanization of the Belarusian proper names in Cyrillic, when either Russian or Belarusian variants are used as a source. Sometimes, however, the choice in favour of either Russian or Belarusian language as a source can be a political message (Kascian 2015).

These ambiguities and identity-juggling, along with other trajectories of Belarusian development, lead the opponents of Lukashenko to call his government an anti-Belarusian formation, destroying the Belarusian national identity. However, the manipulation of various identities is peculiar not only for Lukashenko: many of my interviewees acknowledge this in themselves. For instance, asked about his ethnic identity, one interviewee said:

> I am a manipulator. I act, feel, and talk as a Belarusian, consider Belarus to be my motherland. Yet, in my son's documents I wrote he is a Pole: I have a Pole's card[3] and I want my son to get the same benefits. Yet, I will bring him up surrounded by the Belarusian language and poetry and the feeling that he is a Belarusian. I do not know where we will live, since Belarus is not the comfortable place right now, and we will emigrate if we have a possibility.
>
> (Minsk 2012, male (32))

The country's economic or the personal everyday needs push Belarusians towards juggling their identities too, and it is not surprising that in such a situation so many ambiguities, including those concerning the country's name arise. The arguments for or against this or that usage arise in everyday life, as much of the arguments for choosing this or that identity and the benefits of it.

Still, there are Belarusians who are consistent in breaking the Russian language norm taught at school and reproduced throughout their lives:

> I always write *belarusy* [Belarusians, with copulative a] and *belarusskij*. My hand remembers how to write *belorusskij*, I don't.
>
> (Minsk 2013, male (41))

How to pronounce 'Belarusian'? 143

The Russian factor becomes decisive in shaping the debate over the naming, which is rarely consistent and non-ambivalent. This corresponds to the division of the society and the ambiguities in the political choices the official discourse makes.

Conclusion

Toponyms serve as a system shaping the identity of a society and thus become a vivid expression of power; the renaming process, in turn, usually becomes an act of political propaganda with a great declarative value and public resonance (Azaryahu 1996: 138). While in the majority of cases, and especially in totalitarian regimes, the names are frequently used to underline the state agenda and demonstrate ideology in solid terms (Yeoh 1996), the Belarusian case is quite different, as official Belarus keeps away from a concrete stance. Dictating the standard to Russia – the country most often contradicting the norm by persistently using *Belorussia*, even knowing the difference – would mean undermining the relationship with the most important economic partner and patron. Yet, the adherence to the Soviet name *Belorussia* would mean a declared lack of independence.

Because of this, the struggles over the name remain vernacular and the arenas for them remain rather local. They emerge in informal mundane communication when individual Belarusians correct others (usually those pronouncing *Belorussia*) in oral conversations or internet communication, court cases in the Russian media and individual letters defying Wikipedia. This also remains the discourse of a mainly educated and identity-concerned minority with clear ethnic sentiments and a vision for a fully independent country. It reflects not only the desire to reject the Soviet or longer-term colonial past, but also the wish to change the current political system, which seems indifferent to the unified Belarusian ethnic identity. The adherents of *Belarus* struggle against the civic nationalist system built by Lukashenko – the hegemony of consent; they argue for the country consolidated by the Belarusian consciousness. The usage of the name for Belarus remains inconsistent and confusing reflecting the turbulence within the state and the competing discourses.

Notes

1 Relatively few female respondents volunteered to participate, which suggests that politics in Belarus is considered a male business. Some of those females who still volunteered openly said that the fact they are female makes them uninterested in the political issues.
2 Georgia has been a priority partner for Estonia in development cooperation and humanitarian aid since 2006 (Välisministeerium 2016). The cooperation is very close in the field of education (e.g. student exchange), sports and culture.
3 A document confirming belonging to the Polish nation and providing a Belarusian with a number of benefits in Poland and the European Union.

144 *Anastasiya Astapova*

References

Astapova, A. n.d. Rumor, humor, and other forms of election folklore in nondemocratic societies: The case of Belarus. *Folklore. Electronic Journal of Folklore*, forthcoming.

Azaryahu, M. 1996. The power of commemorative street name. *Environment and Planning D: Society and Space*, 14: 311–330.

Azaryahu, M., Golan, A. 2001. (Re)naming the landscape: The formation of the Hebrew map of Israel 1949–1960. *Journal of Historical Geography*, 27(2): 178–195.

Billig, M. 1995. *Banal nationalism*. London: Sage.

Delfi 2004. [*Tallinn or Tallin*]. *Delfi*, 8 November 2004. Available at: www.delfi.ee/news/paevauudised/eesti/tallinn-voi-tallin-taiend?id=8998754 [accessed 16 June 2016] (in Estonian).

Dittmer, L. 2010. Burma vs. Myanmar: What's in a Name?, in *Burma or Myanmar?: The struggle for national identity*, edited by L. Dittmer. Hackensack, NJ and Singapore: World Scientific, 1–20.

Edensor, T. 2002. *National identity, popular culture and everyday life*. Oxford: Berg.

Foster, B. 2009. Empire and names: The case of Nagorno Karabakh, in *Names in multi-lingual, multi-cultural and multi-ethnic contact. Proceedings of the 23rd International Congress of Onomastic Sciences*, August 17–22, 2008, edited by W. Ahrens, S. Embleton, A. Lapierre. Toronto: York University, 421–433.

Gapova, E. 2008. [On the political economy of the national language in Belarus], in [*Belarusian format: The invisible reality*], edited by A. Usmanova. Vilnius: EGU, 30–70 (in Russian).

Graudina, L., Itskkovich V. and Katlinskaya L. 2001. [*Grammatical correctness of the Russian speech*]. Moscow: Nauka (in Russian).

Isaacs, R., Polese, A. 2015. Between 'imagined' and 'real' nation-building: identities and nationhood in post-Soviet Central Asia. *Nationalities Papers* 43(3): 371–382.

Imenovanie. n.d. [*Naming the Belarusian state in Russian language*]. Wikipedia. Available at: https://ru.wikipedia.org/wiki/Именование_белорусского_государства_на_русском_языке. [accessed 16 June 2016] (in Russian).

Jucho, J. 1968. [About the name 'Belarus']. *Polymia* 1: 182 (in Belarusian).

Kaalep, A. 2005. [*Gruusia or Georgia?*], in *Eesti Päevaleht*, 23 September 2005. Available at: http://epl.delfi.ee/news/arvamus/ain-kaalep-kas-gruusia-voi-georgia?id=51019925 [accessed 16 June 2016].

Kascian, K. 2015. The romanization of Belarusian: An unneccessary dualism. *Belarusian Review*, June.

Leshchenko, N. 2004. A fine instrument: Two nation-building strategies in post-Soviet Belarus. *Nations and Nationalism* 10(3): 333–352.

Pashkevich, V. comp., Shupa S., Bird T. E. eds. 2006. *English-Belarusian dictionary*. Minsk: Z'mitscr Kolas.

Päll, P. 1989. [About the name of the capital of Estonian SSR], in *Eesti keele instituut*. Available at: www.eki.ee/knn/tlnru88.htm [accessed 16 June 2016] (in Estonian).

Päll, P. 2008. [Gruusia or Georgia]. In *Keeleabi*, 27 August 2008. Available at: http://keeleabi.eki.ee/index.php?leht=8&id=113 [accessed 16 June 2016] (in Estonian).

Regnum. 2014. ['Moscow court declined the suit of the Bobrujsk dweller against 'Belorussia'], in *Regnum.ru*. 21 December 2014. Available at: https://regnum.ru/news/society/1879055.html [accessed 16 June 2016] (in Russian).

Rosreestr. 2011. ['Letter from Shestakov S'], *Wikipedia*, 21 April. Available at: https://upload.wikimedia.org/wikipedia/commons/d/d2/Росреестр_-_О_наименовании_некоторых_админ._единиц_в_Казахстане%2C_Эстонии%2C_Франции_и_Абхазии.gif. [accessed 16 June 2016] (in Russian).

Somin A., Poliy A. 2016. [Belarus vs. Belorussia: The structure of a linguo-political conflict in social media], in *Computational linguistics and intellectual technologies proceedings of the annual international conference 'dialogue'*, edited by Selegei et al., issue 15. Moscow: RGGU, pp. 645–659 (in Russian).

Sovetskaya Belorussia. 1994. [Aleksandr Lukashenko: 'I sweat even thinking that i may not be able to keep the promises i gave at the elections']. *Sovetskaya Belorussia*, 1 September: 1–2 (in Russian).

Susha, T. M., Shchuka, A. K. eds. 1989. *English-Byelorussian-Russian dictionary*. Minsk: BelSe.

Tucker, G. R. 2001. Re-naming Texas: Competing Mexican and Anglo placenaming in Texas, 1821–1836. *Names* 59(3): 139–151.

Välisministeerium. 2016. [Georgia], in *Eesti Välisministeerium*, 28 January. Available at: www.vm.ee/et/gruusia [accessed 16 August 2016] (in Estonian).

Yeoh, B. S. 1996. Street-naming and nation-building: Toponymic inscriptions of nationhood in Singapore. *Area* 28: 298–307.

Zaprudnik, J. 1974. The name of *Bielaruś* (Byelorussia). *Facts on Byelorussia. News Bulletin* 1(10): 86–91.

8 Nuanced identities at the borders of the European Union

Romanians in Serbia and Ukraine

Julien Danero Iglesias

Since the 2004 and 2007 enlargements, the European Union (EU) integration process has led to major changes for citizens of Central and Eastern Europe. While most EU citizens live in a borderless Europe, non-EU citizens might appear sometimes to be locked behind what the media of non-EU countries has called a new 'Iron Curtain'. As a consequence of the membership of some of the new Member States in the EU's Schengen area, Europe entered a process of 're-bordering' (Albert and Brock 1996). Therefore, for non-EU citizens, the conditions for border crossings have been made more difficult; these border crossings had previously been easily attainable between neighboring countries. Thus, the accession of countries in the region to the EU has created borders where there was previously fluidity, as between Poland and Belarus and the Russian region of Kaliningrad, or as between Romania and Moldova, Ukraine and Serbia. Resting upon a particular case study of populations living on the non-EU side of the EU border in two different countries, the present chapter sheds light on the influence of this border on the identity constructions at stake in a bottom-up perspective focusing on the way the border influences ordinary citizens' identity and feelings of belonging.

Research on the impact of a border on identity can be found at the intersection of the literatures on borders and nationalism. As for theories on borders, the theme has been scrutinized mainly through individual case studies (Ackleson 1999, Berdhal 1999, Paasi 1999, Klemencic 2000, Migdal 2004) or through strong theoretical emphasis on international relations (Albert et al. 2001). As for theories of nationalism and the construction of identity, while the impact of a particular border is shown by Anderson (1983) and Gellner (1983), the perspective generally adopted by scholars is primarily that of the construction of an identity by political and state actors in a top-down relationship (Breuilly 1982, Brass 1991, Greenfeld 1992, Hermet 1996, Thiesse 2001). Subsequently, following the recommendations by authors like Hobsbawm (1990) for a closer look at how identities are produced and reproduced at the micro level, the chapter follows the line adopted by Billig (1995), Edensor (2002), Brubaker et al. (2006), Fox and Miller-Idriss (2008), Polese and Horak (2015), or Seliverstova (2017), to investigate 'everyday' constructions of identity. The chapter draws particularly on research coordinated by

Wilson and Donnan (1998) to concentrate on 'border identities' that can be approached through a 'border anthropology' inspired by the work of Barth (1969). Such a bottom-up approach seems much needed for research on identity in Eastern Europe (Knott 2015) and has already been used to study issues of trade (Pisano 2009) or contradictions in identity discourses (Galasinska 2006) at Eastern European borders.

The research focuses on everyday constructions of identity as exhibited by ordinary citizens and the way the border impacts such constructions. Nations are 'bounded spaces' (Edensor 2002: 37) where borders enclose definable populations subject to hegemonic administrative and political systems. Such borders can be seen as part of the state 'regulatory apparatus' and 'mundane machinery' that define daily routines and the way members of a nation are (ibid: 91). In Central and Eastern Europe, legal citizenship is generally taken for granted and is seldom a relevant identity. Citizenship comes to matter mainly at borders where it becomes 'visible, salient, indeed inescapable' (Brubaker et al. 2006: 321). Against this background, the chapter is based on a particular case study: a discourse analysis of Romanian-speaking 'ordinary citizens' living in border cities and regions in Serbia and Ukraine a few kilometres away from the Romanian and EU border. Trying to identify those citizens' 'unreflexive' national identifications (20), the chapter looks at their everyday discursive constructions of the nation to which they supposedly belong and at how they 'talk the nation' (Fox and Miller-Idriss 2008: 537) when asked about the border nearby. Data were collected through semi-structured interviews that were undertaken with members of local civil society, journalists, teachers and members of local government. More importantly, focus groups were conducted with such 'ordinary citizens' of Romanian descent. Interviews and focus groups were conducted in Voivodina and Central Serbia in March 2014 (17 interviews and 3 focus groups) and in Bukovina in Ukraine in May and June 2014 (17 interviews and 4 focus groups).[1] In order to avoid overly general answers leading to stereotyped national discourse and to reach their unreflexive constructions of identity, the questions focused on the citizens' daily practices of the border, i.e. their experiences of border crossing, their experiences of what is behind the border and their impressions on the places they live in. All interviews and focus groups were transcribed, coded and analyzed using a discourse analysis software, *Nvivo*.

The chapter aims at interrogating and investigating such 'border identities'. Focusing on the impact of the border on the identity of Romanians living on the other side of the Romanian and EU borders, the aim, following Billig, is not to ask 'what is the Romanian national identity?' but rather to analyze 'what it means for them to claim to have Romanian national identity' (1995: 61). After a few elements of contextual background, the chapter shows how commitment to Romanian identity can be understood as an instrumental attachment. Indeed, the border nearby is often experienced as an unnatural obstacle. Romanian citizenship allows those who hold it to make it less relevant as they enjoy the benefits of EU citizenship and can travel more freely.

148   *Julien Danero Iglesias*

However, the chapter goes further than this simple rational explanation of identity. It shows the emergence of multicultural, multiple and multi-layered identities in regions with a particular past and recent history. The chapter demonstrates how identity constructions are deeply influenced by how Romanians in Serbia and Ukraine compare with, on the one hand, fellow Romanians on the other side of the border and, on the other, with Serbs or Ukrainians, the majorities of the country in which they live. The chapter concludes by showing that in their discourse, ordinary Romanians on the 'wrong' side of the border exhibit a 'nuanced' Romanian national identity. Such identity is deeply influenced by the border nearby and the everyday context of their lives.

Romanians outside Romania

When Romania was created as a country in 1859[2] and 1877-78,[3] numerous ethnic Romanians were to be found outside the newly created country, mainly in the regions of Bucovina, Transylvania and Banat belonging to the Habsburg Empire and in the region of Bessarabia belonging to the Tsarist Empire. After World War I, Transylvania, Eastern Banat, Northern Bucovina and Bessarabia were joined in what has been known as Greater Romania. Romania in its current borders emerged after World War II, losing Bessarabia, Northern Bucovina and Herta to the Soviet Union and Southern Dobruja to Bulgaria. Romanians can be found mainly along the borders of current-day Romania and they form minorities in various countries of Central and Eastern Europe. The exception to it is the Republic of Moldova where the identity of the majority of the population – Moldovan or Romanian – has long been much of a political issue (King 2000, Schrad 2004, Danero Iglesias 2014).

In Romania, these Romanians are considered 'Romanians abroad' ('Românii de Pretutindeni') and a department of the Romanian Ministry of Foreign Affairs is dedicated to handle issues related to them. Autochtonous Romanians in Serbia and Ukraine as well as Romanians who recently emigrated to countries such as Italy, France or Canada are considered 'Romanians abroad'. Therefore, the term 'diaspora' is often used when talking about Romanians in Ukraine and Serbia, even if most of the Romanians that I interviewed in both countries do not consider themselves members of a 'diaspora' (MGUkr, FG4Ukr[4]). If one asks how they would define themselves in national terms, the majority would say they are 'Romanian' in Bukovina and Voivodina, 'Moldovan' at the border with Moldova in Bukovina in Ukraine, and 'Vlachs' in Transcarpathia, Bulgaria or Central Serbia. Nevertheless, despite these different self-declared identities, they all can be analyzed as a Romanian 'national minority' using Rogers Brubaker's triadic nexus (1996) – or quadratic (Smith 2002) - through which the persistence of nationalism in Central and Eastern Europe can be explained by looking at the dynamic relationship between non-fixed and permanently evolving entities: the nationalizing state, the national minority and

Nuanced identities at the borders 149

the external homeland, to which international organizations can be added. The nexus has been largely criticized and further explained (see for example Kuzio 2001, Smith 2002, Commercio 2010, Brubaker 2013) but it still provides a general framework for understanding elements linked to nationalism and identity in Central and Eastern Europe. The framework can easily be applied to the Romanians living outside of Romania in Serbia and Ukraine and proves useful when considering citizenship policies put forward by a country like Romania towards those considered co-nationals abroad and that need protection on the basis of what Iordachi calls 'generalised attempts at reconstructing the national imagined communities against the background of radical post-communist socio-political and territorial reorganization' (2004, 240). While there is much room for commenting on whether Serbia and Ukraine are nationalizing states, this is not the scope of this chapter which only looks at one side of the nexus relationship: the way Romanian citizens outside of Romania and living near the border construct their identity on an everyday basis.

The border as an everyday obstacle

Talking with Romanian ethnic citizens in both countries, one soon finds out that the border, Romania and the EU provoke different feelings, perceptions and representations always linked to and compared with the situation on their Serbian or Ukrainian sides of the border. Comments about the European Union and shared experiences of traveling and living in Europe are generally overwhelmingly positive. The vast majority of the citizens that I had the opportunity to interview see Europe as a hope for Serbia or Ukraine, or even sometimes a 'dream', particularly in Ukraine where the economic situation is described as dire and the political situation as unstable (GUUkr). The EU could help strengthen the protection of minorities in Serbia (MDSer) and support democracy in Ukraine (ABUkr). Europe means 'fresh air' for people who are free (FG1Ukr) and can travel freely (FG2Ukr), without obstacles (VTUkr).

On that basis, even if the situation of Romanians in the two countries under scrutiny is different (see for example Danero Iglesias [2015] for the situation in Bukovina in Ukraine), it is relevant to see whether the border with Romania and the European Union[5] situated a few kilometres away from where they live can influence the way Romanians in both countries construct their identity. Indeed, current regional and international developments seem to push towards a bottom-up construction of an instrumental belonging to the Romanian 'nation' as a whole for Romanians living in Serbia and Ukraine. Border crossing between Romania, Serbia, Ukraine and Moldova was made easy after the collapse of communism. Romanian minorities in Ukraine and Serbia as well as Moldovans from the Republic of Moldova could easily enter Romania without any visa. However, Romania's accession to the EU meant that Moldovans and Romanians from Serbia and Ukraine

150   *Julien Danero Iglesias*

faced new restrictions in conducting trade with and travelling to Romania. The existence of the border and the Romanian membership to the EU can be seen as pushing for an instrumentalization of Romanian citizenship since Moldovan citizens, but also Ukrainian citizens, can easily acquire it. Indeed, claiming a Romanian national attachment and applying for citizenship can be understood in this situation as instrumental to the extent that the prominence of their belonging to the Romanian nation, and in parallel, Romanian citizenship, allow them to enjoy the benefits of citizenship in an EU Member State. This hypothesis aims therefore to test the 'strategic efficacy of ethnicity', drawn from Glazer and Moynihan (1975).

The other side of the border seems to exert an irresistible attraction. Some of the relatives of the citizens that were interviewed had the opportunity to live and work in the European Union and what they say about it also participates in the construction of an imaginary Europe in their home communities. In this Europe, 'salaries are better, you can afford much more, to travel, to go in excursions, much more that what we can with our salaries here' (AUSer). The issue of 'cleaner streets' (AUSer) is recurrent and anecdotes about a European 'culture' (FG3Ukr) of cleanliness are numerous. Europeans are able to carry their rubbish for 'for 2-3 kilometres until they find a bin' (DVUkr). Therefore, when 'Europeans' do not meet these high standards, some are amazed, like this high school teacher in Bukovina who explains that 'There was a German lady visiting our city (...). She smoked a cigarette and then she threw it. Like this, in the street. And I was thinking that I should tell her: "But dear, qu'est-ce que c'est, would you do the same in Germany?"' (FG3Ukr)

These examples show how 'Europe' is built discursively by ordinary citizens in the two countries as a place where the level of 'civilization' is much higher than on their own side of the border. Such perception is to be found when citizens are asked to compare cities on the two opposite sides of the border, like the city of Timisoara, the biggest city in Romania on the other side of the Serbian–Romanian border, which looks like 'Vegas' (VUSer) and where you can go just for a walk, to the mall (AUSer) or take a low-cost flight (Sikimic 2012: 152). Changes in Romania since the country entered the EU are seen in Serbia through a comparison to what Romania was before 1989, when standards of living were much higher in Yugoslavia. Romania had a very bad image in Serbia during communist times (BSSer) and life in there was very hard according to the citizens that were interviewed in Serbia (MPSer). Yugoslavia, for 'famished' Romanians (OMSer), was like the 'West' (FG1Ser) and citizens of Yugoslavia were much richer (NFSer). Therefore, progress since 2007 is seen as 'extraordinary' (ECSer) and can even be seen 'visually' (IBSer) when Romanians cross the border. When one asks about comparing the present-day situation in Romania to the present-day situation in Serbia, Romanians in Serbia feel that Romanians in Romania do not particularly live better than them, but that they do much better than before. On the contrary, in Ukraine, the situation in Romania is seen as much better and the issue of roads in Romania raises as many comments as the issue of cleanliness in Europe because

Nuanced identities at the borders 151

in Ukraine, for example, 'we do not measure roads in kilometres but in time. The time it takes for you to arrive' (FG3Ukr).

These examples show that the perception of Europe and the EU go hand in hand with the perception of the situation of the countries and the places in which people live. When things are moving on the other side of the border, things seem at a standstill in the two countries, or always going down. The impression sometimes is that they live behind closed doors, as demonstrated in an exchange during one of the focus groups in Ukraine:

- People live better in the European Union.
- Yes, well, we don't go there anyway. (FG1Ukr)

This exchange shows that not everyone has the opportunity to cross the border (ECSer) and only 'those who are very rich or those who want to settle there' cross it (OMUkr). Romania's EU accession, and the subsequent securitization of the border, brought feelings of being 'locked up again' (VTUkr) on the 'wrong side' of the border, transforming it into an obstacle against social and economic exchanges of which they are reminded on an everyday basis and that becomes part of their daily lives. Such an impact, even trivial, is shown by this man in his forties who often crosses the border from Romania to Serbia for shopping reasons: 'For example, I go and they ask where I am going to 'I am going to Timisoara.' 'Why?' 'To eat an ice cream!' And they give me a strange look. We should be free to go have an ice cream in Timisoara if we want to.' (MMSer). The situation is comparable in Herta, a small town at the Ukraine-Romania border, where the number of crossing points has been limited to only one (OMUkr). The new border is a place with 'useless bureaucracy and endless queues' (VBUkr, SHUkr) when it is expensive to have a passport (FG2Ukr, LCUkr) and also sometimes difficult to get an invitation (MGUkr).

Citizenship as an exit strategy

As we have seen in the previous section, Romania, from an Eastern European country with which Romanians are ethnically linked, emerges as a state situated imaginarily in an attractive and desired West (Sikimic 2012: 149) mostly conceived as Europe and the European Union by the citizens I met in Serbia and Ukraine. The nearby and securitized European border is both a source of frustration and hope for the future for these citizens who often have the impression of living behind closed doors. The developments citizens have recently witnessed or heard of on the Romanian side of the border, compared with their perceived stagnation of their own border landscape, reinforce their feeling of living at the edges of Europe, in what seems to be its backward periphery. Subsequently their desire to become a part of what can be called a 'European mirage' (Stanculescu and Danero Iglesias 2013) seems to push for the quest of an 'exit ticket' (Bieber 2010) linked with particular exit strategies (Danero Iglesias et al. 2016).

152   *Julien Danero Iglesias*

One of these exit strategies is to regain Romanian citizenship. In Ukraine, in the region of Bukovina where interviews and focus groups were carried out, one can apply for Romanian citizenship if they are able to demonstrate that one of their ancestors was a citizen of Greater Romania between the two World Wars. In this case, the citizenship of the applicant is 'regained' after it was 'lost'. The rule is the same for citizens of the Republic of Moldova and the process seems to have been used widely, even to the extent of being criticized by the European Union.

Legally, Ukrainian citizens cannot hold dual citizenship. However, lots of the persons I met confirmed that they have dual citizenship, even indirectly (DCUkr, VTUkr), or mentioned that lots of people in Ukraine have it (NHUkr). As one of the interviewees puts it, it seems that Ukrainian citizens know that dual citizenship 'is not allowed' but, at the same time, they feel that 'it is not forbidden' (Fg2Ukr). Some explain that even Ukrainian authorities are suspected to have many different citizenships (FG2Ukr). Against this background, it seems that even border guards would be understanding when meeting Ukrainian citizens crossing the border with both Romanian and Ukrainian passports in their hands (VBUkr). The main raison for gaining citizenship seems to be linked with the dire local economic situation (EMUkr). As one of the interviewees puts it, emphasizing the instrumental aspect of regaining Romanian citizenship: 'Citizenship gives you the right to elect and be elected. But I have never seen any Romanian from Bukovina applying for being president or senator in Romania' (NHUkr). Regaining citizenship allows you to get out when you are 'sick of Ukraine' (ABUkr), or to avoid working illegally in Europe:

> Lots of citizens say they are Romanian ... Lots go in for swearing in Romania. This is a joke. They want to enter freely in Europe, they want to be able to work. It is difficult to go to Europe, visas are expensive and, usually, you're only considered a tourist. Therefore, in Europe, you're illegal and you hide. Until they catch you. If they catch you, you're sent back. And here we go again if you don't have a Romanian passport. (VBUkr)

In Serbia the situation is different, as citizens of Serbia are not included in this framework of regaining Romanian citizenship since Vojvodina and Central Serbia were never historically Romanian territories. Subsequently, Romanians from Serbia need to follow the regular process of obtaining citizenship, and some of them do it (ECUkr). Following this situation, some do not understand why Moldovans or Ukrainians can regain citizenship so easily while they are not given such an opportunity (IBSer). Some of them feel that Romania does not care about them and has 'forgotten' them (NCSer):

> I'll die and we won't have Romanian citizenship. Hungary gave citizenship to its citizens, Slovakia gave it, Bulgaria gave it, Macedonia gave it, Croatia

Nuanced identities at the borders 153

gave it. Everyone has given it. We are the only ones who haven't got it from Romania. Our ancestors, 300 years ago, came from Romania and migrated here, we are Romanian, we are parts of the Romanian people. (NCSer)

Again, citizenship from a European Union country is seen as a plus, allowing one to go abroad and to see better things (FG2Ser) and some 'do it' – they apply for citizenship – 'only to leave' as soon as they have obtained it (VPSer) as it means having a chance for a 'better life' (FG2Ser): 'I could obtain 15 times – and I probably will – Bulgarian citizenship. But I have to go twice to Sofia and this is quite bothering as it is quite far' (NCSer). This shows that, for some, if Romania has not given citizenship to Romanians from Vojvodina, they can try to obtain Hungarian citizenship, or Bulgarian citizenship like in the last example, because this is their legal right (FG2Ser).

All these examples show that the main reasons for getting citizenship are mostly instrumental and economic, as demonstrated in the case of other ethnic Romanians in the region (Stoleriu et al. 2011, Danero Iglesias et al. 2016) Since the European border represents, on the one hand, a source of frustration and humiliation and, on the other hand, a hope for the future, Romanians in Serbia and Ukraine can make use of their Romanian ethnicity as an exit strategy to access what seems to be a better life.

The emergence of multiple identities at borders

While instrumentality might explain an important part of the reason why Romanians in neighbouring Serbia and Ukraine apply to Romanian citizenship and activate their Romanian identity in this particular context, some comments on the impact of the border on everyday life hinted that there might be something else behind the citizens' feelings of belonging to the Romanian nation. While numerous citizens in both countries told me that they would not hesitate to take Romanian citizenship, some explained that it would feel strange to apply for any other citizenship, just because they are entitled to it. For example, in Serbia, when asked if they would apply for Hungarian citizenship, some Romanians answer:

> I wouldn't take Hungarian citizenship. Never. For me, this is like selling yourself. Why would I take it if my family is not Hungarian? If my country doesn't give it to me, the Romanian state, then I have Serbian citizenship. (DSSer)

At the same time, some explain that they want to apply to Romanian citizenship just because they are and they feel Romanian (TUSer). Romanian citizenship for Romanians abroad is often perceived as something that is 'historically right' (VTUkr; ABUkr). However, some citizens I met, putting forward the same argument, just do not want to obtain Romanian citizenship, because

154   *Julien Danero Iglesias*

they do not need a passport to feel Romanian (FG2Ukr) or because in their 'soul', they will 'always' be Romanian anyway (GUUkr).

Romanian ethnic citizens in Serbia and Ukraine do not seem to need Romanian citizenship to feel actually Romanian. The unreflexive feelings of belonging that come to the fore when some of them are asked about their main identity are all connected to a strong Romanian identity (MMSer, TUSer, OMUkr, VTUkr) that is treasured and preserved. For these citizens, being 'Romanian' is part of everyday life: 'Me, in the morning, the first thing I do, I make my bed and I put a Romanian hora. I don't know, I like to hear something Romanian' (FG1Ukr). This is the case even if they have never crossed the border to Romania (DSSer) or even if sometimes some feel some shame when speaking Romanian in public (MMSer, FG1Ser, FG1Ukr, FG2Ukr, FG3Ukr): 'We didn't die, we speak Romanian and we are here. And I tell the kids: "You don't have to be ashamed, you have to be ashamed when you do something stupid. When you know several languages, this is pride"' (FG2Ukr).

Being Romanian for these citizens is part of an identity which is strongly influenced by interaction with 'non-Romanians' on their side of the border, with which they share the same 'problems' (VUSer) and, generally, the same experiences of life. The living together is put forward in a proud way in Vojvodina and Bukovina where locals discursively emphasize how their regions are models of peaceful multicultural communities, based on 'tolerance' (IISer):

> I am talking about a regional identity, not especially about a Vojvodinian identity. Romanians from here, they would get along much better with a Serb from Romania. Or, let's put it like this, I would get along much better with a Serb from here than with a Romanian from Bucharest. Because we have the same problems, we live in the same communities. (ECSer)

At the same time, regional identities can be found across borders, particularly in Banat, where people in Serbian Western Banat feel a particularly strong connection with people of the Romanian Eastern Banat (MMSer, OPSer) and particularly for those who identify as Moldovans in Bukovina who feel strong connections with Bessarabia, but also the Romanian region of Moldova. In this regard, some Romanians in Serbia do not feel at home in Belgrade or in Timisoara, but only in Vrsac, the smaller city at the border where they live, or in Timisoara (ECSer), demonstrating a strong 'Banatean' identity put forward by many, sometimes equated with, or integrated into, a more encompassing Vojvodinan identity (IISer, OPSer). Romanians from Ukraine and Moldova also show regional belongings, because of a similar historical experience of the Soviet Union (FDUkr).

By deploying these regional identities, Romanians in Serbia and Ukraine seem to relativize the Romanian 'ethnonational category' (Brubaker et al.

Nuanced identities at the borders   155

2006: 237) by putting forward a tolerant identity in contrast to a Romanian identity to be found on the other side of the border.

Feelings of being different from Romanians in Romania are determinant in everyday identification for the citizens I interviewed. Such feelings of being different are reinforced by the fact that, according to some, Romanians do not know Romanians abroad very well. Sometimes, Romanians seem to take Chernovcy ('Cernauti' in Romanian), the Bukovinan capital, for Chisinau, the capital of the Republic of Moldova (FG2Ukr), or they consider it as a 'suburb' of the latter (ALUkr). They might also ask if by saying that they are 'Romanian', Romanians from Serbia mean that they are actually 'Aromanian' (ECSer), another ethnic minority in the region. Sometimes, Romanians from Serbia and Ukraine would also be called 'Serbs' when they are visiting Romania (MMSer, VPSer, MPSer, TUSer, AUSer, FG1Ukr, FG2Ukr, FG4Ukr). When Romanians from the other side of the border go to Romania, they sometimes have to answer questions about who they are exactly:

> We try to explain that we are Romanian, that our ancestors have come from Romanian territories. Myself I know the history of my ancestors, from where they have come, the native village. And then, it's clearer. Lots [in Romania] are not very well informed and call us Serbs. [...] Anyway, this is not offensive. And Serbs say that we are Romanian but, on the contrary, we rather feel Serb. Because we grew up here, on this territory. (AUSer)

Just like in the case of Hungarians in Transylvania, who found it humiliating that they were not recognized as part of the nation when travelling to Hungary – their supposed Homeland – (Brubaker et al. 2006: 330), Romanians from Serbia and Ukraine often express that a Romanian 'transborder nation' does not actually cross the border next to which they live.

When they cross the border, the national habitus and the embodied habits Romanians from Serbia and Ukraine have developed in the places they live in become clear and they are 'dumbfounded by the range of everyday competencies' which they do not possess. Indeed, even though they are 'Romanian', when in Romania, they 'come across a culture full of people who do not do things the way [they] do them, who draw on different practical resources to accomplish everyday tasks' (Edensor 2002: 93):

> [In Romania,], I don't feel like home. In a foreign country. But not like it in Germany. In 2007 I went to Germany [...]. There, it's different, I don't know the language, I don't know anything, I don't know the peoples' mentality, I cannot talk with the people. There, [I express myself] with my hands and with the English I haven't learned [...].

These examples all seem to show that the strategic efficacy only tells one part of the story and that the national feelings and identities that I have observed

156   *Julien Danero Iglesias*

are not hardly part of a 'choice'. On the contrary, these examples demonstrate once again that 'nationhood operates as an unselfconscious disposition: it underwrites people's choices without becoming a self-conscious determinant of those choices' (Fox and Miller-Idriss 2008: 544, following on Bourdieu and Foucault). As evidence of the fact that 'nationhood defines the parameters, but not the contents of people's choices' (ibid), what seems to be 'true' attachments to national identity have been often identified during my field research. In Serbia and Ukraine, the persons I talked with all showed loyalty to the state they live in: 'Even if I love the motherland, I am loyal to this country which feeds me, which raised me, which gives me a salary. (...) This country, I love it. This is where I grew up' (VUSer). However, such loyalty does not prevent them from being Romanian, as explained by this Romanian 'Ukrainian patriot': 'I am a great Ukrainian patriot, and I am Romanian, but a huge Ukrainian patriot. I was raised in this state, and this has a big importance for me. (...) When the Ukrainian anthem starts, I stand up and I feel good' (GHUkr). Such loyalty seems to demonstrate that identity and feelings of belonging are closely linked to past and present experiences of the citizens in the region under scrutiny. Such citizens have grown up outside of the Romanian national bounded space. Different historical experiences of people living in different nationalizing states with different nationalizing policies have created 'nuanced identities' for these Romanian ethnic citizens outside of the borders of Romania (Stanculescu and Danero Iglesias 2013) that are often not fully understood by Romanians in the External Homeland.[6]

Some might say that all those 'multiple identities' (Hall 2002, Spickard 2013) lead to a general 'confused identity' (MMSer) of Romanians outside of Romania which is best exemplified by the national football teams they support. One person I met in Serbia explained that he indeed supported the Yugoslavian team until the break up and the civil war in the 1990s, then Romania because he felt suddenly Romanian but now supports Serbia because 'in the end' he feels more attached to Serbia than Romania. This seems to show that identities can be 'context-specific' and 'experiential' (Brubaker et al. 2006: 210). Romanians from Serbia and Ukraine are 'Romanian' when they are home, but they can sometimes be Serbian or Ukrainian, depending on the situations they encounter, the person that is in front of them or the country they visit.

Conclusion: the border as an identity marker

The aim of this chapter was to investigate 'border identities' in the case of Romanian populations in Serbia and Ukraine living a few kilometres away from the Romanian and EU border and measure the impact of this border on their constructions of identity. Following a bottom-up perspective inspired, among other authors, by Billig (1995), Edensor (2002) and Brubaker (2006), and looking at what it means to claim to have Romanian national identity (Billig 1995: 61), the chapter started by determining whether the presence of such a border could have an instrumental impact on the way Romanians put forward and activate their belonging to the Romanian nation on the other side of the border.

Indeed, following Glazer and Moynihan's hypothesis of the strategic efficacy of nationalism, commitment to Romanian national identity could be explained as an instrumental attachment to the extent that Romanian citizenship allows those who hold it to enjoy the benefits of EU citizenship and get rid of the border nearby, often experienced as an unnatural obstacle. Looking at unreflexive constructions of identity and the way the nearby border is constructed in their speech, I observed during interviews and focus groups at the border between Serbia, Ukraine and Romania that on the basis of a general positive image of Europe and the European Union and on the basis of generally economically low conditions of living in the two countries, sometimes in situations of political instability, Romanian citizenship is perceived as a plus and as an exit ticket which can make life better. Reasons for activating feelings of Romanian belonging and regaining Romanian citizenship through a simplified procedure supported by the External Homeland seemed to be mainly instrumental for citizens of Ukraine and the situation of citizens of Serbia applying for Hungarian citizenship even if they are not Hungarian shows the same pattern of explanation. It seems consequently that Glazer and Moynihan's hypothesis might play a huge role in explaining why Romanian-speaking citizens outside of Romania apply for Romanian citizenship.

This conclusion confirms criticisms of the European Union towards Romanian citizenship policies and shows that, contrarily to some official Romanian discourse, regaining citizenship relates more to present-day pragmatism than to redressing a historical wrong. Nevertheless, the present chapter also demonstrates that such strategic efficacy only tells one part of the story of the emergence of multicultural, multiple and multi-layered identities in the two regions under scrutiny that exhibit a particular past and recent history. On the other side of the border, outside of the Romanian nation understood as a bounded space, Romanian feelings of belonging have developed under different historical and political circumstances that led to the creation of particular identities that are strongly influenced by living together with other communities in multinational regions like Bukovina and Vojvodina. Such experiences have a strong influence on feelings of belonging that can only be explained by the existence of the border, that have separated and still separates Romanians from both regions from their External Homeland in Brubaker's terms. This shows, in line with Billig, that national identities do not develop in 'social vacuums' (1995: 60) but are highly dependent on situational and contextual aspects.

In their discourse, when they 'talk the nation' by relating it to the nearby border, ordinary Romanians outside of Romania constantly put forward an 'us' that seems very different from the Romanians on the other side

158 *Julien Danero Iglesias*

of the border. The different historical circumstances seem to lead to the creation of nuanced Romanian identities, which can be compared to Romanian identity in Romania but that exhibit a series of different traits: Romanians outside of Romania feel for example that they are more tolerant (VPSer) or that they are culturally 'richer' than their counterparts in Romania, because they speak and practice on an everyday basis more languages (OPSer) and because they feel that they have actually preserved their traditions better than in Romania (NTUkr). Such feelings can be best exemplified in this excerpt of a conversation with a Romanian cultural officer in Serbia explaining how Romanians in Serbia have kept their traditions 'better':

> I would never say that we are higher than Romania, God forbid, this is the motherland. I want to say that [culture] is a bit better preserved here, maybe because we have been in another country, somehow isolated, or I don't know how to say, and we have striven to preserve it. We are not higher, but we are not lower. We preserve it. (VUSer)

Consequently, even if the border sometimes seems to block the Romanian citizens I met in Serbia and Ukraine, the border has also created the conditions for the emergence of nuanced and particular multiple Romanian identities that all are meaningful in the current context of both Bukovina and Vojvodina and that evolve following the different situations that ordinary citizens encounter in their everyday lives. Living a few kilometres away from the border and Romania, the border seems one of the main identity markers in their everyday lives, a marker that came to the fore when Romania became a member of the EU. Even if borders seem to exert an influence long after they are gone (von Hirschhausen et al. 2015), the influence we observed could evolve, and maybe diminish drastically, if the social, economic and political situations of the places the ordinary citizens I met were to change.

Notes

1 I would like to thank warmly all the colleagues in Serbia and Ukraine who have made this research possible, particularly Laura Spariosu and Marina Puia-Badescu at the University of Novi Sad and Daniela Bicer and Felicia Vranceanu at the National University Y. Fedkovich, and Vasile Bâcu at the Society M. Eminescu in Chernovcy. I also want to thank Maria-Philippa Wieckowski at the ULB who spent hours transcribing interviews and focus groups from Ukraine. The research would not have been possible without the financial support of the Faculty of Social and Political Sciences at the ULB and the Fonds national belge pour la Recherche scientifique (FNRS).
2 First time the principalities of Wallachia and Moldavia were united to form the Romanian United Principalities, which later became officially known as 'Romania'.
3 When Romania was declared independent from the Ottoman Empire.

4 References to interviews and focus groups have been made as following: initials of the person and number for focus groups, followed by the first three letters of the country in which the interview took place.
5 During interviews in the three countries, it soon appeared that 'Europe' and the 'European Union' are the same thing for citizens we talked with, particularly in Ukraine but also in Serbia.
6 Damian, George. Cazul Irina Tarasiuk. Basarabia din suflet și Basarabia reală, Personal blog, 5 August 2014, www.george-damian.ro/cazul-irina-tarasiuk-basarabia-din-suflet-si-basarabia-reala-5905.html (last accessed August 2016).

References

Ackleson, J. 1999. Discourses of identity and territoriality on the US-Mexico border. *Geopolitics* 4(2), 155–179.

Albert, M., Brock, L. 1996. Debordering the world of states: New spaces in international relations. *New Political Science* 18(1), 69–106.

Albert, M., Jacobson, D., Lapid, Y. (eds). 2001. *Identities, borders, orders: New directions in international relations theory*. Minneapolis, MN: University of Minnesota Press.

Anderson, B. 1983. *Imagined communities: Reflections on the origin and spread of nationalism*. London: Verso.

Barth, F. 1969. *Ethnic groups and boundaries: The social organization of cultural difference*. Oslo: Universitets forlaget.

Berdhal, D. 1999. *Where the world ended. Re-unification and identity in the German borderland*. Los Angeles: University of California Press.

Bieber, F. 2010. Dual citizenship can be a solution, not a problem, in *Dual citizenship for transborder minorities? How to respond to the Hungarian-Slovak tit-for-tat*, edited by R. Bauböck. Fiesola: EUI Working Papers, RSCAS, 757.

Billig, M. 1995. *Banal nationalism*. London: Sage.

Brass, P. 1991. *Ethnicity and nationalism. Theory and comparison*. New Delhi: Sage.

Breuilly, J. 1982. *Nationalism and the state*. Chicago: The University of Chicago Press.

Brubaker, R. 1996. *Nationalism reframed. Nationhood and the national question in the New Europe*. Cambridge: Cambridge University Press.

Brubaker, R., Feischmidt, M., Fox, J., Grancea, L. 2006. *Nationalist politics and everyday ethnicity in a Transylvanian town*. Princeton, NJ: Princeton University Press.

Brubaker, R. 2013. Nationalising states revisited: Projects and processes of nationalisation in post-Soviet states. In *New nation states and national minorities*, edited by J. Danero Iglesias, N. Stojanovic and S. Weinblum. Colchester, ECPR Press, 11–38.

Commercio, M. 2010. *Russian minority politics in post-Soviet Latvia and Kyrgyzstan. The transformative power of informal networks*. Philadelphia: University of Pennsylvania Press.

Danero Iglesias, J. 2014. *Nationalisme et pouvoir en République de Moldavie*. Brussels: Editions de l'Université de Bruxelles.

Danero Iglesias, J. 2015. Ukraine, Romania and Romanians in Ukraine. *Südosteuropa: Journal of Politics and Society* 62(3), 372–383.

Danero Iglesias, J., Sata, R., Vass, A. 2016. Citizenship and identity: Being Hungarian in Slovakia and Romanian in Serbia and Ukraine. *Minority Studies* 18, 15–32.

Edensor, T. 2002. *National identity, popular culture and everyday life*. New York: Berg.

Fox, J., Miller-Idriss, C. 2008. Everyday nationhood. *Ethnicities* 8(4), 536–563.

Galasinska, A. 2006. Border ethnography and post-communist discourses of nationality in Poland. *Discourse and Society* 17, 609–626.

Gellner, E. 1983. *Nations and nationalism*. Ithaca, NY: Cornell University Press.

160 Julien Danero Iglesias

Glazer, N., Moynihan, D. 1975. *Ethnicity. Theory and experience*. Cambridge: Harvard University Press.

Greenfeld, L. 1992. *Nationalism. Five roads to modernity*. Cambridge: Harvard University Press.

Hall, S. 2002. Political belongings in a world of multiple identities, in *Conceiving cosmopolitanism: Theory, context and practice*, edited by S. Vertovec and R. Cohen. Oxford: Oxford University Press, 25–31.

Hermet, G. 1996. *Histoire des nations et du nationalisme en Europe*. Paris: Le Seuil.

Hobsbawm, E. 1990. *Nations and nationalism since 1780. Programme, myth, reality*. Cambridge: Cambridge University Press.

Iordachi, C. 2004. Dual citizenship and policies toward kin-minorities in east-central Europe: A comparison between Hungary, Romania, and the Republic of Moldova, in *The Hungarian status law syndrome: A nation building and/or minority protection*, edited by Z. Kantor, B. Majtznyi, O. Ieda, B. Vizi and I. Halasz. Sapporo: Slavic Research Center at Hokkaido University, 239–269.

King, C. 2000. *The Moldovans. Romania, Russia and the politics of culture*. Stanford: Hoover Institution Press.

Knott, E. 2015. Generating data. Studying identity politics from a bottom-up approach in Crimea and Moldova. *East European Politics & Societies* 29(2), 467–486.

Kuzio, T. 2001. Nationalizing states' or nation-building? A critical review of the theoretical literature and empirical evidence. *Nations and Nationalism* 7(2), 135–154.

Klemencic, M. 2000. The boundaries, internal order and identities of Bosnia and Herzegovina. *Boundary and Security Bulletin* 8(4), 63–71.

Migdal, J. (ed.) 2004. *Boundaries and belonging*. Cambridge: Cambridge University Press.

Paasi, A. 1999. Boundaries as social practices and discourse: The Finnish-Russian border. *Regional Studies* 33, 669–680.

Pisano, J. 2009. From Iron Curtain to Golden Curtain. Remaking identity in the European Union borderlands. *East European Politics and Societies* 23(2), 266–290.

Polese, A., Horak, S. 2015. A tale of two presidents: Personality cult and symbolic nation-building in Turkmenistan. *Nationalities Papers* 43(3), 457–478.

Schrad, M. 2004. Rag doll nations and the politics of differentiation on arbitrary borders: Karelia and Moldova. *Nationalities Papers* 32(2), 457–496.

Seliverstova, O. 2017. 'Consuming' national identity in Western Ukraine. *Nationalities Papers* 45(1), 61–79.

Sikimic, B. 2012. Romanians in the Serbian Banat: Imagining Romania and the West, in *Migration and identity. Historical, cultural and linguistic dimensions of mobility in the Balkans*, edited by P. Hristov. Sofia: Bulgarian Academy of Sciences Paradigma, 232–245.

Smith, D. 2002. Framing the national question in Central and Eastern Europe: A quadratic nexus? *The Global Review of Ethnopolitics* 2(1), 3–16.

Spickard, P. 2013. *Multiple identities: Migrants, ethnicity, and membership*. Bloomington, IN: Indiana University Press.

Stanculescu, C., Danero Iglesias, J. 2013. Identités nuancées à la frontière de l'Union européenne. Cahul, Moldavie. *Studia Politica: Romanian Political Science Review* 13(3), 457–475.

Stoleriu, M., Groza, O., Dimitriu, R., Turcanasu, G. 2011. Visions of Europe at the European Union eastern border. Focus on Moldavian migration to Romania. *Eurobroadmap*, 1–36.

Thiesse, A. -M. 2001. *La Création des Identités nationales*. Paris: Le Seuil.

von Hirschhausen, B., Grandits, H. Kraft, C. Müller, D., Serrier, T. 2015. *Phantomgrenzen. Räume und Akteure in der Zeit neu denken*. Berlin: Wallstein.

Wilson, T., Donnan, H. 1998. *Border identities: Nation and state at international frontiers*. Cambridge: Cambridge University Press.

9 Can nation building be 'spontaneous'? A (belated) ethnography of the Orange Revolution

Abel Polese

Introduction

November 2004 saw nearly a million Ukrainians take to the streets to protest against election falsification – the first major protest of this form in the country. In Autumn 2016, this might not sound as fascinating as it was more than a decade ago, given that mass protests have become a common means of contestation in the country, with the occupation of the main square happening regularly over the last decade. The 2004 events also had very little drama, if compared to the recent Euromaidan that saw the deaths of over hundred people and the destruction of the centre of the city of Kyiv.

However, the importance of the 2004 events, and in many respects the other protests that would follow, reaches well beyond its narrow political significance. Millions of words have been used to describe the Orange Revolution, its consequences and Ukraine's political evolutions after 2004, celebrating the change in national politics, illustrating the growth of civil society or attempting to emphasize the democracy-related aspects (D'Anieri 2005, Kurth and Kempe 2005, Kuzio 2005, McFaul 2005). Little has been said, though, on the relationship between the events and the new Ukrainian identity, or identities, that have resulted from this. The main point of this chapter is that the 2004 events have a crucial role in identity construction.

In this respect, it is worth mentioning that this chapter is not an attempt to provide a framework to understand current Ukrainian events. This clarification goes against any advice students would get at academic writing training workshops (never say what a paper is not about) but is needed at this stage. This is not to deny any connection between the 2004 and further development in the social and political destiny of the country. But the current work does not seek any correlations either. The research that informed this article happened to be carried out at a given moment of the story of the country where politics and identity started to be intertwined. However, the message of this chapter is simply that there are phenomena that, born out of certain intentions, transform and go beyond those initial intentions. In 2004, what started as a political protest action happened to play a major role in the identity construction of the country and its people and this perspective is perfectly in

162 *Abel Polese*

line with the argument we make throughout this book. For the same reason, this work avoids referring to politicians by name and minimizes the focus on political events. They are certainly the background that allows us to understand the context. But the main goal of this chapter to explain how identity could be affected by its (often unaware) everyday performance and reproduction. In particular, language attitudes, political activism and perception of the other (Russia) will be surveyed to show how their change affects the self-perception of Ukrainians at the daily and then national level.

In order to do this, the concept of 'spontaneous nation building' (Polese 2009a, Polese and Horak 2015) is borrowed. Nation building has been considered, since its conceptualization, a top-down process, performed by political elites for the inculcation of a domestic identity in all the inhabitants of a given administrative territory (Connor 1972, Deutsch and Folz 1964). Scholars have debated whether this is an inherently ethnic process or whether civic elements can also be transmitted through a standard nation-building process (Brubaker 1996, Kuzio 2001). However, the starting idea is that political elites define and develop measures for the construction and reproduction of national identity through top-down political measures. In contrast, the idea behind spontaneous nation building is that, in line with the main approach of this book, identity can be constructed through elements and by actors other than the political elites. Following Eriksen's distinction between formal and informal nationalism (1993) we identify several channels for the production and dissemination of a national identity. This approach follows the debate on the role of the elites in a nation-building project (Gellner 1984, Smith 1991) to look at the role of 'minor' actors in the construction of national identity.

Appaduraj has pointed at the role of groups over a territory or institution to construct the local in a given context (1995). As a result, historical change can be regarded as the result of a synergy between local and translocal dynamics (Ortner 2006) to argue that people do not just observe and passively receive instructions to obey them but have agency, while the elites attempt to 'build the nation' (Gramsci 1971).

This chapter is part of this stream analyzing phenomena that have gone unnoticed, underreported or ignored, in a continuation of the critical approach suggested by Hobsbawm and Rude ([1968] 2014) and that has recently been rediscovered as approach for the study of the informal or the 'invisible' (Knott 2015, Pawłusz and Seliverstova 2016, Pawłusz and Polese 2017, Polese 2008, 2016). In particular, this chapter looks at the Orange Revolution as a crucial moment of identity construction in post-independence Ukraine. It proposes it as a new moment of consciousness of being Ukrainian and an historical moment in the creation, identification or invention of identity markers that were not used before. Like a number of other scholars of post-socialist identity building (Bilaniuk 2005, Isaacs 2015, 2016, Knott 2015, Morris 2005, 2007), we will use a focus on the everyday to illustrate how Ukrainians started living their everyday identity in a different way to construct or identify markers that were not used before. These markers have then migrated from ordinary people

Can nation building be 'spontaneous'? 163

to society at large and were tacitly accepted, or even endorsed by the elites through public narratives or simply behaviours that confirm the importance of these markers to contemporary Ukrainian identity.

Inspired by the above approaches, we suggest that nation building can be conceived, performed and engaged in with by people or organizations of people (Kulyk 2014, Metzger et al. 2016). Previous studies have documented participation in and performance of popular culture elements that may impact national identity (De Juriew 2003, Pawłusz 2016, Seliverstova 2017, Ventsel 2012, 2016), a process that can happen independently from, and regardless of, the role of a state. In addition, nation building has also been used to refer to the fact that just as nation-building measures might not have the desired effects and impact on a given population, there might be some measures that, conceived of at the central level, were not intended to primarily influence identity construction – this is the case of elections, opposition movements, and mega events (Danero Iglesias 2015, Militz 2016, Ó Beacháin and Kevlihan 2015, Ostapenko 2010, Persson and Petersson 2014, Issacs and Polese 2016) – but nevertheless end up substantially affecting the perception of identity, its construction and reproduction among the local population (Gronskaya and Makarychev 2014, Horak and Polese 2016, Knott 2015, Polese 2014).

The case study presented here stems from the above considerations and is a re-interpretation of what became known as the Orange Revolution from a distinct angle. The overwhelming majority of studies have tended to frame the Orange Revolution within a democratization, social movement and in general political action framework. Works published immediately after the events have analyzed the evolutions and dynamics of top politics, with the competition for power, electoral fraud and democratization attempts (Aslund and McFaul 2006, Forbig and Demes 2007, Wilson 2005). Alternatively, in an attempt to provide a more bottom-up view on the events, scholars have looked at the way civil society has evolved and informed politics and political decisions to become an integrated part of the political actors and arena of the country (Kuzio 2006a, 2010, Stepanenko 2006). Subsequent studies have looked at the failed democratization process and the broken promises by politicians, parties and in general political actors (Christensen et al. 2005, Kubicek 2009, Lane 2008). Only a few, and often overlooked, works have engaged with what can be considered as 'side effects' of the Orange Revolution (Beissinger 2011, 2013, Kuzio 2006b, Polese 2009b).

The context: 'comerade revolutionaire please close the door behind you'

22 November 2004. A slow snow whitens the centre of Kiev and falls on the bags, boxes and people that are now occupying ulitsa *Kreshchatyk* at the level of *Maidan nezalezhnosti*, the Independence Square now famous worldwide for the dramatic killings of 2013. A crowd of protesters has taken the streets, blocked the centre of the Ukrainian capital and is getting ready to stay there.

164   *Abel Polese*

Tents are camped all over the place. A screen is being mounted on Independence Square and opposition figures are already there, crying out against falsification of elections and pushing people to action. Some policemen approach and fine the protesters for illegal occupation of public soil, the equivalent of 3 euro in local currency. Then they let them complete the construction. Opposition parties have, for the first time, successfully coordinated between one another and with civil society organizations in the country. A network has been constructed at the national level and participation of several thousand people is expected, at least in the first days of the occupation. As planned, people start converging into Maidan and the crowd starts thickening. What was less planned is that an action, initially foreseeing involvement of around one hundred thousand people, would eventually bring nearly a million of Ukrainian citizens into the centre of Kiev at its peak (Wallander 2005). The words of a businessman to his subordinates are quite telling to understand the general mood: 'Colleagues, I am unable to work whilst in Ukraine I see happening what is happening. Each one of you do what they believe is most opportune. I go to Maidan.'

The first place to be occupied was the area near Maidan that hosted an underground shopping centre with a number of luxury shops. At the entrance of the centre a sign was hung: *Uvazhaemye gospoda revolutsioniery, zakrivaite za soboy dver pozhaluista (Respectful comrades revolutionaries, please close the door behind you)*.

This can, in some respects, be seen as the turning point. Until that day the word 'revolution' brought to the memory bad images and ideas. Official narratives depicted participation in a revolution as a way to be reactionary, against the stability of the country and, eventually, against its institutions and citizens. The free use of the word revolution is, here, emblematic and represents the beginning of a different standpoint that will unleash all the well-known dynamics of the Orange Revolution, with long occupation of the centre of Kiev and picketing of governmental buildings, and contribute to the pressure towards political elites to accept the change in the country. It represents also a pragmatic stand of common people working in the shopping centre. Knowing that they cannot stop the movement they try at least to regulate it, show some respect and ask for some respect (closing the door to avoid heat loss). Unable to participate, they express moral support for what is the quietest revolution of the CIS in the period. Occupation of public buildings does not culminate in violence, people still pay to enter the metro underneath Maidan and do not break into shops to devastate and rob them (as will happen a few months afterwards in Kyrgyzstan) and shop staff often invite protesters into shops to warm up or use the toilets.

The quiet movement of thousands of people, in a city that otherwise keeps on functioning as it was, changes some dynamics of the capital. Louder than the people is, however, colours. The colour chosen by the main opposition candidate was orange so that wearing orange came to symbolize support for anti-regime forces or ideas. As days pass, orange becomes a predominant

Can nation building be 'spontaneous'? 165

colour in the streets of Kiev, and all across Ukraine, making immediately recognizable the supporters of the protests. Some people move to the centre and remain for several weeks. Some others simply go to see what is happening after finishing their working day. The 'revolution' becomes an immense social event with concerts, free food and drinks and a solidarity mood that was rarely, if ever, seen before.

There has been a lot of speculation as to why people were able to stay in the centre of Kiev for so long under freezing winter conditions, why so many people kept on going there from other regions, how the whole revolution was organized and what the motivation was of each of them to participate. Pro-Western analysts would look at the democratic nature of the events whereas pro-Russia accounts emphasized the artificial nature of the events (see Lane 2008, Ó Beacháin and Polese 2008, 2009, 2010a, McFaul 2007). It is well beyond the scope of the chapter to endorse either version. The point here is that the very existence of a space where people could meet, discuss politics and the very fact that politics was part of their everyday life created the opportunity for increased political awareness. In turn, this gave Ukrainians a place to perform, develop and reproduce their national identity through several channels.

The people of Maidan become an extended family, what Anderson would call the imagined community or horizontal comradeship. Except with people from the east, west, north and south of the country converging into Kiev the imaginary becomes real. They get used to going to the main square in the evening to receive the latest updates, feeding or getting fed, and enjoy the show that artists, intellectuals and other main figures appearing on stage regularly prepare for them. The stage at the centre of the city provides revolutionaries with music, intellectual debates, shows and other forms of entertainment. Romances mushroom across the tent town; some decide even to marry on the spot or move their wedding ceremony to the place where nobody is short of friends. Groups of people coming from different cities label their tents and join the crowd claiming to represent Odesa, Zaporizhzhya, Sumy but also Ukrainians. Cultural and linguistic differences that seemed to divide the Ukrainians now unite them. It could almost be said that a number of Ukrainians would go to Maidan in search of a meaning of 'being Ukrainian'. Those looking for a prototype, for a unique way of being Ukrainian, quickly learned that Ukraine was also about diversity and different (political, social, cultural) views on common features but the very fact of being interested in these features could make them Ukrainian. Discussions happen in Russian or Ukrainian with little attention for the language and more for the content. The important thing is to communicate to discover that, in the end, someone from 600 km away and a different native language has much in common with you. Social communication is possibly more important than language when it comes to identity (Deutsch 1966) but this is something that not everyone realized, at least not immediately.

The cold temperature takes the first victims and a growing number of protesters get a cold or flu. The problem is met with enthusiasm by doctors,

166   *Abel Polese*

nurses and practitioners from a number of Ukrainian hospitals who arrange temporary medical points to take care of anyone who needs it. Several points emerge around the city and become another meeting point between people who would never meet otherwise. Patients are looked after regardless of their language, regional origins or political ideas.

The city administration quickly becomes an immense canteen where meals are prepared. A reception service is set up at the central station to meet, and give directions to, the groups of people coming from the various corners of the country. A home stay service is organized with Kiev residents giving availability to host anyone from outside the city looking for a temporary shelter. Music is played at several places in the city around improvised bonfires, and tea and food points become more and more numerous to meet the demand of an increasing number of people converging into Kiev.

Orange, the colour of the opposition, is quickly accompanied by blue, the colour of pro-regime forces who, after some days, also converge into Kiev. In a fashion that one will learn to appreciate during future colour revolutions, the authorities attempt to counterbalance the protesters by using their strategy and encourage the creation of pro-regime groups. An alternative tent town is set at around 500 meters from Maidan and is mostly coloured in blue. Opposition supporters largely outnumber pro-regime ones and rarely, if ever, respond to any provocations. What is more interesting, however, is the fact that within a number of days the two groups start mingling together; people from one place visit the other one and vice versa, they take pictures and go eat together at the canteens organized all over the place.

Some attacks are reported but they seem to be rather sporadic episodes, by people who had been instructed to act this way, rather than by the general mood. Other than that, it becomes relatively common to see 'blue' and 'orange' people drinking tea or discussing politics in a fashion that had rarely, if ever, been witnessed in the country before.

Much has been written about the broken promises of the colour revolution (Arel 2005, Hale 2006, Tudoroiu 2007). However, there have been a number of points that have passed almost unperceived but have, to various degrees, affected the social and cultural history of the country. In particular, they have helped redefine and reconstruct identity markers that had not been comprehensively employed or developed before.

Marker 1: language

Pre-2004 Ukraine hosted a very peculiar situation. Ukrainian had been embedded as the sole state language in the 1996 constitution; it had been fairly accepted as the language of politics, public administration and of school education. Nevertheless, there were numerous accounts of the role of Russian and its use in a high number of contexts. Indeed, the race between the two main candidates of the 2004 elections was also a linguistic competition, with the pro-government candidate using Russian, the language of the most populated eastern region, and the main opposition candidate using Ukrainian, the official language of the country. The current president, Leonid Kuchma, prioritized the use of Russian, his native language. In contrast, a new generation of politicians and activists were ready to use Ukrainian as the language of public speaking in spite of being Russian speakers to show their commitment to a new ideology and a rupture with the regime.

This dualism was, although not necessarily politicized, visible in other parts of the country. In Kiev, a train going to Odesa, and its staff, would mostly sound Russian whereas the same train, going in the opposite direction, would see the growing importance of Ukrainian. A train going to L'viv would, almost automatically and organically, have Ukrainian spoken in most places but on its way back to Kiev Russian would sound more familiar in some coaches. Indeed, an independent study conducted by the Kiev International Institute of Sociology (Khmelko 2004) showed the relationship between identity and language illustrated in Table 9.1.

Starting from 22 November, a permanent show is staged on a screen placed on Independence Square and things radically change. First, whatever the language spoken around or on Maidan, the language spoken on the stage was predominantly Ukrainian. The use of Ukrainian was more a political stand than a matter of convenience (Arel 1995), an attitude already noticed by Shevel (2002) when declaring one's native language during the census interviews.

This sudden change of attitude towards Ukrainian, and choice of the language of political discourses, did not change the attitude towards Russian language. Russian speakers supporting the Orange Revolution were many and they could not change their language overnight. Eventually, what changed was the attitude towards Ukrainian language and culture, which started being perceived as more positively Ukrainian in many places (Polese and Wylegala 2008). Russian was widely spoken around Maidan, Kiev and Ukraine and little, if any, discourses promoted a negative attitude towards it. It was important to create distance from a Russia that was often accused of invading the sphere of competence of a sovereign state. However, there seemed to be a conscious distinction between Russian elites, Russians and Russian language, with hostility displayed only towards the former.

Table 9.1 Use of languages in Ukraine

Language used	1991–1994	1995–1999	2000–2003
Ukrainian (Ukrainian speakers)	41.2%	46.3%	45.4%
Ukrainian (Russian speakers)	32.6%	28.2%	30.9%
Russian (Russian speakers)	19.7%	17.0%	16.5%
Other	6.5%	8.5%	7.2%
Total	100%	100%	100%

168   *Abel Polese*

During the occupation of Maidan languages were switched in the most natural way. It was understandable that those politically committed to support the opposition would start a conversation in Ukrainian. However, a good number of them were ready to switch to Russian if needed or simply bilingual conversations (each of the interlocutors speaking their preferred language) were frequent (Polese 2009a).[1]

Much has been written about the cultural and linguistic differences between the east and the west of the country (Birch 2000, Katchanovski 2006, Kubicek 2000). Still, the revolution seemed to level down all this, allowing a space where people could meet, discuss, become friends or fall in love, as demonstrated by the numerous marriages, including matching people from different regions.

Emotions count and contribute to the construction of one's identity and attitudes (Pawłusz 2016). The fact that most messages from the Maidan scene were delivered in Ukrainian contributed to the creation of a version of the events narrated in Ukrainian. This was not only done through political speeches; a vital role was played by bands and singers performing in Ukrainian and thus creating an emotional connection between performing arts and the use of Ukrainian. Several informants admitted that they rediscovered their interest in Ukrainian as a result of the events. A Russian speaking Odessa businessman confessed that, during the events, in the morning he would try to remember the words of the Ukrainian anthems. Some other NGO workers I was working with told me that their Donetsk partners started, all of sudden, writing emails in Ukrainian. It was not the best-written Ukrainian but it showed a change of attitude towards the language (Polese 2009a).

Two examples can perhaps better illustrate the change of attitude during and after the events so to provide a better view on a phenomenon that is easy to perceive but difficult to report.

Maria met Andrey a few months before the 2004 events, when they were both students in Kiev. Their first language is Russian, which was also the language of communication they used. What's more, Andrey had always been fascinated by Moscow, which he saw as a very dynamic place where one day he might live. A few months after the Orange Revolution they formalized their relationship but switched to Ukrainian. They eventually married but, since 2005, made a point of only speaking Ukrainian between themselves. The same is true with their daughter, who is now brought up in a totally Ukrainian speaking environment, with Russian only spoken when they visit grandparents. They underwent several transformations. Andrey initially refused to speak Russian at all, then became comfortable with both. Maria went on with her studies and completed a degree in Ukrainian.

Pavel was a Ukrainian-speaking student in 2004. For a number of reasons, he had made a point of only speaking Ukrainian. Being a shy and smiley person, he would not impose the language of communication but his idea was that being Ukrainian means that one has to be able to speak Ukrainian. He would simply answer in Ukrainian whatever language he was addressed in,

Can nation building be 'spontaneous'? 169

thus allowing his interlocutor to answer in Russian but never using it himself. A few months after the events his attitude changed. While still preferring Ukrainian, he never declined to speak Russian again and told me he now accepted the fact that some Ukrainians might not speak Ukrainian, while still being Ukrainian.

The November 2004 events were bilingual, not in the use of language but in the attitude towards languages. Identity and language become less entwisted in the imaginary of many. There is an unfounded but highly civic assumption that the use of Russian is contextual and incidental, while Ukrainian could be used if needed. The political discourse changes in the same direction. After 2004 Ukrainian becomes predominant in political speeches, with Russian being accepted in a variety of cases. The word of a maths teacher from Odessa about his pupils I interviewed possibly say a lot: 'They are not Ukrainian speakers. I am neither but we all do our best.'

Marker 2: identity and civic engagement

Most pre-2004 reports on political activism in Ukraine, and in general in the post-socialist region, claimed a low level of civic and political activism in the region (Kuzio 1997). This has been criticized from several angles (see the discussion in Ó Beacháin and Polese 2010b). However, it is possible to say that the general perception on domestic activism showed a relatively low level of civic participation and interaction between civil society and politics.

There are, however, some segments of the population that show some interest. The protests after journalist Georgi Gongadze's beheading and, previously, the 1990 granite revolution, showed that Ukrainian civil society was somehow present. However, the number of active people was low and ordinary people were not interested in politics. November 2004 marks the passage from a society that is uninterested in the general mood of politics to a society where people feel that they can make a difference. It is the moment when fast food restaurants and other popular places started broadcasting political information, and people would gather and go to the city council to wait for a political decision (Polese 2009a). Hairdresser conversations could turn into political debates with people taking a position for either of the candidates but nonetheless discussing politics. Orange started colouring the streets, the building and the cars of Kiev, then the rest of the country. It was sometimes contrasted by blue gadgets. At any rate, displaying a colour was also a sign of political activism. The day of the political debate between the two presidential candidates the city of Kiev looked as empty as it would look during a World Cup football match. People were leaving the workplace earlier to be sure they would arrive home on time to follow the debate. The occupation of Kiev also served as a crash course on Ukrainian political institutions since people had to know where to go to picket governmental buildings and had to learn the centre of power. This was not a phenomenon limited to those living in the street. Continuous broadcasting from all centres of power also gave

170 *Abel Polese*

Ukrainians a better idea of the institutions present in the country. Political participation was at unprecedented levels. Yuri Shevchuk, the singer of the Moscow-based rock band DDT, declared on TV during the protests that he had come to Kiev to see with his eyes what was going on in Kiev since he did not trust Russian media. 'A new generation is born', he said a few hours after arriving in Ukraine. The enthusiasm of the protesters infected also people close to the current regime. Viktor Pintchouk, President Kuchma's son-in-law, after an evening spent in Maidan, stated 'had I been a student, I would certainly have spent the night here in Maidan with you'.

This is not to claim that being Ukrainian means to be active politically, or to claim that all Ukrainians are engaged with or interested in politics. However, the massive interest in the November 2004 events prompted the authorities to create a lieu de memoire with the 22nd of November being called the anniversary of the Orange Revolution. An unprecedented number of Ukrainians, not necessarily from the elites or intelligentsia, became interested in politics. This becomes visible with the frequency street protests are used, and abused, after the events. Occupation of a part of the city becomes a mode to express discontent with a particular decision, like in the case of the park near the Shulyavska metro station, occupied to stop the construction of two tall buildings in autumn 2005, and the attempts to stop IKEA from cutting part of the Borispyl woods to build a store.

Political involvement of popular figures, like the boxer Klichko, the Okean Elzy singer Sviatoslav Vokarchuk or even Ruslana, winner of the 2004 Eurovision contest, made it easier to picture the revolution as a pop event. This is the link between the social, the popular and the political that was missing and that prompts people who had not been interested before into forming at least a vague political opinion.

Much has been written about the civic movement PORA, its different components, the network that it managed and its role in the Orange revolution (Beissinger 2011, Laverty 2008, Polese 2009a, Wilson 2006). However, this was just the tip of the iceberg. A further effect of the Orange Revolution is the emergence of a number of civic movements and political platforms. For one thing Yuri Lutsenko, after leaving the Socialist Party, created, with some other activists of the Orange Revolution, including Taras Stetskiv et Oles Donii, activist of the 1991 protests, the movement *narodna samooborona* that would eventually register for the 2007 elections.

The most striking aspect of the protests was not necessarily its political aspects. It became quasi natural almost overnight to see people wearing different colours debate in the street. This implied two things. First, that people had political preferences and started expressing them in their everyday interaction with other people. Second, that people started actively debating political ideas and showing respect and tolerance towards other individuals with different political preferences. This may be regarded as a new feature introduced by the Orange Revolution. No matter your political ideas it is

Can nation building be 'spontaneous'? 171

possible to share and debate them in a fashion that was unprecedented in the country.

Marker 3: othering Russia

Moscow, Russia and Russian culture, whatever this means, have often been located in a grey zone for Ukrainians. Nationalists would see Russia as an alien culture to the Ukrainians while for the population of the eastern regions Russia was an economic opportunity and a place with which they would share a language, TV channels and much more. This is to say that Russia could be considered abroad or 'nasha' (ours) depending on the context. Soviet, and post-Soviet cinema, often shot in Russia, and bands created and developed in Moscow were not unambiguously considered 'foreign' in the country so that Russia was in a place in between abroad and domestic.

The 2004 events start the placement of Russia as away from many domestic issues. This is not to deny the common features that Russian and Ukrainian societies might have in common such as the use of language, TV channels and cultural linkages and also the fact that many Ukrainian families have Russia-born relatives. However, something in the Russia–Ukraine relationship changes.

By taking a clear stand in favour of one of the presidential candidates, and de facto putting pressure on Ukrainians to prompt his election, Moscow made a statement that nearly half of the Ukrainian population found difficult to agree with. How would you react if the political elites of a country that claims to be your best neighbour, your bigger brother, explains to you how to vote? As soon as electoral frauds are uncovered, anti-Russia manifestations start in L'viv and Kyiv. On 28 November the fact that a Moscow major goes to Donetsk to openly support a candidate contributes to a further escalation. Further attempts to destabilize Ukrainian politics include threats to close the gas transit through the country or the rise of gas prices from a 'friend's level' to the market price.

If all this may be said to have had an effect on Ukrainian politics, it has had little (positive) effect on the perception of Russia as big brother, as friend or as anything positive. There is a limit to what one can endure. If you prefer to listen to Russian news for language proximity but this news constantly goes against your beliefs and perceptions then it is possible that you will move to a different information source and will look critically at this source of information. There are few things so effective in aiding identity construction than the existence of a common enemy. Although it is not possible to claim that all Ukrainians would see Russia as the enemy, it is possible that Moscow's excessive attempts to influence domestic politics have pushed a growing number of Ukrainians, while acknowledging the common past or culture, to see Russian political elites as a potential threat and, in turn, to develop a different awareness of the self and the other.

172 *Abel Polese*

Final remarks on revolutions and awareness

By defining and describing the rapports between memory and identity at the group scale (Candau 2005) the Orange Revolution can be regarded, in a Norian fashion (Nora 1984), as a lieu de memoire in itself. The November 2004 events have complemented an increased awareness of the political history of the country. For one thing, an immediate result has been the recognition of the 1932-33 famine as a genocide allowing reflection on the reappropriation of political categories and their new function of redefining, and reproducing, a national identity under a new light (Amselle 2001, Verdery 2000).

National identity is constantly lived, reproduced and renegotiated through a series of actions, positions and attitudes complementing the construction of the political by the national elites with everyday construction of iden- tities (Billig 1995, Edensor 2002, Skey 2011). In this respect, the narrative presented in this chapter has been an attempt to illustrate the way identity is reproduced and renegotiated at the everyday level. It has also illustrated to what extent identity construction originated in people self perception can eventually influence mass-scale perceptions of identity at the regional or national level.

The rapid evolution of perception and reproduction of a Ukrainian iden- tity illustrates the transformation of a political discourse that can originate at the bottom of the society and be influenced by the production and evolution of locality. By doing this, we have made an attempt to explore the different dimensions, and layers, of ethnographic landscapes influencing identity at all the levels of a society so to suggest the need of a cultural intimacy approach (Herzfeld et al. 2014) giving equal importance to micro processes and elevat- ing them in worth to what political science focuses on (macro processes).

Note

1 This was, however, not the attitude of the totality of the staff. I once had to conduct an interview in Ukrainian with someone who, to the best of my knowledge, knew that my Russian was much better but insisted on speaking Ukrainian

References

Amselle, J. L. 2001. *Branchements: Anthropologie de l'universelle des cultures*. Paris: Flammarion.
Appaduraj A. 1995. *Après le colonialisme*. Paris: Payot
Arel, D. 1995. Language politics in independent Ukraine: Towards one or two state languages? *Nationalities Papers* 23(3), 597–622.
Arel, D. 2005. Is the Orange Revolution fading? *Current History* 104(684), 325–330.
Åslund, A. and McFaul, M. (eds.). 2006. *Revolution in orange: The origins of Ukraine's democratic breakthrough*. Washington, D.C.: Carnegie Endowment.
Beissinger, M. 2011. Mechanisms of Maidan: The structure of contingency in the making of the Orange Revolution. *Mobilization: An International Quarterly* 16 (1), 25–43.

Can nation building be 'spontaneous'? 173

Beissinger, M. 2013. The semblance of democratic revolution: Coalitions in Ukraine's Orange Revolution. *American Political Science Review* 107(03), 574–592.

Bilaniuk, L. 2005. *Contested tongues: Language politics and cultural correction in Ukraine.* Ithaca, NY and London: Cornell University Press.

Birch, S. 2000. Interpreting the regional effect in Ukrainian politics. *Europe-Asia Studies* 52(6), 1017–1041.

Brubaker, R. 1996. *Nationalism refrained: Nationhood and the national question in the new Europe.* Cambridge, UK: Cambridge University Press.

Candau, J. 2005. *Anthropologie de la mémoire.* Paris: Armand Colin

Connor, W. 1972. Nation-building or nation-destroying? *World Politics* 24(3), 319–355.

Christensen, R. K., Rakhimkulov, E. R., Wise, C. R. 2005. The Ukrainian Orange Revolution brought more than a new president: What kind of democracy will the institutional changes bring? *Communist and Post-Communist Studies* 38(2), 207–230.

Crescente, J. 2007. 'Performing Post-Sovietness: Verka Serduchka and the hybridization of identity in Post-Soviet Ukraine. Conference paper presented at the Soyuz Symposium, 25-28 April 2007.

D'Anieri, P. 2005. The last hurrah: The 2004 elections and the limits of machine politics. *Communist and Post-Communist Studies* 38(2), 231–250.

Danero Iglesias, J. 2015. Eurovision song contest and identity crisis in Moldova. *Nationalities Papers* 43(2), 233–247.

De Juriew, D. 2003. *Mythes politiques et identité en Ukraine post-soviétique: passé composé et reconquête du sens.* Paris: L'Harmattan.

Deutsch, K. 1966. *Nationalism and social communication: An inquiry into the foundations of nationality.* Boston: MIT Press.

Deutsch, K. and Foltz, W. J. 1964. *Nation building.* New York: Atherton Press.

Edensor, T. 2002. *National identity, popular culture and everyday life.* Oxford: Berg.

Eriksen, T. H. 1993. Formal and informal nationalism. *Ethnic and Racial Studies* 16(1), 1–25.

Forbrig, J., Demes, P. (eds.). 2007. Reclaiming democracy: Civil society and electoral change in Central and Eastern Europe. Washington, DC and Bratislava: German Marshall Fund.

Gellner, E. 1984. *Nations and nationalism.* Cornell University Press.

Gramsci, A. 1971. *Selections from the prison notebooks.* London: Lawrence and Wishart.

Gronskaya, N., Makarychev, A. 2014. The 2014 Sochi Olympics and sovereign power: A political linguistic perspective. *Problems of Post-Communism* 61(1), 41–51.

Hale, H. E. 2006. Democracy or autocracy on the march? The colored revolutions as normal dynamics of patronal presidentialism. *Communist and Post-Communist Studies* 39(3), 305–329.

Herzfeld, M., 2014. *Cultural intimacy: Social poetics in the nation-state.* London: Routledge.

Hobsbawm, E., Rudé, G. 2014. *Captain swing.* London: Verso Books.

Horak, S., Polese, A. 2016. Personality cult and nation-building in Turkmenistan. In Isaacs, R., Polese, A. (eds.), *Nation building in the post-Soviet space: New tools and approaches,* edited by R. Isaacs and A. Polese. London: Routledge.

Isaacs, R. 2015. Nomads, warriors and bureaucrats: Nation-building and film in post-Soviet Kazakhstan. *Nationalities Papers* 43(3), 399–416.

Isaacs, R. 2016. Cinema and nation-building in Kazakhstan, in *Nation-building and identity in the post-Soviet space: New tools and approaches,* edited by R. Isaacs and A. Polese. London: Routledge.

Isaacs, R., Polese, A. 2016. *Nation-building and identity in the post-Soviet space: New tools and approaches.* London: Routledge.

174 Abel Polese

Katchanovski, I. 2006. Regional political divisions in Ukraine in 1991–2006. *Nationalities Papers* 34(5), 507–532.

Khmelko, V. 2004. *Lingvo-ethnichna struktura Ukrainy: regionalni osoblivosti ta tendentsii zmin za roki nezalezhnosti.* Kiev: Kiev International Institute of Sociology.

Knott, E. 2015. Generating data studying identity politics from a bottom-up approach in Crimea and Moldova. *East European Politics and Societies* 29(2), 467–486.

Kubicek, P. 2000. Regional polarisation in Ukraine: Public opinion, voting and legislative behaviour. *Europe-Asia Studies* 52(2), 273–294.

Kubicek, P. 2009. Problems of post-post-communism: Ukraine after the Orange Revolution. *Democratization* 16(2), 323–343.

Kulyk, V. 2014. Ukrainian nationalism since the outbreak of Euromaidan. *Ab Imperio* 2014.3: 94–122.

Kurth, H., Kempe. I. (eds.). 2005. Presidential election and Orange Revolution: Implications for Ukraine's transition, Kiev: Zapovit.

Kuzio, T. 1997. *Ukraine under Kuchma.* London, New York: MacMillian

Kuzio, T. 2001. 'Nationalising states' or nation-building? A critical review of the theoretical literature and empirical evidence. *Nations and Nationalism* 7(2), 135–154.

Kuzio, T. 2005. Ukraine's Orange Revolution. The opposition's road to success. *Journal of Democracy* 16(2), 117–130.

Kuzio, T. 2006a. Civil society, youth and societal mobilization in democratic revolutions. *Communist and Post-Communist Studies* 39(3), 365–386.

Kuzio, T. 2006b. Everyday Ukrainians and the Orange Revolution, in Åslund, A. and McFaul, M. (eds.), *Revolution in orange: The origins of Ukraine's democratic breakthrough.* Washington, DC: Carnegie Endowment for International Peace, 45–68.

Kuzio, T. 2010. Nationalism, identity and civil society in Ukraine: Understanding the Orange Revolution. *Communist and Post-Communist Studies* 43(3), 285–296.

Lane, D., 2008. The Orange Revolution: 'People's revolution' or revolutionary coup? *The British Journal of Politics and International Relations* 10(4), 525–549.

Laverty, N. 2008. The problem of lasting change: Civil society and the Colored Revolutions in Georgia and Ukraine. *Demokratizatsiya* 16(2), 143–161.

McFaul, M. 2005. The second wave of democratic breakthroughs in the post-communist world: Comparing Serbia 2000, Georgia 2003, Ukraine 2004, and Kyrgyzstan 2005. Danyliw/Jacyk Working Papers No.4. Toronto: University of Toronto.

McFaul, M., 2007. Ukraine imports democracy: External influences on the Orange Revolution. *International Security* 32(2), 45–83.

Metzger, M. M., Bonneau, R., Nagler, J., Tucker, J. A. 2016. Tweeting identity? Ukrainian, Russian, and Euromaidan. *Journal of Comparative Economics* 44(1),16–40.

Militz, E. 2016. Public events and nation-building in Azerbaijan, in Isaacs, R. and Polese, A. (eds.), *Nation-building and identity in the post-Soviet space: New tools and approaches.* London: Routledge.

Morris, J. 2005. The empire strikes back: Projections of national identity in contemporary Russian advertising. *The Russian Review* 64(4), 642–660.

Morris, J. 2007. Drinking to the nation: Russian television advertising and cultural differentiation. *Europe-Asia Studies* 59(8), 1387–1403.

Ó Beacháin, D., Kevlihan, R. 2015. Imagined democracy? Nation-building and elections in Central Asia. *Nationalities Papers* 43(3), 495–513.

Ó Beacháin, D., Polese. A. 2008. American boots and Russian vodka: External factors on coloured revolutions in Georgia, Ukraine and Kyrgyzstan. *Totalitarismus und Demokratie* 5(1): 87–114.

Ó Beacháin, D., Polese. A. 2009. From roses to bullets: The spreading of the colour revolutions to the post-Soviet world and its rapid decline, in Backes, U., Jaskulowski, T., Polese, A. (eds.), *Totalitarismus und Transformation - Defizite der Demokratiekonsolidierung in Mittel- und Osteuropa.* V&R: Gottingen

Can nation building be 'spontaneous'? 175

Ó Beacháin D., Polese, A. (eds.). 2010a. *The colour revolutions in the former Soviet Union: Successes and failures*. London and New York: Routledge.

Ó Beacháin, D., Polese. A. 2010b. 'Rocking the vote': New forms of youth organization in post-communist spaces. *Journal of Youth Studies* 10(2), 1–16

Ostapenko, N. 2010. Nation branding of Russia through the Sochi Olympic Games of 2014. *Journal of Management Policy and Practice* 11(4), 60–63.

Pawłusz, E. 2016. The Estonian song celebration (Laulupidu) as an instrument of language policy. *Journal of Baltic Studies*, 1–21. Published online first. Available at: www.tandfonline.com/doi/abs/10.1080/01629778.2016.1164203

Pawłusz E., Polese, A. 2017. "Scandinavia's best kept secret": Tourism Promotion as a Site of nation-building in Estonia (with a free guided tour of Tallinn airport). *Nationalities Papers*. Published online first. Available at: www.tandfonline.com/doi/abs/10.1080/00905992.2017.1287167

Pawłusz, E., Seliverstova, O., 2016. Everyday nation-building in the post-Soviet space. Methodological reflections. *Studies of Transition States and Societies* 8(1), 69–86.

Persson, E., Petersson. B. 2014. Political mythmaking and the 2014 Winter Olympics in Sochi: Olympism and the Russian great power myth. *East European Politics* 30(2), 192–209.

Polese, A., 2008. Does civic nation-building exist? An answer from Ukraine. Paper presented at the ASEN annual conference, London School of Economics, UK.

Polese, A. 2009a. Une version alternative de la 'révolution orange': transformations identitaires et 'nation building spontané. *Socio-logos 4*. Available at: http://socio-logos.revues.org/2315.

Polese, A. 2009b. Dynamiques de nation building et évolution d'une identité nationale en Ukraine: le cas d'Odessa. PhD Thesis, Universite libre de Bruxelles.

Polese, A. 2014. Between official and unofficial temperatures: A complication to the hot and cold ethnicity theory from Odessa. *Journal of Multilingual and Multicultural Development* 35(2), 59–75.

Polese, A. 2016. *Limits of a state: How informality replaces, renegotiates and reshapes governance in post-Soviet Ukraine*, Stuttgart: Ibidem Verlag.

Polese, A., Horak, S. 2015. A tale of two presidents: Personality cult and symbolic nation-building in Turkmenistan. *Nationalities Papers* 43(3): 457–478.

Polese, A., Wylegala, A. 2008. Odessa and Lvov or Odesa and Lviv: How important is a letter? Reflections on the 'other' in two Ukrainian cities. *Nationalities Papers* 36(5): 787–814.

Shevel, O. 2002. Nationality in Ukraine: Some rules of engagement. *East European Politics and Societies* 16(2), 386–413.

Smith, A. D. 1991. *National identity*. Reno, NV: University of Nevada Press.

Stepanenko, V. 2006. Civil society in post-Soviet Ukraine: Civic ethos in the framework of corrupted sociality? *East European Politics & Societies* 20(4), 571–597.

Tudoroiu, T. 2007. Rose, orange, and tulip: The failed post-Soviet revolutions. *Communist and Post-Communist Studies* 40(3), 315–342.

Ventsel, A. 2012. This is not my country, my country is the Gdr: East German punk and socio-economic processes after German reunification. *Punk and Post Punk* 1(3), 343–359.

Ventsel, A. 2016. Language, economy and nation-building in the Republic of Sakha, in Isaacs, R. and Polese, A. (eds.), *Nation-building and identity in the post-Soviet Space: New tools and approaches*. London: Routledge.

Verdery, K. 2000. *The political lives of dead bodies: Reburial and postsocialist change*. New York: Columbia University Press

Wallander, C.A. 2005. Ukraine's election: The role of one international NGO. *International Affairs* 51(3), 92–103.

Wilson, A. 2005. *Ukraine's Orange Revolution*. New Haven, CT: Yale University Press.

Wilson, A. 2006. Ukraine's Orange Revolution, NGOs and the role of the West. *Cambridge Review of International Affairs* 19(1), 21–32.

Conclusion
Identities for the everyday

We have conceived this book as a dialogue between empirical approaches and cases with the goal of contributing to the burgeoning number of studies of nation building in post-Soviet states. It offers in-depth case studies that use methods from a wide variety of disciplines with no limitations in the way the subject matter should be approached. Our task has been facilitated by the fact that the breakup of the Soviet Union and Yugoslavia have offered one of the quickest accelerations in nationalism studies, yet most extant works focused on institutional and administrative aspects of nation and state building.

This is why we have conceived of this book in order to turn attention to those aspects of identity creation which have not been so well documented or often overlooked and underreported in initial studies (Polese 2016). These are everyday, situational, uneventful choices, practices and interactions in which identity is being settled, or to the contrary, gradually challenged, but which do not make the headlines (Morris and Polese 2015, Seliverstova 2017). We move the focus from top political actors and decision-makers to the agency, or even unconscious drift towards understandings of nation by, and of, ordinary citizens.

Methodologically, our goal has been to contribute to a greater epistemological shift – focusing on the complex, underreported, uncountable phenomena that matter for people's identifications and cognitive schemes (how they makes sense of the world around them) but remain largely unattended by mainstream social science (Thompson 2001, Knott 2015, Polese 2016). In line with this, this volume has been an attempt to engage with some major debates on nation building and identity construction. Although producing evidence from a variety of cases from post-socialist spaces, our ambition has been to go beyond our region to engage with a dialogue on global theories of nationalism. By force of our chapters, we suggest that nation building is an ongoing practice in both states 'in construction' and stable ones (Bonikowski and Gheihman 2015). Modalities and approaches may be different but one can consider all states 'nations' in the making or remaking. Identity is constructed, confirmed and performed in the everyday and thus it rapidly evolves and adapts to ever-changing demographic, geographical and cultural factors that are reproduced and lived by the people through their conscious and non-conscious actions, practices and co-lived lives.

Conclusion 177

This understanding has also informed our approach and attempts to contrast, or better complement, the study of top-down factors, as they have been analyzed by a number of scholars (Brubaker 1996, Smith et al. 1998, Kolstø 2000, 2014, Mole 2012). We believe that, in spite of a growing attention to the everyday and everyday construction of identities (Fox and Miller-Idriss 2008, Skey 2011), there is still little emphasis on people's agency and daily choices of non-political actors. This has also led nationalism and identity studies to focus on events of great social and political magnitude – wars, conflicts, breakups of empires – at the expense of micro processes and routine practices in which identities are sustained (Thompson 2001, Edensor 2002), and which in the longue durée may have just as much impact.

This volume has been a first attempt to bring back the agency of people in construction, negotiation and reproduction of identity. In this respect, the focus on the everyday proves valuable when formal identity proposed by the state and top political actors is contested in various social or cultural groups (Isaacs and Polese 2015). Inquiry into the everyday allows us to unpack this contestation and unravel alternative identity choices or alternative sources of its production that are meaningful for some parts of the society. By doing this, we have attempted to propose that identity construction is also a mundane, quotidian practice that individuals engage with in their everyday lives, sometimes unconsciously and unintentionally. We may choose a certain product, hobby or cultural activity (such as making music about one's own perceived folk heritage) without the explicit intention to declare our national identity or for other reasons, yet such choices often reveal taken-for-granted assumptions about the nation and its inclusion/exclusion dynamics and contribute to their reproduction.

The authors in this volume have engaged with debates on the everyday and regular construction of identity. They have suggested that identity construction is maintained by routine actions, choices and practices we all conduct in our everyday lives, and this is an important extension to Michael Billig's (1995) banal nationalism thesis which focused mostly on people as passive receivers, presented with banal forms of nationalism such as flags displayed in public spaces or the use of speech terms like 'us' and 'them', reminding us about the tangibility of the nation and present in all media forms. As such, our intention has been to propose a further step towards theorizing the uneventful, banal and everyday forms of nation building and identity creation.

We thus propose to complement existing definitions of nation building, and in general the debate on identity construction, by taking into account several factors that have not received sufficient attention thus far. First, we propose the existence of a spectrum of formal and informal actors, markers and factors that frame people's understanding of the nation and inclusion-exclusion mechanisms which are crucial for the definition of national community; political, popular and quotidian actors matter. Second, we wish to emphasize the study of practice over teleological process with an end goal, going beyond the functionalist assumption that once saw national identity as

178   *Conclusion*

stable and uncritically reproduced by the people. By doing this, we increase attention on the contested aspects of identity construction, production and reproduction and on the fractures generated by the contrasting agency of a variety of actors and processes, with an interaction between 'hot' nationalism events and routine, mundane and apparently uneventful ones.

Ultimately, our idea is that identity is a mix of what's there in the wider society and what's there in one's own local or contextually nation-specific experience (for example, such as a person's exposure to food and foodways or popular music, both of which lie at the very edge of state-informed processes of formation). Identity is an individual and community practice and experience, we cannot experience it otherwise, and this is why to understand identity construction and negotiation we need to attend to the individual and community at a level below the 'nation' as a whole.

In addition to our attempts to address some urgent questions on the study of identity formation our expectation is that this book will open the way to new possible horizons for further research by ourselves or other scholars. In particular, it might be worth exploring socio-psychological aspects of identity construction, like emotional attachments and affects that are socially constructed and learnt. We acknowledge the reluctance with which we, social scientists, seem to engage with other disciplines such as sociobiology, or even cognate disciplines such as psychology of human experience. But we are confident that new directions could be found by expanding beyond traditional approaches.

Moreover, we would like to emphasize the value of in-depth, embedded studies in unpacking how identities work in practice. If census results, however problematically, provide the overview of final identity choices people make (like 'I am X'), in-depth studies can shed light on the changing content of identity declarations ('what it means to be X', and how and when one experiences, accepts or challenges it). By attending to the complexity of practiced and individually experienced national identity, we gain insight into its cognitive schemes, practices and fractures, which are often overlooked if identity is measured as a declaration.

Finally, social media and the Internet in general have given a voice to many who were allegedly absent from public debates. A tweet or a post may gain notoriety or fame; ideas that would remain confined to discussions among friends may be translated into a national debate on identity. The study of social media and ICT-related social phenomena has exponentially increased over the past years. Still, it is possible that more attention to the increasing importance of popular culture, Internet and social media as political arenas may produce important findings for a better understanding of the self, but also official identity construction narratives. This is especially true in the context of contestation of what the state 'says' about national belonging and identity.

References

Billig, M. 1995. *Banal nationalism*. London: Sage.

Bonikowski, B., Gheihman, N. 2015. Nation-state as symbolic construct. *International Encyclopeadia of the Social and Behavioral Sciences*, 2nd edition, 309–314.

Brubaker, R. 1996. *Nationalism reframed: Nationhood and the national question in the New Europe*. Cambrige: Cambridge University Press.

Edensor, T. 2002. *National identity, popular culture and everyday life*. Oxford: Berg.

Fox, J. E., Miller-Idriss, C. 2008. Everyday nationhood. *Ethnicities* 8(4), 536–563.

Isaacs, R., Polese, A. 2015. Between 'imagined' and 'real' nation building: Identities and nationhood in post-Soviet central Asia. *Nationalities Papers* 43(3), 371–382.

Knott, E. 2015. What does it mean to be a kin majority? Analyzing Romanian identity in Moldova and Russian identity in Crimea from below. *Social Science Quarterly* 96(3), 830–858.

Kolstø, P. 2000. *Political construction sites: Nation-building in Russia and the post-Soviet states*. Boulder, CO: Westview Press.

Kolstø, P. (ed.) 2014. *Strategies of symbolic nation-building in south eastern Europe*. Farnham: Ashgate.

Mole, R. 2012. *The Baltic states from the Soviet Union to the European Union. Identity, discourse and power in the post-communist transition of Estonia, Latvia and Lithuania*. New York and London: Routledge.

Morris, J., Polese, A. (eds.) 2015. *Informal economies in post-Socialist spaces: Practices, institutions and networks*. New York: Palgrave Macmillan.

Polese, A. 2016. *Limits of a state: How informality replaces, renegotiates and reshapes governance in post-Soviet spaces*. Stuttgart: Ibidem.

Seliverstova, O. 2017. "Consuming" national identity in Western Ukraine. *Nationalities Papers* 45(1), 61–79.

Skey, M. 2011. *National belonging and everyday life*. Basingstoke: Palgrave.

Smith, G., Law, V., Wilson, A., Bohr, A., Allworth, E. 1998. *Nation-building in the post-Soviet borderlands: The politics of national identities*. Cambridge: Cambridge University Press.

Thompson, A. 2001. Nations, national identities and human agency: Putting people back into nations. *The Sociological Review* 49(1), 18–32.

Index

belonging 8, 9, 29, 31, 35, 37, 41, 57, 61, 73–76, 80–81, 86–87, 91–93, 95–96, 98, 101–102,109–116,118,121,123,132, 143, 146, 148, 150, 153–154, 156–157, 178
border 11, 54, 61, 103–104, 119, 133, 146
border identity 147–156
bordering 10–142
bottom-up approach 109, 111, 147,160,174
boycott 1, 9, 73–74, 77, 81, 82–88, 118, 121
buycott 82, 85

choral singing 38, 44
citizenship 1, 7, 9–11, 45, 55, 73–76
consumer citizenship 1, 9–10, 13, 73–77, 89, 111
consumer movement 73–75, 82

diasporic 10, 91–98, 101–105

Estonia 8–10,34–47, 80,103–104, 109–124, 135–136; Estonian identity 35, 40, 43, 46; Estonian language 39, 46, 135–136
Estonianess vi, 10, 43–44, 46, 109–110, 113, 121, 123

foodways 10, 94–96, 101, 104, 178

Georgia v, vii–viii, 9, 20, 52–57, 59–69, 101, 103, 122, 143, 144–145, 174

heritage 8, 34, 38–39, 40–41, 44–46, 48–50, 53–56, 59, 68–69, 104, 177

Imaginary Europe 80, 150
independence, independent (about the state) 11, 17, 19, 21, 40, 42, 45–46, 52–53, 59–61, 65, 76, 118, 131, 133–137, 139, 141, 143
instrumental/ization 11, 53, 136, 147, 149–150, 152–153

memory 27–28, 32, 36, 52–54, 67–69, 89, 96–97, 102, 104, 112, 127, 164, 172
metal 34, 39, 46–47
Metsatöll 9, 34–47
migrants 9, 10, 91–100, 102–106, 133
minority 10, 45, 139–140, 143, 148, 155
museum 8–9, 52–63, 65–69
music 17, 19–20, 24–25, 27–30, 34–38, 40, 43, 45–47, 60, 103, 139, 165–166, 177–178

name 10–11, 25, 26, 40, 61, 81–82, 83, 100, 131–145, 162
national 1–14, 17–25, 27, 30–41, 43–57, 60, 61, 64–69, 73–82, 84–95, 97–119, 121, 123–127, 132, 136–140, 142–150, 154–165, 167, 171–179
nationalization 17, 23, 47
Nordicization 119
nostalgia 91–93, 96–99, 101–104, 106, 134

official (vs. oppositional/unofficial) discourse 4–5, 7–11, 17–19, 22–24, 26–27, 30–31, 35, 38–41, 53, 55, 61, 64, 110, 112, 114–115, 117–119, 121, 124, 131–133, 137–143, 157
Orange Revolution 11, 77, 78, 161–164, 167–168, 170, 172

patriotic consumption 9, 81–82, 85–87, 95
performance 3, 9, 10, 17–19, 24, 26–30, 34, 36–37, 39, 42, 43–44, 47, 81, 93, 103–104, 110, 162–163
political elite 3, 4, 9, 18, 52–53, 61, 66–67, 111, 119, 140, 162, 164, 171

Index 181

political ideology 19, 31
post-soviet 3, 9–10, 12–13, 19,
   31–33, 37–39, 45–46, 49–52,
   54–55, 68–69, 77–78, 80, 89–92,
   96–97, 101–105, 109, 111–113,
   123–127, 135, 137–138, 144, 159,
   171, 173–176, 179

rebordering 11–146
rock 8, 26, 35–47, 170
Russian speaker 104–105, 110–113,
   115–122, 124, 126, 135–137, 167
Russianness 92–93, 97–102

social status 27–30
Soviet 20, 30–31, 40, 43, 52, 60–62,
   79–80, 92, 96–97, 102–104, 112, 114,
   119–121, 133–135, 138
spontaneous (nation building) 1, 3, 162
strategic 56, 86, 150, 155, 157
strategy/ies 67, 69, 73, 76–77, 83, 85, 96, 100

transborder 155

Ukraine 1, 9, 11–12, 73–74, 76–82, 84–88,
   93, 103, 105, 106, 110, 134–135, 138,
   146–159, 161–162, 164–167, 169, 170–171